# A Cobra Pilot in Vietnam

## True Tales and Otherwise

### Ira McComic

AMIRADO PUBLISHING

CP232A

Amirado Publishing
Plano, TX 75075
www.AmiradoPublishing.com


ISBN 978-0-9887574-4-8

To all helicopter crew members who served in Vietnam
and in memory of WO-1 Larry Bodell,
CW-2 Glenn Fetterman, and
CW-2 Gary Weatherhead.

# Contents

# Introduction

This book is an attempt to preserve a small piece of history: my experience related to flying helicopter gunships in Vietnam. Although some of my experiences may parallel those of other Vietnam helicopter pilots, I don't claim that all of my experiences were typical of them. As I believe is the case for anyone who served in Vietnam, I doubt any helicopter pilot's experience was exactly like anyone else's. Each person's experience was unique to him, shaped by his specific job, the unit in which he served, the people with whom he served, the time of his tour, the missions he performed, and other influences. Most importantly, a person's experience was shaped by his own perceptions.

My experiences are those from the perspective of an Army helicopter gunship pilot, a Cobra pilot specifically, who flew Cobras in the southernmost part of Vietnam, the Delta, for a one-year tour of duty between August of 1968 and August of 1969, serving with the 235th Aerial Weapons Company, the "Delta Devils", and for most of that time as a fire team leader.

The accounts are all based upon actual events, but they aren't all totally factual. Some of what I've written was reconstructed from letters I wrote and tapes I recorded during the time I was in Vietnam—preserved by my long persevering wife— yet those letters and recordings are spotty, leaving many of the details that have been filled in subject to flawed recall. Furthermore, some accounts have been purposely stretched beyond the strict truth, ones that adhere to a long revered tradition among those aviators who ask, "Why bother to tell a war story unless you can improve it?"

I've attempted to arrange these accounts in mostly chronological order, but I haven't been rigid about it. Some of them are composites of a thread of occurrences over a period of time and are melded together to reflect a theme or summarize particular kinds of operations.

Regarding names, I've used "Aerial Weapons Company" consistently throughout the book although the 235th changed its descriptive designation during the time I was with it. Also, not all

1

the names of individuals are their real names; some actual names I don't remember and I've purposely changed some names.

I've attempted to provide some detail about specific circumstances and to convey some of the practical technical issues related to flying Cobras in combat for the particular time and place of my service. By doing so, I hope to help persons understand the problems associated with specific situations and to offer some insight into why things were done the way they were, not that all those actions produced the results intended. To help that comprehension, I've included a glossary defining some of the words and terms I've used. The glossary isn't a universal one; its definitions are brief and focused on their use in the context of this book. It's likely that the accounts make reference to some things that may have little meaning to some readers and that aren't included in the glossary or not explained fully enough for those readers. It's for cases like those that we have Google, and if perhaps you don't know what Google is, it could be you're a Luddite or you're reading this long after I'm dead and gone and Google has perished from the earth.

Finally, for those persons who urged me to write this book, perhaps thinking it might have some merit, I hope they may find forgiveness; I'm sure their intentions were good.

Ira McComic
235th Aerial Weapons Company
Republic of Vietnam 1968-69

# Preface

I didn't realize it at the time, and it was only upon reflection, that I came to appreciate how privileged I was to have been a gunship pilot, to fly Cobras, and to have served as a fire team leader.

I understood how I came to be a helicopter pilot; that was a choice I made and that fate allowed me to fulfill. But for a long time, I pondered how I came to be a gunship pilot in particular.

Part of my puzzlement came from reading an article in an Army publication that characterized Vietnam helicopter gunship pilots as "personally aggressive and coldly calculating." I admitted that I might have some degree of personal aggression—anyone who's ever seen me elbow my way to the head of a buffet line would attest to that—but as far as being coldly calculating, I considered myself closer to room temperature. Since I didn't recognize those qualities as being extraordinarily innate to me, I thought perhaps the Army had erred in assigning me to be a gunship pilot. But then I remembered what I had been so forcefully taught during my military tenure: the Army never makes mistakes.

What I came to realize is that I wasn't selected to be a gunship pilot because of a natural inclination for that job, but rather it was because the Army chose to make me one. It was a corollary of Chuck Yeager's axiom that there is no such thing as a natural-born pilot; the particular corollary is that there's no such thing as a natural-born combat helicopter pilot, including a gunship pilot.

It's not at all natural for a person to fly a helicopter in any circumstances; persons aren't born to do that. It's not natural for a person to purposely risk himself by taking into the air such a loud, vibrating machine with a large, turning air beater overhead. And, especially, flying helicopters in combat isn't a natural instinct. It's not a natural instinct for a person to fly a helicopter into lethal places. It's not a natural instinct for a slick pilot, bullets buzzing around him, to fly into an Landing Zone and to sit there waiting until his passengers are off and the rest of the flight is ready to take off together. It's not a natural instinct for a

Chinook pilot or a Crane pilot or any other cargo pilot delivering essential supplies to a threatened outpost to hold on to the valuable load until it can be delivered to the desperate troops even though his helicopter is straining at the weight, the rotor rpm is bleeding down, and panel warnings are screaming at him to let the load go. It's not a natural instinct for a medevac pilot, called to extract a critically wounded soldier, to race to some remote spot and land in pitch darkness to the light of a single match. It's not a natural instinct for a scout pilot to fly at tree-top level doggedly following the tracks and signs of the enemy when he knows the enemy likely has a bead drawn on him and is ready to blast him from the sky. And it's not a natural instinct for a gunship pilot to fly into an enemy threat, putting himself between it and the persons he's responsible for protecting.

No, there's no such thing as a natural-born combat helicopter pilot. If so, the Army wouldn't have had to spend so much time training persons to become one. Those pilots had to be trained to do things that aren't natural, things counter to their instincts. In fact, they had to be over trained. In a combat situation, training had to be stronger than natural instincts. Not just equal, but stronger. In the face of danger, a combat helicopter pilot had to react immediately. There was no time to listen to his natural instincts debating the counter arguments to his training. His duty required him to do what he was trained to do, not what he was born to do.

So, if it's true that a Vietnam helicopter gunship pilot was personally aggressive and coldly calculating, it could have been partly due to his nature, but it was more a matter of training. In my case, being coldly calculating meant doing what I was trained to do despite what my nature may have wanted me to do.

By extension, a fire team leader is a gunship pilot trained for that specific role. He isn't any more important to a fire team than any other member. He's simply the representative of the team. The Army's chain-of-command requires that any operational unit needs a point of authority, someone who represents that unit, someone who can speak for it and speak to it, someone entrusted to shoulder responsibility for the unit, including taking the blame when things go wrong.

The reality of being a gunship pilot was contrary to a dime novel notion of a shoot-em-up aerial gunslinger. As a fire team leader, my essential responsibility wasn't to wreck havoc, but to protect. I was entrusted to use good judgment and expected to coolly evaluate, decide, and act. My fear was seldom of the enemy, but more the fear of failing to fulfill my responsibility. I didn't take a life needlessly, and I never failed to pull the trigger when it was necessary. In the first case, I was doing my job. In the second case, I believe I was doing my duty.

# A Ball of Fire: The Beginning of the End

The first mission that day for our fire team of two Cobra helicopter gunships had taken us to the eastern edge of the Vietnam Delta, the southernmost part of the country. At the Soc Trang airfield, we had met up with an air assault company's flight of Huey helicopters for a first-light insertion of South Vietnamese troops into a Landing Zone thirty klicks south. Our Cobras added more firepower, if needed, to the company's own pair of Huey gunships. The insertion had been uneventful, but we remained on station after the Hueys left, flying protective cover for the troops. After a while, the troops had encountered no resistance, so we were dispatched on another mission. This one took us deeper into the heart of the expansive Delta, to the Ca Mau province, where we escorted a single Huey on an ash and trash mission carrying supplies to a company of troops already in the field.　After we saw the Huey safely off, we flew to the landing strip just outside the town of Ca Mau to refuel. Afterwards, we parked beside the runway, shut down the aircraft, and while awaiting our next mission, chowed down on the C-Rations we carried behind the back seats of the two-place tandem Cobras.

The next mission came in the afternoon when we were called to the south coast to provide air cover for a Navy Riverine Force patrol. We flew to the rendezvous point and watched over the three boats as they approached from the sea, entered the mouth of a small river, and slowly slipped along a route of winding waterways until, an hour later, they made their way back to the open sea. From there, we flew to Rach Gia, near the southwest edge of the Delta—and of Vietnam—where we hot fueled quickly before our next assignment, escorting a Medevac extraction near Long Xuyen. When that mission was completed, it was late afternoon and I pointed our fire team toward our home base, Can Tho Army Airfield, fifty klicks away. We still carried the full load of armament with which we had started the day.

Typically, I led our fire team from place to place at fifteen hundred feet, but as the number of days remaining for my Vietnam tour grew fewer, my chosen altitude had crept up to two

thousand feet, closer to the upper limit for effective small arms
fire, adding more distance between us and some reckless Viet
Cong who might be tempted to take a shot at a pair of cruising
Cobras. I was only twenty-seven days from completing my
yearlong tour.

When we were within radio range, I contacted my
company's Operations. "Devil Ops, Satan One-Three."

In a moment, I heard a voice. "One-Three, Devil Ops."

I clicked the mike switch again. "Delta Ops, One-Three is
inbound with a team of two. ETA one-five. Full armament. We'll
only need to top off with fuel."

"One-Three, say current fuel status."

"Seven-five minutes to bingo."

"Roger, One-Three. Standby"

Standby? What was there to standby for? It was a simple
report that we'd soon be home. It would be close to sunset by the
time we got back to Can Tho. I wanted to have a decent meal at
the mess hall before it closed, and then relax at the Officers'
Club, after which I would go back to my compartment in the
platoon hootch and scratch off this date on my wall calendar,
marking one more day closer to my return to the States.

I heard the radio again in the headphones of my helmet.
"Satan One-Three, Delta Ops." I recognized the voice of the
captain who headed Operations. I answered, "One-Three."

"One-Three, I need you to divert. There's an outpost that's
requested an aerial surveillance. Ready for the coordinates?"

I pulled the grease pencil from the sleeve pocket of my
Nomex flight shirt. "Go," I said.

As the captain called them out, I wrote the map coordinates,
identifying the location of the outpost, on the Cobra's Plexiglass
canopy, jotting down also the call sign and contact frequency for
the outpost. I read back what I had written and the captain
acknowledged.

I switched the transmit switch to the Cobra's VHF radio and
keyed the mike to talk with my wingman. "Did you get that?"

"Yeah," he said, "I got it." He sounded like he needed a beer
as much as I did.

I keyed the intercom before handing the Cobra to my copilot/gunner in the front seat. "You've got the aircraft," I said. "Turn to two-eight-zero."

I felt a wiggle on the controls and heard the copilot's voice on the intercom. "I've got it," he said as he began a turn to take up the heading I'd given him. I looked back and saw the wing ship following.

From a few key digits of the coordinates I had been given, I knew the location of the outpost was toward the northwest, but I had to consult my map to determine its location more precisely. Using the full coordinates, I found it. We were being sent to a place twenty klicks north of Chau Doc and near, very near, the Cambodian border. Thirty klicks from where we were, it would take ten minutes at our typical cruise speed to get there. I had time for a smoke while the copilot flew the aircraft.

A few minutes later, I stubbed out the cigarette butt and took the controls again. As we neared the location, I keyed the radio transmit switch on the cyclic's handgrip. "Tango Fox, Satan One-Three. Over."

In a moment, the squelch on the FM receiver hissed open the channel. "Satan One-Three, Tango Fox."

"Tango, I've got a light fire team of Cobras at your disposal. ETA: three. Say situation."

Tango was vague. "We're hearing noises outside the perimeter. Could you check it out?"

I collected some more information. What direction was the noise? How close? Any friendlies outside the perimeter? The answers came back: northwest, not sure, negative.

A minute later, I spotted the small compound sitting on a slender finger of land squeezed between two crooked rivers. The FM radio spoke. "One-Three, I have you in sight."

I keyed the mike. "Roger, Tango, I have your location. We'll check things out for you."

Sometimes, at remote outposts like this one, especially at night or as nightfall approached, active imaginations could magnify noises so that a loose water buffalo might sound like a regiment of Viet Cong. A flight of Cobras overhead could be reassuring, or if there actually were Viet Cong in the area, the appearance of a pair of Cobras, bristling weapons, could persuade them to alter their intent on the outpost.

I had the wing ship stay up as high cover while I dropped down to treetop level to scout the thicket of dense growth between the compound and the rivers. Starting close to the compound, I made circles around the area northwest of it, gradually enlarging them, looking for anything that didn't belong there.

I didn't see anything suspicious until the fourth circle when I caught a glint from something within the growth of trees. I didn't know what it was, but the glimpse was worthy enough to take further actions, the first of which was for me to get farther away from where I had seen the possible threat.

I climbed back to two thousand feet and the wing ship joined up with me again. I clicked the mike. "Tango, I saw something, not sure what, a half klick to your northwest, near the edge of the river. Confirm there are no friendlies out there."

"Confirm that, One-Three, negative friendlies outside the compound. And be advised we've got a free fire zone for the entire perimeter as far as the river."

I didn't know if there was anything, or anybody, down there, but I decided I'd put in a few rockets and see if anybody might possibly rise to the bait and shoot back. It was a tactic called recon-by-fire, always somewhat of a gamble, but the odds were usually on our side. A Cobra could nearly always outgun small arms ground fire and that was mostly all we encountered in the Delta.

"Okay, Tango, it may be nothing, but I'll put in a strike. To be on the safe side, tell your folks to keep their heads down."

"Roger, One-Three. Will do."

The advice for persons in the compound to keep their heads down was cautionary, but needful. Sometimes a rocket took a mind of its own. Once out of the tubes, a tail fin might not spring into position, skewing the aerodynamics of the rocket and sending it off course. Other mishaps could cause a renegade rocket to stray from its intended path. In any case, the advice would likely go unheeded; the entertainment of a Cobra shooting rockets was usually too enticing for spectators to keep their heads down.

The location of the compound presented a problem. It sat on a narrow appendix shaped piece of land bounded on three sides by two rivers, on the north and east by a sharp bend of the Bassac River and on the west by the smaller Binh Di River that branched from the Bassac a short distance upstream from the bend. The particular problem was that the courses of these ravines of muddy water marked an international boundary. The political geography was such that the few dozen acres of appendix was national territory belonging to the Republic of Vietnam, and just on the other sides of the rivers was another nation, Cambodia. Because the rivers marked the boundary of another sovereign nation on the other sides, we were forbidden to cross them. Not only were we prohibited from flying over those rivers, we couldn't allow our ordnance to cross them.

Taking the political boundary into consideration, I analyzed how to set up the rocket run. I visualized the appendix as a narrow horseshoe within which the compound sat. On three sides of the compound, a thin, cleared perimeter separated it from the wider, dense tangle of trees that grew along the banks of the rivers. On the fourth side, toward the open end of the horseshoe, lay open rice paddies. I didn't want to fly directly over the compound inbound on the run; the loud swoosh of rockets overhead would likely further unnerve the already antsy friendlies down there. More importantly, rockets, rather than streaking out of a tube toward a target, sometimes simply fell out of the tube, landing on whatever or whoever happened to be below. Neither did I want to make the run toward the compound; an errant rocket might run long and impact there. Plus, there was the political boundary to contend with. To avoid flying over the rivers and to keep our ordnance on the Vietnamese side of them, I decided to initiate our target runs from the open end of the horseshoe, squeeze our Cobras between the south side of the compound and the river on that side, make a hard right turn to swing around the compound in a half circle, and then angle toward the target, a convoluted pattern that would allow us to shoot toward the open end of the horseshoe and with the larger expanse of Vietnamese territory downrange.

A problem with that plan was that, because of the tight maneuvering to accommodate the slim confines around the sides of the compound, I would have only a few seconds to line up on the target before firing the rockets and too little time to have the gunner lay down suppressive fire from the turret's minigun. But, given the restrictions, I didn't see a better way to get at the target.

I transmitted to the wing ship. "Let's come in from the east, stay left of the compound, turn one-eighty, and shoot east. Break will be to the right. Let's be careful not to cross the river and not let anything impact on the other side of it."

A double click on the radio from the wingman indicated he'd heard me.

I flew to the open end of the horseshoe, made a reverse-course turn while dropping down to fifteen hundred feet, and flew back toward the compound, hugging the Vietnam side of the river. Just past the compound, I made a hard right turn while nosing up to bleed off airspeed, trading it for altitude, and allowed the Cobra to climb to twenty-five hundred feet. At the peak of the climb, I added more right pedal and the Cobra's nose spun in that direction. I pushed the cyclic forward and the gunship's nose came down, pointing toward the cluster of trees where I'd seen the glint. I looked through the rocket sight atop the instrument panel and eased up the cyclic to establish a straight dive line toward the target. I added slight pressure on a pedal to better streamline the aircraft and improve the rockets' tracks when they shot out of the pods underneath the gunship's wing stubs.

The Cobra was quickly picking up speed in the dive and I had only a moment to tweak the aim before I punched the button, sending a pair of rockets racing from the tubes. I watched the rockets briefly as they sped toward the target; then broke right and began climbing. I turned my head to follow the rockets and saw where they hit. I radioed the wing ship. "I'm long, about thirty feet." My wingman hadn't seen the glint in the trees and could only judge the location of the target from where my rockets had hit.

He was already in position when I had made my break. Still climbing, I banked hard right, racing to get in close behind him and be in position for another run when he made his break. I saw his rockets impact, the first pair closer to where I intended mine. His second pair was even closer. There was no return fire.

As the wingman made his break, I nosed into a second run. I was coming in from the same direction as our previous run, not usually a preferred practice, but given the geography, there wasn't another reasonable choice.

I had the target in the rocket sight. I inched the Cobra's nose down to improve the sight picture, my thumb on the button that fired the rockets. That's when a flash erupted from the ground and a ball of fire came rushing up toward me, appearing to swell larger as it grew closer. This wasn't small arms fire; it was something big, something coming my way fast, and I had nowhere to go.

## Life Before Slipping the Surly Bonds

On one sun filled day when I was three years old, I was standing in the back seat of my folks' two-door Ford, my dad and mom in the front. We were at an airfield and I was gaping in wonder at the airplanes, most of them sitting with their tails on the ground, when a man walked up to the open window where Dad sat behind the wheel. I didn't pay much attention to the man until I heard him say, "Well, then, how about the boy? Would he like to go up in an airplane?"

When I dove headfirst for the open window so I could go with the man who was offering me a ride in an airplane, Dad was caught by surprise, but Mom was quicker; she managed to grab one of my legs. She hung on to it as I squirmed to get loose. "No," she said, "I don't think he would want to do that." The man tipped his hat and walked away. It would be a long time before I got another chance to fly.

I grew up on a small farm in Texas and airplanes often flew over it. The farm, in a rural community called Climax, lay under a pathway in the sky. Planes flying from the east toward Love

Field in Dallas, forty miles away, followed a navigational radio beam that led them directly over the farm.

I was a farm boy and I tended the livestock, milked the cows, slopped the hogs, fed the chickens, and worked in the fields. The farm grew hay and corn but cotton was the cash crop. In the early summer, I hoed the rows of cotton plants, and whenever I heard a plane coming, I stopped to lean on the hoe handle and watch the plane pass over, gliding across the sky, its bright metal sparkling in the sun. In the late summer and fall, I picked the cotton, and when I heard a plane, I took a moment from stooping over the bolls to stand and watch it pass lazily over me. I wiped the sweat from my face on a shirtsleeve, imagining how much cooler it must be up there. I stretched my aching back, imagining how soft the seats must be. I felt the calluses on my hands and imagined how smooth the controls must be in the pilot's hands.

When I was in the ninth grade, I found a book in the school library, *Eight Hours to Solo.* It was about a young man, not many years older than me, who was learning to fly a yellow airplane, a tail dragger. I read the book and studied the pictures over and over. Sitting in a yellow vinyl chair in the kitchen, the book open on the table beside me, I flew the airplane in my imagination. Just as the book described it, I climbed into the cockpit, fastened the safety belt around me, set the throttle, switched the magnetos from off, and yelled "contact" before the prop was turned through. I taxied to the runway, revved the engine, and started my takeoff run. I gained speed, eased the stick forward to lift the tail wheel off the ground, gained more speed, and then pulled back on the stick. The plane lifted off the runway, and sitting in the kitchen chair, I could almost hear the wind rushing over the wings and feel the breeze in the cockpit.

By the next year, though, flying seemed too distant a prospect for a farm boy like me, yet I didn't want to be a farmer. I wanted a more glamorous life, one like that of a rodeo bronc rider. However, the mumps steered me in a different direction.

When I got the mumps in the tenth grade, my dad learned that a possible side effect for someone my age was sterility, and because any activity was believed to increase that risk, he ordered me to stay strictly in bed. I was the only one who could continue the family name.

For two weeks, I wasn't allowed to do anything except listen to the radio, and that's what I did, day and night. By the end of that time, I had determined there was a life even more glamorous than a rodeo bronc rider's. I decided I wanted to be a radio disk jockey. Besides, between those two choices, I figured a disk jockey was likely to incur a lesser number of broken bones.

Determined to become a disk jockey, I learned everything I could about radio, and when I earned enough money during the summer before my senior year in high school, I spent most of it for a correspondence course that prepared me to pass the series of tests for an FCC first-class radiotelephone license, which I believed would give me an advantage for being hired to work at a radio station.

My parents had always expected me to go to college, which I wanted to do, and to have a traditional, respectable career, for which I had less desire. Considering their expectations for me, instead of telling them I wanted to be disk jockey, I announced that I wanted to go to college and study electrical engineering. It wasn't a lie; I was also interested in the technical side of broadcasting, though privately I felt a degree in electrical engineering would enhance my job opportunities in radio and boost my prospects for becoming a disk jockey. With that thought in mind, I applied to Texas Tech College in Lubbock, three hundred miles away, to pursue a degree in electrical engineering. Meanwhile, the desire to fly lay dormant.

I doubt there were many freshman students less prepared for a college like Texas Tech than I was. Even though I had made good grades in high school and graduated near the top of my class of thirty-six students, I was out of my class at Tech. I ended the first semester with a grade point average that put me on academic probation. Since I didn't want to get kicked out of college, I decided to boost my grades by taking easier courses. I looked through the college catalog and found a major related to radio: Radio and Television Speech, which sounded more aligned with my desire to be a disk jockey. Officially declaring that as my new major, I was allowed to enroll in courses leading to that degree.

The ploy worked. When the second semester ended, I was no longer on academic probation. Instead, I was on the dean's list for academic achievement. I had, at least for that semester, avoided being booted from Texas Tech, and as a corollary, I could retain a student deferment, a safeguard against being drafted into the military.

I used that tactic for the remainder of my college career at Texas Tech. For the fall semester, I declared my major as electrical engineering, took courses consistent with that major, and watched dismally as my grades plummeted. Then, in the spring, I changed my major to Radio and Television Speech, lounged through the classes, and exulted as my grades soared.

The spring of my freshman year, as part of my new degree plan, I became an announcer for the college radio station. Then, shortly after beginning my sophomore year, I landed a paying job with a commercial radio station in Lubbock, the most popular one among college students. My first-class radiotelephone license proved to be an advantage in getting hired because the station was required by the FCC to have a "first phone" license holder present at all times to log the transmitter meter readings and adjust the equipment if necessary. But my job was mostly on-air work, including disk jockeying.

I had reached my goal of becoming a disk jockey, and to my delight, I discovered that a disk jockey got to meet a lot of girls. In fact, it helped me meet the girl I eventually married. And this was in spite of the fact that she held a generally low opinion of disk jockeys, me being the closest example she knew. I suppose her eventual decision to marry me could have been influenced by the example of her grandmother, the one who married a fiddle player. More likely, though, it was because that decision came later, when I was no longer a disk jockey. By then, I had set my sights on becoming an Army helicopter pilot; surely there was nothing more glamorous than that. But that was after the Navy had its shot at me.

## The Navy Had the First Shot at Me

After almost four years at Texas Tech, I had accumulated enough hours for a senior ring, but I had fluctuated between majors so often that I was still at least a year short of a degree of any kind. Toward the end of the spring semester of that fourth year, a Naval Aviation recruiter came to campus and I happened to meet him. When he discovered I worked at a radio station, he asked if I would place some announcements on the air promoting his recruiting effort and I agreed. I did so purely because of my responsibility as a professional broadcaster and the obligation I had to serve the public's interest—and for no other reason. After all, there were laws forbidding payola, and his offer to take me for a ride in an airplane had no influence whatsoever.

The day after the announcements aired, I met the recruiter at the Lubbock airport where he had parked the Navy T-34 trainer he had flown to the Texas High Plains for the recruiting trip. After he explained to me some of the airplane's different parts, he helped me strap on a parachute and showed me where to step as I climbed into the back seat of the tandem airplane.

When he finished explaining some of the controls and instruments in the cockpit, he asked me if I had any questions. I had lots of questions, but I didn't ask a one; I was eager to go. I felt the same way I did when I was a tot in the back seat of my folks' car, squirming to get a chance to fly in an airplane.

The recruiter left open the canopy's sliding covers, climbed into the front seat, and started the engine. He taxied to the runway and in the earphones, I heard the radio conversations with the tower. I could hardly believe it; I was in a real airplane, behind a real pilot who was talking to a real airport control tower.

We took off, climbing above the long stretched plains of West Texas. I tried to look everywhere at once: ahead where we were going, behind where we had been, the cars on the highway below, the clouds above, the buzzard circling a mile away, the instruments in the cockpit, the ailerons on the wings as they moved gently up and down, and the wings ever so slowly rising and falling as the pilot leisurely S-turned above a dusty road that stretched beyond the horizon.

After a while, the recruiter asked if I wanted to fly the airplane. Following his directions, I positioned my feet on the pedals and grasped the control stick. "You have it," he said. And I did have it. I had my cowboy boots pressed on the pedals as firmly as if they were in the stirrups of a saddle aboard a snorting bronco. My hand choked the control stick like I had a live rattlesnake by the neck. I didn't know what to expect. Maybe the airplane would try to fly out from under me, or it might all of a sudden try to flip upside down. I held on, waiting for the slightest quiver from the straight and level path it was flying.

The airplane flew along serenely, just where it was pointed. I watched the altimeter; it didn't budge. After a while, I began to relax. A little while longer, I still had my hands lightly on the controls and the airplane held its straight and level course even though I hadn't moved anything.

The recruiter said, "Now, turn all the way back around and we'll head back to the airport."

Although I wasn't ready to go back, here was a chance to really fly the plane myself, I mean, really move something. I had watched the control stick when the pilot was weaving along the road and I thought I knew how to turn the airplane. I pushed the control stick to the left and the airplane banked in that direction. And as it banked, it began to turn.

The recruiter spoke to me. "Push the left rudder pedal a little."

I did that and I felt the tail line up. I thought, this is easy.

But the airplane kept banking further over, and then the nose fell, and we began to lose altitude.

The recruiter spoke calmly, "Just ease back on the stick and push it a little bit to the right."

I did that and the airplane straightened up. It had lost some altitude, but I had it turned around in the opposite direction. I felt like a regular Sky King.

As we flew back toward the airport, above the hot, dry fields below, I held the controls, relaxing in the cushioned seat, feeling the cool breeze through the open canopy, listening to the wind rushing over the wings. At one point, I looked down and thought I saw a young boy, leaning on something that could have been a hoe, looking up at me.

That flight stirred anew my desire to fly, and it suggested to me a possible avenue to achieve that desire sooner than I had imagined. I had thought a college degree was necessary before becoming a military pilot, but I learned from the recruiter that the Navy had an aviation cadet program that required only two years of college. When I told him I was interested in that, he arranged for me to take a flight physical as a prelude to the possibility of flying with the Navy.

A couple of weeks later, on a weekend, the Navy flew me on a commercial flight to the Dallas Naval Air Station for a flight physical, a series of tests to determine my physical fitness for the Navy's program. At the end of the all-day testing, I was informed that one of my teeth had a cavity and the Navy would only consider me for its aviation cadet program after I had the cavity filled. I went back to Lubbock to think it over.

## The Conspiracy that Got Me Into the Army

The day after returning to Lubbock from my flight physical with the Navy, one of my apartment roommates asked me to drive him downtown on an errand.

After I parked and he had left, I noticed a sign for an Army recruiting office down the block. I thought I would drop in there, mostly to kill time, yet curious about what the Army might have to offer in the way of flying.

When I entered the small office, a sergeant— sitting at a desk, his feet up, reading a newspaper and sipping coffee— glanced at me and nodded; I nodded back.

The posters on the walls attracted my attention and I moved slowly from one to another, looking at them. All the time, I felt the sergeant's eyes on me. Eventually, my perusal of the posters brought me to him. On the wall behind his desk was a poster picturing a helicopter and, standing beside it, a young man in a flight suit. I craned my neck over the top of the sergeant's head to get a better look at this poster. He turned and studied the poster with me as if we were two art connoisseurs admiring a masterpiece.

From over his shoulder, the sergeant said, "You like helicopters?"

I really hadn't thought much about them before, but instantly I decided that, yes, I did. "Yep," I said, still studying the poster.

He turned back around and appraised me. "Do you think you'd like to work on them?"

"I was thinking more about flying," I said.

"Why, sure," he said, "there's no better place than the Army if you want to fly helicopters."

He pointed to the chair next to the desk. "Have a seat."

I sat down.

"I'm Sergeant Dinger," he said. "What's your name?"

I told him my name.

He smiled. "Want some coffee?"

"No, thanks," I said. "I don't have much time."

He glanced at the ring on my hand. "I'll bet you go to Tech."

"That's right," I acknowledged.

"And you're about to graduate. Right?"

"Well, actually," I said, "I don't know if I'm going to stay in school."

Sergeant Dinger seemed concerned about that, in an almost fatherly way. "If you're not going to stay in school, what are you going to do?"

"I don't know. I've been thinking that I might join some branch of the military—if I could fly. I've been talking to the Navy about doing that."

"The Navy?" he said. I thought I detected a bit of scorn in his tone.

"Yeah," I said. "They gave me a flight physical and told me to come back and see them after I had a cavity filled."

Sergeant Dinger rolled his eyes. "That's the Navy for you. Picky, picky, picky."

"But," I said, "I've been thinking. Maybe I should stay in school, finish a degree, and fly with the Air Force."

Sergeant Dinger eyed me, squinting like a poker player studying his hand. "Sure, I suppose you could do that."

He glanced at my senior ring again. "How long have you been in college?"

"Four years," I said.

Sergeant Dinger rubbed his chin. He had a concerned look. "Four years, huh? And during all that time you've had a draft deferment?"

"Yeah," I said apprehensively. "Why?"

"Oh, it's probably nothing to worry about," he said. He sipped his coffee, looking at me from a corner of his eye.

"What would I have to worry about?" I said, shifting in the chair.

Sergeant Dinger seemed reluctant to even bring it up. "Well, it's just that some draft boards don't extend a college deferment more than four years."

"And so?" I said, feeling a little nervous.

"And so," he said, "after four years, a draft board sometimes just ups and drafts a young man like you, and with hardly any notice at all."

"You mean, it could be that I'm about to be drafted?" I said. Suddenly, this conversation had become serious.

"Oh, it's probably nothing to be—too—concerned about," said Sergeant Dinger.

"What would happen if I got drafted?" I said. "Is there a chance I could get to fly?"

"Well, I'll level with you," Sergeant Dinger said with a deep sigh, as if he regretted what he was about to tell me. "If you got drafted, you wouldn't have a lot of choices."

He sipped his coffee as I mulled that over, and then added, "On the other hand, if you were to voluntarily enlist in the Army, you could control the shots. You could choose what you wanted to do, and the Army would agree to that as a part of your enlistment."

He nodded his head back toward the poster behind him, the one I was facing while sitting in the chair. "For example, say you wanted to fly helicopters, you could enlist specifically on the condition that you'd go to flight school."

I was cautiously interested. "But wouldn't I have to have a college degree to get into flight school?"

Sergeant Dinger had the answer. "Not with the Army, you don't."

He winked as if he had a little something he wanted to share with me, but first he glanced over his shoulder, obviously to make sure no one might be eavesdropping, before he leaned across the desk and whispered, "The Army has this thing called the Warrant Officer Rotary Wing Aviator Course."

I looked around to confirm there was no one in the whole place other than the two of us. "What's that?" I said, whispering also.

"It's something a lot of people don't know about," said Sergeant Dinger. Then he added, as if passing along a secret password, "It's called WORWAC."

I nodded, confirming that I grasped the importance of this vital bit of information.

He said, "With that, you could learn to fly—and without a college degree."

Sergeant Dinger continued. "Of course, the Army likes it better if you have some college. By the way, how much college did you say you have?"

"Four years," I reminded him.

Sergeant Dinger leaned over the desk even farther. He smiled knowingly as if he was revealing to me a secret known only to a forty-third-degree Mason. "That would probably get you in for sure."

I found myself leaning over the desk also. We were almost head-to-head in this collusion. I studied the coffee stains on the desk, thinking over this information, undoubtedly classified, that Sergeant Dinger had imparted to me. I wanted to confirm something. "This WORWAC you mentioned has something to do with 'rotary wing'? Does that mean helicopters?"

"Exactly," he said, arching an eyebrow as if I had just discovered a key link in this little known conspiracy.

I hadn't really thought about flying helicopters before I had walked into this office a few minutes before. I looked at the poster again. The clear-eyed, wavy haired pilot had a strong-jawed, determined look.

"How could I get into this?" I said.

Sergeant Dinger leaned back in his chair. I had a momentary impression of him holding a bended rod, reeling in a fish he had just hooked. He said, "Oh, I might could arrange it for you." He took a sip from his coffee cup. "Of course, there are some things you would have to do."

"Like what?" I said.

He waived his hand in the air as if dismissing these trifling matters. "Well, you would need to enlist in the Army, of course, but ...," he said, raising a finger in the air for emphasis "... specifically for flight school. You'd have to pass some tests, and as I mentioned, you'd need to complete basic training."

Before I had time to think much about that, he thumbed toward the poster behind him. "And then you'd be in flight school, flying helicopters."

Sergeant Dinger watched me closely as I stared at the poster behind the desk. He said, "Now, if I could get you a slot for flight school—and I'm not promising I can because those are pretty hard to get, you know—but if I could, you would take it, wouldn't you?"

I was still staring at the poster. "Sure," I said.

He pulled out a pad of paper and a pen. "Spell your name for me," he said. I did that.

"What's your phone number?" he said, and I gave him the number.

"Okay, I'll tell you what I'll do," said Sergeant Dinger. "I'll see when the next openings for flight school are."

He stood up and I stood up with him. He held out his hand and I shook it. It reminded me of shaking hands with the car salesman after we had settled on a deal for my new Mustang.

I walked out of the recruiting office to my car. My roommate was standing beside the Mustang. "Where have you been?" he said.

"Talking to a guy from the Army."

"Why?" he asked.

"Just curious," I said.

The summer was approaching. I had spent four years at Texas Tech, more often chasing a good time rather than pursuing a degree. I still wanted a degree, but the notion of flying was enticing. I considered my options.

During my first two years at Texas Tech, I had taken Air Force ROTC, for which I had mediocre enthusiasm, yet I concluded the Air Force was the most logical choice of services for someone who wanted to fly. Since I knew I would need a degree to fly with the Air Force, I mapped out a plan. I would stay in college, take my chances with the draft, finish a degree in electrical engineering, join the Air Force, and become a jet jockey. There was an outside chance I could complete a degree in one more year, if I went to school that summer taking a maximum load of courses, and if I took a maximum load for the following fall and spring semesters—and if I passed all the courses. I would have to do that while working nearly full time and it would curtail my social life, but it was possible.

The next day, the day before registration for the first summer session at Texas Tech, the phone rang early that morning. Still groggy from working at the station until midnight and hanging out with friends for several hours after that, I reached for the phone. "Hello."

The caller identified himself as Sergeant Dinger. He said, "Congratulations!"

Sergeant Dinger, I thought, who's that? Then I remembered: oh yeah, the Army recruiter.

"Congratulations for what?" I yawned.

"You've got a slot for a flight school," said Sergeant Dinger. "I knew how much you wanted it, so I pulled some strings and got you into a class at the earliest date possible."

"Oh?" I said, rubbing my eyes.

Sergeant Dinger said, "Of course, you'll have to enlist immediately."

Now I was awake. "You mean enlist in the Army?"

"Of course," he said. "The flight school begins in August and you'll need to finish basic training before that. It's a tight schedule. Come on down to the office and I'll help you complete the paper work to get everything rolling."

I said, "Well, you see, I'm thinking I should go back to school and finish a degree."

There was a long silence before Sergeant Dinger spoke again. He sounded wounded. "Do you know how much trouble I went to so I could get you into flight school?" I was about to speak, but before I could, he said, "I thought we had a deal. We shook on it." I thought back. That was true; we had.

I went back to the recruiting office that afternoon. I learned that I would need to take some tests to determine my aptitude for flying and I would need to take a physical test. The tests would be given in Amarillo the next day. After the Army evaluated the tests, and if I passed them, I would be inducted into the Army where I would complete basic training, a stepping-stone toward the Warrant Officer Rotary Wing Aviator Course. I signed some papers and Sergeant Dinger shook hands with me again. He was smiling; I tried to.

For the tests, I had to be in Amarillo at 7 o'clock the next morning. Sergeant Dinger, assuming I would spend the night in Amarillo, had already arranged a room at a hotel within walking distance of the Army induction center in downtown Amarillo where the tests would be given. Since he had already gone to the trouble, I didn't tell him that I would likely have little use for the room. I would be working at the radio station until midnight and would still have to drive to Amarillo after that.

I finished my shift at the radio station and, as usual, went with a couple of friends to our favorite late-night truck stop where we hung out for several hours. After consuming a complete seven-item Mexican plate, a slice of pecan pie, four cups of coffee and three cigarettes, I was ready to travel.

Highway 87 stretched directly north from Lubbock across the flat West Texas plains to Amarillo, more than a hundred miles away. Only a few small towns, none with stoplights, lay between. After clearing the city limits of Lubbock, I kicked the Mustang up to ninety-five and pulled into Amarillo a little before seven that morning.

I would have made it sooner if I hadn't been stopped in Tulia, midway between Lubbock and Amarillo. I had already zoomed past the little town when I saw the red light in my rearview mirror nearly two miles back. I dutifully pulled over and it took the ancient cruiser, with its bubble-gum-machine-shaped red light on the roof and a long whip antenna bolted on the rear bumper, almost two minutes to arrive where I waited. When the elderly constable came to the window, I handed him my driver license. He looked at it and asked me where I was going in such an all-fired hurry. I explained I was bound for Amarillo and didn't want to be late for my Army tests. The gray haired gentleman looked up from the license, studied me a moment, gave my license back to me, and said, "Good luck, son."

At the Army induction center, I completed a battery of tests. The flight aptitude test consisted of looking at a collection of illustrations with views of the horizon from an airplane cockpit and matching each view with another one from a set of illustrations showing airplanes in different combinations of flight attitudes: climbing, diving, and turning. The physical test consisted of a medical professional asking me some questions, tapping my knee, looking at my arches, and scrutinizing private parts of my body. The physical exam included a vision and a hearing test, but no one looked at my teeth.

The testing and finger probing were finished by noon and I sped back to Lubbock, slowing as I went through Tulia.

Two days later, Sergeant Dinger called to congratulate me on passing both the flight aptitude test and the physical exam. He gave me a date, just a few days away, on which I was to return to Amarillo to be sworn in and begin my military service. On that date, once again back in Amarillo, I raised my right hand along with a couple of dozen other young men, mostly draftees, and repeated the words that bound me to the Army.

We were bussed to the airport in Amarillo where we boarded a Trans Texas Airways DC-3. The plane, after a few engine backfires and other symptoms of its age, took off and eventually delivered us to Fort Polk, Louisiana, between Shreveport and Baton Rogue. We arrived at ten o'clock that night and were bossed onto a bus that took us to the processing center within the interior of the facility. I surrendered my new blue jeans, my Gant button-down shirt, and my saddle stitched, oxblood, tasseled loafers for a set of baggy fatigues and a pair of stiff, black, lace-up boots.

## Fort Polk Purgatory

At Fort Polk, the eight weeks of basic training during July and August were like being swallowed by a fevered beast. It was hot and humid, and we were soon made to feel like excrement.

Growing up on a farm, the custom of awakening early in the morning wasn't foreign to me, but I had never learned to like it. In college, I was exposed to the more civilized concept of sleeping in late and I found that it suited me much better. The Army, however, apparently had never adopted that concept. We trainees—as we were officially designated, though more commonly called other names—were awakened before dawn, greeted by a symphony of frogs croaking in the Louisiana bayous and a chorus of drill sergeants barking in our faces. We ran two miles before breakfast and were already well into the intricacies of the oblique-right close-order drill movement before the sun troubled itself to rise and begin its daily duty of roasting us.

I discovered that when encouraging trainees, drill sergeants not only expressed themselves with great volume, yelling loudly enough to drown out Mount Vesuvius in full eruption, they also used exceedingly expressive language. Furthermore, it became apparent to me that drill sergeants weren't selected for their profession because of their charm, tact, and delicacy of expression. On the contrary, I discovered that, when ministering to the young men in their charge, drill sergeants often forgot to use kind, pleasant words. Instead, they often voiced rather harsh opinions about these young men's fitness for Army duty and more generally their overall worthiness to draw the breath of life. Perhaps they felt our shortcomings were a lack of parental influence since they often suggested that our mothers had conceived us without the benefit of matrimony. I felt it important to retain these discoveries so that I could share them some time if I ever chanced upon an innocent individual who did not have any experience with drill sergeants and who might be considering inviting one to afternoon tea at a ladies social.

Drill sergeants administered basic training, whether it was physical drills or classroom instruction, all in the same mine-blasting amplitude, and they supplemented their admonishments with inspiring invectives of loathing directed toward the recipients of their administrations. The purpose of the drills and instruction was to teach us essential soldiering skills. These essential skills included, in part and in no special order, the ability to march in perfect formation for marathon distances; pummel a combatant with a pugil stick; tear down and reassemble an M-14 rifle while blindfolded; split a bulls eye with the same said rifle using a bullet or, with a bayonet attached to the end of the rifle, filet a combatant; toss a live grenade far enough so that it didn't dismember the tosser himself; field strip a cigarette; and recognize the three most common symptoms of syphilis.

I felt that many of these skills were of no permanent value to me since I would be a warrant officer flying helicopters. Of course, I knew I had to participate in the training and satisfy the drill sergeants by demonstrating to them that I had sufficiently mastered these skills, yet I considered most of the training to be simply an inconvenience, especially since it began so early in the morning.

Apparently, another one of the essential skills of becoming a soldier was the ability to high step through automobile tires. One morning, we were marched to a field where two dozen old automobile tires lay on the ground in two rows next to each other. We were lined up at one end of the two rows and encouraged to run through the rows of tires, being careful to step into the center of each tire with our leading foot and to lift our trailing foot high enough to clear the tire we were abandoning. If someone made a misstep, there was a chance he could sprain an ankle or even break a leg. At the very least, he'd be trampled underneath the herd of high steppers behind him who were being stampeded through the tires by our pitiless taskmasters.

This was a drill with which I was familiar, having done it when I was on the high school football team. Except this time, I had to do it while wearing a steel pot rather than a football helmet, while wearing combat boots instead of football cleats, while carrying a heavy M-14 instead of an inflated ball, and while lugging a back pack weighted with essentials such as a mess kit, a first aid kit, a gas mask, a poncho, a blanket, a flashlight, spare batteries, spare underwear, spare socks, an entrenching tool, a pup tent with stakes, a five-pound bound volume of abridged Army regulations, and a half dozen melted Hershey bars.

At first, I didn't see the value of this used-tire hopscotch, but upon reflection, I realized a skill such as this could be potentially useful in a civilian occupation; for instance, if there should ever come a time when I found myself in a salvage yard doing some midnight requisitioning and encountered a junk yard dog. In that circumstance, with a slobbering, big-jawed Rottweiler at my heels, I could see the advantage of such a skill, if it so happened that my escape route was hindered by old automobile tires—ones laid out in two carefully arranged, parallel rows—and assuming the Army had not taught the dog similar skills.

I also spent some time in basic training hanging onto pine trees. Since pine trees were plentiful at Fort Polk, and drill sergeants could readily find one nearby when they needed it, the drill sergeants habitually used these evergreens as disciplinary aids. If a trainee violated some infraction, he was sentenced to shimmy up a pine tree and wrap himself around the trunk like a koala bear clinging to a eucalyptus and the trainee was required to hang there until he had sufficient time to ruminate upon his transgression.

From personal experience, I was so well acquainted with this pastime that I became somewhat of an expert at the practice. I learned two fundamental lessons about hanging around a pine tree trunk. First, it was important to choose a tree that was just the right size. It should have a trunk thin enough so that a person could wrap his arms and legs around it completely; it was too difficult to hang on a pine tree with just boot toes and fingernails. But it was also important that a person not pick a tree trunk that was too thin; a sapling would simply bend over with his weight and leave him clinging to it, his bottom dragging the ground. This was not good form.

Second, I learned that a person should not climb too high. If a trainee climbed much above eye level, the drill sergeants might overlook him. To them, a trainee hanging on a pine tree became just another unripened pinecone. It was an easy mistake for them to make since trainees all wore an olive drab uniform, which was color coordinated to blend with trees and shrubbery. If a trainee climbed too high, the drill sergeants might forget him, walk off, and leave him there. A trainee could miss meals this way. Or worse, if the drill sergeants forgot the trainee for so long that they left him up there overnight, the next morning he could be counted AWOL. Then, when the drill sergeants eventually remembered where they had left the trainee hanging, it irritated them so much, because the trainee had created more paper work for them, that they put him up a tree again. Then, if they once again forgot they had hung him on a pine tree and he turned up missing at roll call yet again—well, it was easy to see how a situation like this could compound on itself, resulting in a trainee spending quite a length of time with his face in the bark. Although it may have been only a rumor, I heard of one trainee who went more than halfway to a twenty-year retirement even though, from the second day of basic training, his feet had never touched the ground. I was told, when he was finally discovered still hanging onto the pine tree, the trunk had grown around him like he was a rusty nail.

About midway through basic training, I was called out of a training exercise and told to report to the company quarters. There, I was given directions to report to a building on the base. I wasn't told the purpose, nor did I ask. I felt it best not to ask questions of anyone in authority since it might lead to me becoming a rusty nail.

I found the building and discovered it was a medical facility. After a wait, I was handed a small bottle, told to produce a urine sample, directed to strip down to my underwear, and sent down the hall to a room. There, a medic began strapping my arm in preparation for drawing blood. He looked about my age and appeared to have no real authority, so I ventured to ask him why I was there. When I spoke, he looked as surprised as if a white lab rat had just spoken to him, one asking the purpose of running through a maze. But after his shock, he glanced at a sheet of paper on a clipboard and explained, "This says you're here for a flight physical."

"But I've already had a physical," I said. "I took one in Amarillo."

"Oh," he said, tightening the strap, "that was just an induction physical."

As we both watched my blood being sucked up into the gallon-sized syringe attached to the needle, he added, "An induction physical isn't very thorough. If you've got a pulse, you're good enough for the Army. Even if you don't have a pulse, the Army can still pass you with a waiver if rigor mortis hasn't set in. But for flight school, you need a more thorough physical."

A chill raced up my backbone. "What happens if I don't pass this flight physical?"

Having drawn enough blood to feed a litter of newborn vampire bats to maturity, he began loosening the strap on my arm. "Then you don't get to go to flight school," he said with what I deemed too much of a tone of triviality for such a firm finality.

"So, in that case," I ventured, "I'd just go back home, right?"

"Naw," he said, "since you're already in the Army, they'd want to keep you."

"Keep me? They couldn't do that. We had a deal," I said, and then added, "We shook on it."

"Oh, the Army wouldn't keep you forever," he said, "only a couple of years." He probably intended those words as a comfort, but if he had been taking my blood pressure or pulse at that moment, I would have flunked the flight physical right then.

I hardly remember all the rest of the things that various other specialists and practitioners did to me while I was there. It was a blur of dilated eyes, lights in the ears, thumpings on the knee, turnings and coughings, and standings on one leg with my eyes closed. In other words, it was very much like a highway sobriety test.

After they all completed their area of specialty, whether it was collecting different fluids or examining parts of my body of a reproductive nature, I was directed to return to the company area of my basic training unit. When I asked with some desperation if I had passed the flight physical, I was told I would learn the outcome later.

As I trotted back to the company area—no trainee walked—I considered the possibility that I might not have passed the flight physical. Instead of being a pilot, my occupation could become that of an infantry rifleman. It could be that, instead of flying over the Commies in Vietnam, I might be mud wrestling them in the rice paddies. As a consequence of that possibility, I began to take basic training a lot more seriously. Instead of gentlemanly tapping my opponent with a pugil stick, I clobbered him. And because I feared I might come to experience my entire Army career as an enlisted man, I began to pay more attention to honing my potato peeling skills.

In this suspenseful state, Fort Polk had become my military purgatory. I awaited judgment on whether or not I could ascend to flight school. It was almost two weeks later when a memo came to me stating that I had passed the flight physical, and it was with relief that I resumed my previous slacker attitude, becoming more tolerant of dirty spots on the plates when pulling dishwashing duty during KP.

Eventfully, basic training ended. We trainees were mustered onto a parade ground where we marched in review under the gaze of officers, NCOs, and other dignitaries who likely were even more eager than us to get this over. We stood at parade rest while various personages spoke. The keynote address was especially memorable to me. I remember the flags, in the absence of even the slightest breeze, hanging limply on the poles and I remember thinking I could become permanently cross eyed from watching sweat droplets drip off the end of my nose, but as for the admonishments the speaker insisted it was important that we heed, I don't remember a single one of them, even though it was obvious he had practiced very much to impart them to us.

Fort Polk and basic training, the worst the Army could throw at me—so I thought—was over. I had orders to report for primary flight training at Fort Wolters, Texas, a place that would be, surely, one of gentlemanly *bon vivant*, a genteel setting suited to cultivating the charm, character, and culture of aspiring young airmen.

# Fort Wolters: A WOC in a Hard Place

For me, one of the attractions of the Army's helicopter flight school was its location. The first several months of training was at the Army's Primary Helicopter Training Center at Fort Wolters, Texas, which was within a few-hours driving range of my home in Climax as well as Lubbock, both places where I still had connections with young ladies.

Fort Wolters, fifty miles west of Fort Worth, was spread near Mineral Wells, a small town of bustling commerce with an economy based upon hard scrabble ranching, oil royalties, and the purchasing power of persons associated with the military base. Those persons included Warrant Officer Candidates.

As a WOC, I was elevated to the pay rank of Specialist Fifth Class, a jump of several pay grades from the Private E-1 rank that I held in basic training. Even though I would be making more money, I pledged to myself that I would handle my increased earnings in no less responsible a way than I had before; that is, I would spend it all.

I pledged also to give the Army a fair return for my paycheck. Monday through Friday, I would expend a good, honest eight hours a day learning to become the world's best helicopter pilot. The evenings, however, I expected would be mine. Some of them I would share with my fellow flying lads, quaffing mugs of beer and singing jolly songs around a piano. Other evenings, I planned to venture into Mineral Wells and delight young ladies.

On the day I was told to report to Fort Wolters, I drove to Mineral Wells, which wasn't hard to find. It only required driving to Fort Worth, turning west, and continuing until I came to the town. I found Mineral Wells easily enough, but as for Fort Wolters, I almost overlooked it.

I expected that Fort Wolters—home of the soon-to-be best helicopter pilot in the world, namely me—would be a rotary wing Camelot, sitting loftily apart from a land wherein dwelt a populace of lesser ambition. In actuality, the Army base abutted the very edge of Mineral Wells and its main entrance was just down the road from a pawnshop and a laundry.

My first impression was a letdown similar to the first time I saw the Alamo in San Antonio. I had imagined this historic monument as an isolated outpost standing proudly alone, a setting appropriate for its legendary defenders' impelling desire for independence. I expected to see the walls still scarred by the canon blasts and, above the pinnacle of the mission, a tattered flag still rippling defiantly in the breeze, just as it was when Fess Parker, playing the role of coonskin capped Davy Crockett, went down swinging his long rifle, Ol' Betsy.

Instead, what remained of the fortress sat amid the bustle of downtown San Antonio, on a street crowded with stores and a hotel. The walls, though weathered with age, were intact. And over the entrance, stirring gently in a breeze that carried the smell of snow cone syrup and cotton candy from the vending carts along the sidewalk, was a tidy Texas flag identical to the ones atop any schoolyard flagpole in the state.

Yet despite that initial letdown, when I realized I was indeed looking at the famous facade of the mission I remembered from Texas history schoolbooks, the historic Alamo soon materialized before me. Its pedestrian surroundings melted away and I visualized the fortress as it was on that day in 1836, its scarred walls standing in the dawn after the final assault, and on its ramparts, a flag whipped by the March wind that carried the smell of gunpowder and spilled blood. With that visualization, even in its urban setting, I judged the Alamo a majestic shrine, a worthy symbol of bravery, honor, and sacrifice.

Likewise, Fort Wolters at first sight was so far from what I had expected that, rather than driving in, I stopped across from the entrance to reconcile what I saw. On either side of the wide entrance was a helicopter, on one side an OH-23 and on the other side a TH-55. The helicopters sat on pedestals of stone, the pedestals supporting an arch that spanned the entrance. Embedded within the arch were words that heralded "U S Army Primary Helicopter Center" and atop the arch was a large, silver replica of master Army aviator wings. After viewing the portal for a while, I judged it not just satisfactory, but inspiring.

As I drove under the arch and onto the base, I was in high spirits, expecting to commence flight training the next day, perhaps soloing before noon. I imagined how pleasant it would be to focus on flying, free from the distractions of the demeaning demeanor exhibited toward me in basic training, and which I assumed would soon become a forgotten memory, lost in the blissful environs of flight school.

Reality turned out to be different. After reporting to Fort Wolters, it was four weeks before flight training began. Those weeks were termed "preflight" and were much like an extension of basic training, filled with early morning rigors of physical training, daylong military indoctrination, and thoroughly disciplined regimens, all enforced by verbal lashings and liberal demerits. We cleaned and scrubbed our barracks, picked up trash around the base, and painted the "WOC rock." We spit polished our boots, carefully hung our tailored and starched Army fatigues in our lockers all facing the same direction and precisely spaced evenly apart, and ensured our foot lockers were kept in perfectly arranged order, each item in its prescribed place.

We moved in unison wherever we went, marching in formation, running in synchronization. In the line to the mess hall, we stood at parade rest, and to fill an open gap in front of us, came to attention, took one step precisely twelve inches long with our left foot, drew our right foot beside it, then returned to parade rest. At the mess table, we sat with our backs rigid, picked up a fork beside the tray, stabbed a morsel, placed it our mouth, and returned the fork to the precise same place beside the plate, where it rested until we were ready for another bite, which required repeating the ritual.

Our every movement, our every minute, was scrutinized by TAC officers who hovered around us like energetic horse flies, eagerly pouncing on any deviance from a prescribed procedure so they could lavish us with pushups and demerits. This intensive intimidation was intended to weed out those Warrant Officer candidates who lacked sufficient perseverance, an objective that our supervisors appeared to relish. For them, it was their recreation. As for our recreation, we plotted revenge on these horse flies that doled us misery and demerits.

We had a weekly allowance of forty-five demerits to avoid being restricted to the base during the following weekend and from suffering other repercussions. The first week, I accumulated a hundred and forty-seven, which may not have been an all-time record but probably qualified for at least an honorable mention.

At the end of those weeks of preflight, the WOCs who had persevered to that point moved from the wooden barracks near the base's entrance to "the hill" and the three-story cinder block barracks that were closer to the flight line. Along with two roommates, I was assigned a room on the topmost, third floor of a barracks that had a spectacular view of the helicopters at the main heliport less than a mile away.

After moving to the hill, we were still ridden hard by TAC officers but who were now aided by a population of upperclassmen, student pilots in classes ahead of us in training, most of whom took delight in enforcing their superiority by standing us at attention while they verbally lashed us or, as was their prerogative, having us drop and give them twenty or more pushups for such serious infractions as having a flight suit zippered two-and-a-quarter inches from the neck rather than two. Generally, though, these zealots bothered us only in the barracks area. The classrooms were safe harbors, and the flight line a refuge, from their pestering.

A typical day of flight school consisted of half a day of classroom courses and the other half of the day with a flight instructor. An instructor usually began flight training with three students, but the number he retained was often less. The Army's flight school was a continuing process of elimination, progressively culling out student pilots who failed to achieve the required standards for flying, academics, and fortitude. Some would-be pilots had already been eliminated in preflight. Once flight training began, many of these earliest eliminations were a result of student pilots who didn't gain sufficient proficiency quickly enough to solo.

We were expected to solo with no more than sixteen hours and twenty minutes of dual instruction. This amount of time may have been generously adequate for soloing an airplane but it wasn't for a helicopter. A student pilot flying airplanes didn't have to come to grips with learning how to hover the aircraft before he could solo.

## Learning How to Hover

I immediately came to realize that I had been mistaken to assume that as soon as I got to Fort Wolters the Army would give me a helicopter to fly around. The Army insisted that I must first learn how to fly one. I conceded that was a reasonable expectation, and I also acknowledged the Army's generosity in providing me with an instructor pilot to help me get started, even though I was sure it would soon discover that I didn't really need one of those since I was a natural-born pilot.

To get started toward flying my own helicopter, my IP said that one of the first things I had to learn to do was how to hover. We flew out to a stage field in an OH-13 helicopter, one of the bubble domed, vintage helicopters from the Korean War that our class had been assigned for training. As the helicopter sat there running, my IP said he would explain to me how to hover and then would show me how to do it.

He explained that to coax a helicopter to hover, the aircraft had all these different controls that I was supposed to move around. For instance, there was a long stick jutting up from the floor of the helicopter, right in front of me, that the instructor said I was supposed to use to encourage the helicopter to go forward, to back up, and even to go sideways. He called that stick a "cyclic." I was supposed to hold on to it with my right hand. Then there was another control that I was to hold on to with my left hand. He said this control, which looked to me like a pump handle, was called a "collective", and I was supposed to move it up or down when I wanted to convince the helicopter to go in those directions.

In addition, my IP showed me that on the end of the collective was another control. This control was a throttle, a thing used to give the engine more or less gas. Its function was similar to an automobile's gas pedal, except that with a helicopter, I didn't use my foot to control the throttle; I had to use my hand. And I didn't push on the throttle; I had to twist it. He explained that I was supposed to twist the throttle in one direction to give the engine more gas and twist it in another direction to give it less. The twist grip throttle on the helicopter operated somewhat like the one on a motorcycle, except I discovered I was supposed to twist the throttle on the helicopter in opposite directions from ones on a motorcycle to give it more or less gas, and I had to use a different hand for the throttle on a helicopter than the hand I was accustomed to using with a motorcycle's throttle. So, essentially, whatever habits I had already formed for feeding gas to an engine when I was driving a car or riding a motorcycle were pretty much useless for the purpose of flying a helicopter.

My IP informed me that the presence of a throttle among the helicopter's controls wasn't just an afterthought. On the contrary, he said that it was an essential device because the throttle determined how fast the helicopter's rotor turned, clarifying for me that a rotor was that big, spinning thing on top that kept the helicopter in the air.

My IP told me that when hovering, as well as in flight, a helicopter's rotor had to be kept turning at a fairly constant speed—within a narrow range of rpms. If the rotor was allowed to spin too slowly, the rotor blades could fold up like an umbrella whose underside got turned up in a stiff wind, and in that case, the helicopter would come crashing down. On the other hand, if the rotor was allowed to spin too fast, the rotor blades could become so independently minded that they would decide to go flying off on their own, leaving the majority of the helicopter behind, and consequently the forsaken helicopter would, as in the case of its rotor spinning too slowly, likewise come crashing down.

There were some other controls in the helicopter to which he drew my attention. When sitting in the helicopter, out in front of me, at the end of my legs, were these two things to put my feet on. I thought perhaps the Army had provided these things as convenient foot rests, but my instructor informed me that they had another purpose. They were called "anti-torque pedals" and I was supposed to push one or the other of these pedals with one foot or the other when I wanted to suggest to the helicopter, when it was hovering, that it turn its nose to the left or to the right.

I learned that all the controls were used to "suggest" to the helicopter what I wanted it to do. I discovered that a helicopter is exceedingly temperamental and if I attempted to demand that it do something—for instance, by yanking on one of its controls—the helicopter would just get all persnickety and go storming off in some direction beyond any normal limits of reason. Instead, I had to suggest what I wanted it to do with gentle, persuasive touches on the controls.

My IP explained all these controls to me and asked me if I had understood all of them. The way he had explained the controls individually, I thought I had the grasp of how they worked. So, he brought the helicopter up to a hover over a spot on the ground and showed me how to do it. The helicopter stayed right there on that spot, pointing straight ahead, and remained at exactly the same altitude a few feet off the ground. Then he said, "Okay, now you do it."

I took the controls in hand—and feet—and the helicopter hovered right there on that spot as smooth as could be—for about two seconds. And that's when I learned that in order to hover a helicopter with all these different controls—cyclic, collective, throttle, and pedals—I couldn't just move them around one at a time at my convenience. No, I had to move them all around at the same time. That was because, when I changed one control, it affected the helicopter in so many ways that I had to change all the others too.

For example, I was hovering over that spot, but the helicopter started sinking toward the ground, so to suggest to the helicopter that it return to its former height, I pulled up on the collective. But when I did that, the engine needed more power, so at the same time I was pulling up on the collective, I needed to twist the throttle to give the engine more gas. And when I gave the engine more gas, the rotor on top of the helicopter turned harder, which meant the nose of the helicopter tried to turn in the opposite direction, so then I needed to push on one of the pedals at the end of one my legs to tell the helicopter that I wanted it to keep pointing where it was before I told it I wanted it to go higher. Then the helicopter decided that, even though I had asked only that it go up a little higher, it would move over to a different place. So, when the helicopter began drifting over to that other place, I yanked on the cyclic to remind the helicopter that I wanted it to stay where it was, but as I have suggested before, a helicopter doesn't like for its controls to be yanked. When I yanked on its cyclic, the helicopter became so agitated that it flew off the handle (that's as a manner of speaking and not to be confused with the collective, which is a different kind of handle) and the helicopter went skittering off way over to some other place where I didn't intend for it to go at all. Then, to compound the problem, when the helicopter moved from the spot where it was, it lost the little cushion of air it had under it and began to sink toward the ground again. So, I pulled up some more on the collective, which required me to twist the throttle—nope, not that way, the other way—and then push on one of the pedals to keep the nose pointed where I wanted it and, whoops, there it went off somewhere else. Then, it started sinking toward the ground again and I yanked up on the collective. And because I yanked its collective, then the helicopter was in a perfect snit. It jumped way up higher than I ever wanted it to be—plus I discovered that somehow the helicopter had swapped ends. Its nose was back where its tail once was, and the tail was around where I had intended the nose to be.

I tried to get the ends back around in their right places by pushing on a pedal, the right pedal. But when I pushed on that pedal, I needed to give the engine less gas, which meant I had to twist the throttle—whoops, not that way—and then because I had twisted the throttle the wrong way, the helicopter misunderstood my intention and went up even higher yet, so I pushed down on the collective to ask the helicopter to consider descending a little bit, but when I did that, the rotor started spinning too fast and I had to twist off some gas to the engine. And when I did that, there was less torque on the rotor, which caused to the nose to swing around in the other direction, so I stepped on a pedal to try to fix that. Then I noticed the helicopter was dropping toward the ground far faster than was healthy, so I pulled up on the collective again, and the helicopter started back up, but because I forgot to twist in some more gas with the throttle, then the rotor blades were beginning to spin too slowly and the nose was turning back the other way, so I kicked a pedal to fix that—and the helicopter swapped ends again.

I pushed, pulled, twisted and wiggled all the controls, and by holding my tongue just right, I eventually managed to get the ends back around in the right order. So, there I was, the helicopter pointed in the general direction I wanted it to point, hovering somewhere near the altitude I wanted, and its rotor spinning at a reasonable speed. But then, I looked around and discovered I'd been so occupied with trying to prevent these individual and cumulative disasters that the helicopter had drifted off somewhere so far off that I didn't know where I was anymore.

In short, it took more than just that one time—or even several times—of trying it, but eventually I did learn to hover a helicopter. The only person more surprised by that accomplishment than me was my IP.

## Solo and So Long, Fort Wolters

It hadn't taken more than my first flight in a helicopter for me to relinquish the notion that I was a natural-born pilot. And even though I had learned to hover a helicopter, I was acutely aware of all the other skills for which I had to demonstrate competency before I was deemed worthy to solo.

When I first began my flight training, I had worried that my instructor might not allow me to solo; then as I became better acquainted with the difficulties I had flying a helicopter, I became worried that he would. And that day did come. We landed at a stage field beyond the main heliport and the instructor got out of the helicopter, threw in some sandbags to partially compensate for the absence of his weight, and told me to take the helicopter around the stage field's traffic pattern three times and make a takeoff and landing with each lap, reminding me that it was the expectation that the number of takeoffs and the number of landings equal each other.

He assigned me the task; then walked away, leaving me alone in the helicopter. I waited awhile to see if he might change his mind and come back, but when he didn't, I undertook to perform the task. I picked the helicopter up to a hover and managed to make the first takeoff and landing. During the second lap, I even gained some confidence, but on the third downwind leg in the pattern toward the last landing, my confidence was shaken when I saw the base's medevac helicopter less than a mile away and it appeared to be flying in my direction. I didn't think I was doing that badly. When I landed, completing my solo flight, I learned the medevac Huey was actually on its way to another site where a student pilot had flown into electrical power transmission lines.

Pilots rarely forget the day they first soloed. It's a momentous event. In my case, though, some wags claimed that I didn't solo that day in the true sense of the word, but rather my instructor had abandoned the aircraft for his own safety.

Though there was some degree of risk associated with a first solo, the greater danger of soloing at Fort Wolters may have been the ritual that followed. After a student soloed, which was at a stage field, the bus back to the base would stop at the Mineral Wells Holiday Inn so everyone could celebrate the occasion. The entire celebration consisted of the other student pilots hauling the fresh soloee to the motel's swimming pool, throwing him in—flight suit, ten-pound combat boots, and all—and waiting to see if he bobbed back up to the surface.

Instead of the Holiday Inn swimming pool, and if it was more conveniently conducive to the attempted drowning of a new soloee, a local rancher's livestock pond would serve the same purpose. The bus would stop on a county road where, just across the fence in a pasture, there was an earthen pond to accommodate the ritual immersion. With this alternative site for a solo baptism, the victim enjoyed the added risk of tetanus, resulting from being raked through a rusty barbed wire fence when his fellow classmates dragged him to the pastoral baptistery. In addition, when dunked in an earthen pond, the fresh solee might have the unique experience—rarely encountered at the Holiday Inn swimming pool—of being bitten by a water moccasin. Water moccasins, as a species, generally have little tolerance for the customs of student Army helicopter pilots.

Soloing was only an early milestone for being allowed to remain in flight school; there were more in the months to come. There were also tragedies.

On my first night flight, one with my instructor, we were the first ones to land at the site of a TH-55 crash that killed the student and the instructor. We were the only ones who witnessed the aircraft coming down in a flat spin.

Two other student pilots were unscratched even when the TH-55 they occupied shook itself to pieces as a result of ground resonance.

Two classmates survived being downed by either a flying duck or a goose—it couldn't be determined from the partial remains—that shattered the plastic bubble canopy and knocked unconscious the student pilot who was flying. He slumped over the controls sending the OH-13 into a dive. With effort, the other student pilot pulled his classmate from the controls in time so that, although the helicopter pancaked onto the ground, he managed to save the two of them.

There were inadvertent mishaps and some that were self-induced. During one flight with my instructor, the fog became so thick after departing the main heliport that we couldn't find the outlying stage field to which we had been assigned and neither could we find our way back to the heliport. We wandered around in the fog until we were practically out of fuel before finding a prominent landmark that led us to another stage field where we landed safely. On my first solo flight from the main heliport, I discovered I hadn't fully closed one of the helicopter's doors and had to land in a cornfield to secure it.

After flying solo a few times, I came to enjoy flying alone and the freedom for some extracurricular fun sometimes. One time, I dashed—if flying in an OH-13 could ever be termed that—outside the confines of our assigned flying area so I could explore Possum Kingdom Lake. Another time, after making a landing on one of the lofty ridges designated for practicing pinnacle landings, I thought that since I was already up that high and had a start at the attempt, I would see if I could coax the tired, old OH-13 to climb as far as a mile high. As it got higher, its rate of ascent kept getting slower and slower, but eventually it got there even though it took the rest of my assigned flying time.

Our days at Fort Wolters were filled with academics, flying, and learning how to become a warrant officer. It was a process of classroom lectures; testing; autorotations; testing; day and night cross country flights; testing; landings and takeoffs to and from pinnacles and confined areas, the tightness of each area depicted by a old tire painted either white, yellow, or red; and more testing. We endured weather extremes of burning sun, torrential rain, blinding snow, wind driven sleet, threatening tornadoes, and pelting hail, which Texans bragged sometimes occurred during the same day. Besides bird strikes from feathered flyers that failed to yield the right-of-way to their mechanical brethren, there were rumored threats of disgruntled deer hunters targeting our helicopters after their four-legged targets were scared away by our loud machines. And throughout it all, there were the continual plagues inflicted upon us by TAC officers.

Our class lost several members during the next months, most of them for failing to meet standards, some from their own voluntary withdrawal, and some from accidents. Eventually, the remainder of us completed primary flight training at Fort Wolters and we were passed on to the next series of testings in the process of learning to be helicopter pilots. For that, a portion of our class was assigned to Hunter Army Airfield in Georgia, but most of us, including me, were assigned to the proving grounds at Fort Rucker, Alabama.

## Mother Rucker

Called "Mother Rucker", sometimes derisively, but more so because it birthed so many Army aviators, Fort Rucker, Alabama, was the center of Army Aviation. A hundred miles southeast of Montgomery, the base encompassed more than ten square miles.

I found the environment for WOCs at Fort Rucker different from Fort Wolters. At Fort Rucker, it was more about flying. The upperclassmen were too busy to have any time for us, and as long as we kept out of trouble, our officer and NCO custodians didn't bother us. We had nearly every weekend off to lounge around, take in a sport car race in Montgomery, or more often drive to Panama City, Florida, for the sun, the beach, and the dog races. We had most evenings to ourselves, and although there were hours of studying, I found time to frequent the NCO club, which was conveniently located right next door to the barracks.

The sixteen weeks of flight training at Fort Rucker were divided into four phases, each of which required passing an end-of-phase flight test, called a "check ride." Those check rides were in addition to ones in the Link instrument trainer and separate from the volume of written tests we had to pass in the classroom.

During the first eight weeks we faced two phases of instrument training—basic and advanced—where we flew new TH-13T helicopters, a modernized version of the OH-13 that I had flown at Fort Wolters. The TH-13 was equipped with a full panel of instruments necessary for flying without outside visual reference. The training in instrument flying was designed to give us a chance of surviving if we had to fly in instrument conditions in places like Vietnam, but was less than what was needed to qualify to fly under instrument condition rules in US airspace.

The third phase of training at Fort Rucker was four weeks long. That's where we learned to fly Hueys, the iconic helicopter of the Vietnam War. Toward the end of that phase, the two students and I who shared the same IP had already passed our check rides but we still had some flying time remaining to meet the twenty-five hour minimum for that phase. Mister Melette, our obliging civilian instructor, let us fly to Panama City and buzz the beach. That was after he took the precaution of selecting a Huey with a smoky engine whose residue had blacked out the aircraft's tail number.

The last phase of flight training was divided into two parts, ending in "TAC-X" where we quartered at a remote camp within the confines of Fort Rucker and dealt with a series of field problems, exercises similar to missions we might experience in Vietnam. As part of that training, I flew as a pilot gunner in a B-model Huey gunship, firing the side-mounted M60 machine guns. The experience hadn't fostered for me any great enthusiasm for flying gunships. Burdened with the armament, the B-model Huey felt slow and sluggish.

We flew days, nights, short hops, cross country, and things in between. My head was filled with new terms: ADF, OMNI, RMI, DECCA, EGT, OAT, ACP, LZ, OPORD, ISUM, SOP, SOI.

We also dealt with subjects and training exercises not directly related to flying: unit organization, Army regulations, court martial proceedings, artillery fire adjustment, the gas chamber, pistol qualification, and Escape and Evasion.

For the E&E training, we were divided into small groups. My group was hauled by truck, dumped deep within the piney woods of Fort Rucker, told to prepare a meal; then when signaled by a shot in the distance, simulating the approach of an enemy force, we were to "escape" and find our way to a designated rendezvous point several miles away through the thick woods.

For the meal preparation, we were handed the main courses: chicken and rabbit, both alive. The majority of our group, more tenderhearted than hungry, elected to roast only the chicken and let the rabbit escape. Before roasting, though, the chicken required dispatching. I was nominated for the office of chicken dispatcher and, since I was unopposed on the ticket, elected.

I must have been the only one with the practical know-how for the job. My grandma had taught me how to wring a chicken's neck when I was a youngster. Many families in Climax, Texas, had practitioners who were accomplished at this form of meal preparation, most of them women. Men more often provided wild game. For them, hunting and fishing weren't recreations; they were necessities. Furthermore, to help bring home meat for the table, fathers put guns in the hands of their sons at an early age.

When the shot rang out signaling it was time for us to escape, we embarked on a trek through four miles of Alabama tick-infected woods, which had been specially populated for this occasion by "aggressors" eager to capture us. The aggressors, enlisted personnel promised a reward for each one of us they caught, were strategically staked out in the woods near any direct or easy path we might take.

The last of the uncaptured escapees straggled to the rendezvous point late that night, and even though some escapees had forgone the meal—preparing it was part of the requirement of the E&E exercise, but not eating it—we were all heavier than when we began this exercise due to the differential weight of all the ticks that had latched onto us.

Although some Warrant Officer Candidates had entered the Army's WORWAC program with months or years of military service, most of them, like me, were an "enlisted option", a new recruit who had joined the Army specifically for flight training. The enlisted option carried the obligation of serving an additional three years in the Army from the date of graduation from flight school, concurrent with being warranted an officer. It also had the provision that if the training was discontinued, the enlistee was obligated to remain in the Army in the enlisted ranks until completing two years of service from the date he joined the Army. Near the end of flight training, most enlisted options had been in the Army about a year, counting their time in basic training, leave time, and possibly other delays.

Throughout flight school, I had heard talk about a ploy to drop out of flight school shortly before graduation, finish the remaining months of military obligation in the enlisted ranks, and take advantage of the Army-paid training to land a civilian flying job. Nearing graduation, there was increased talk about this loophole with the added speculation that the Army was unlikely to send someone to Vietnam with only months of service remaining. As for me, I didn't want a civilian flying job when I could fly in the military. Although I was sure the military wasn't going to be a career for me, I felt the Army was giving me a chance to do something not all pilots had the opportunity to do: fly in combat, and even more rarely, fly helicopters in combat.

While at Fort Rucker, I saw someone I hadn't seen in several months, a student pilot in the flight class immediately ahead of mine. During the time when we were both at Fort Wolters, he rode with me to Lubbock one weekend to visit his wife and two small girls who lived in Brownfield, a small town near Lubbock.

After he went to Fort Rucker, a few weeks before I did, I lost contact with him until I happened to bump into him one day just three weeks before he was scheduled to graduate from flight school. He told me he had gotten orders to the First Air Cavalry in Vietnam, and he talked about having a week with his family, who had remained in Brownfield, before leaving. The next week, he and three other student pilots were killed in a midair collision.

Eventually, my graduation date arrived. I donned the dress blue uniform I had special ordered and sat through a formal program that led to awarding me wings and warrant officer bars. I was now a WO-1 Army aviator and, as one cynic put it, ready for "flying and dying."

My classmates and I had completed the Warrant Officer Rotary Wing Aviation Course. We had endured months of intense training devoted to learning the skills of helicopter flying. We had passed the scrutiny of check rides and written tests. We had endured physical conditioning, tactical exercises, the discipline of TAC officers, white glove inspections, and the demands of military requirements of performance. Among other dangers, we had escaped the lethality of hazardous weather, the fatality of failed equipment, and the terminal consequences of our own mistakes. Many who had started with us had not finished. The demands of the course and other circumstances had culled them from us. We were the survivors, and on that day in June, we celebrated our survival, unaware that many more of us would not survive what was still to come in Vietnam.

## The Army Knew Best

I had joined the Army for the opportunity to fly—and I knew the price for my training would likely be a tour in Vietnam—but it hadn't been a goal of mine to become a gunship pilot specifically.

At Fort Rucker, a few months before our projected date for finishing flight school, the Army circulated a questionnaire to each of us in our class. It asked us, if we were selected for advanced training after flight school, to name our choices for that training. There were three choices. One choice was advanced training to qualify for flying the Army's twin-engine, twin-rotor CH-47 (Chinook) helicopter. A second choice was special training to fly Hueys in medevac operations. A third choice was transition training to fly Cobras, the aircraft that had begun service in the Army about the same time I had. The form directed us to list those three choices in the order of our preference. On the questionnaire, in the three spaces for those choices, I wrote: Medevac, Medevac, Medevac.

A month before my projected graduation from flight school, I received orders for my next assignment. I supposed the orders were to report to Vietnam, but I was surprised to learn I had been selected for advanced training, and I was even more surprised to learn I had been selected for Cobra gunship training. I suppose the Army knew best.

I didn't object to gunship school because not everybody was selected for advanced training and I was happy to have been selected for anything. Besides, it would allow me a few more weeks in the States before going to Vietnam. That was especially important to me because I had become engaged shortly before leaving Fort Wolters and going to Fort Rucker, and I was getting married right after graduating from flight school. Advanced training would give me more time with my new bride before I shipped off. And who knew; maybe those extra weeks would be enough time for everybody to think it over, conclude that the whole situation with Vietnam was just a misunderstanding, and call off the hostilities.

The Army had helped make my life simpler in many ways. I no longer had to decide what to wear each day, I no longer had to decide how to style my hair, and I no longer had to decide whether or not I wanted to sleep in until after sunrise. However, the Army did force me to make one important decision: what was I going to do about that cute girl I was dating?

Midway through flight school, as I neared completion of the primary flight training at Fort Wolters, the reality of my situation became clear to me. In a few months, the Army was going to send me to Vietnam, and I felt it was highly unlikely that my employer was going to let me return home on weekends just so I could date this lovely girl with a perpetual smile and eternal optimism and who's only flaw was the misjudgment of choosing to date the likes of me. I was certain, though, that this girl had the good sense that she wasn't going to wait a whole year for me. She would no longer be on the market when I returned—she had too many other opportunities—so I took preemptive action; I asked her to marry me. And, amazingly, she said, "yes." I suppose she simply couldn't refuse my romantic proposal.

I remember that proposal as if it were just yesterday. I was on Christmas leave and she was home from college. It was evening and we were sitting in the almost leather-like bucket seats of my beloved Mustang, and though separated by the gearshift console, I felt our hearts were united. There in the darkness, I turned to her and she turned to me. I watched the faint light flickering on her soft face as if from a fluttering candle flame, but which actually was coming through the windshield from the drive-in movie screen where "Attack of the Killer Shrews" was being projected.

I smiled at her romantically as I lifted the plastic pouch of peanuts to my lips. Romantically, I opened it with my teeth. Suavely, yet romantically, I gently tapped the package, plopping the peanuts into the neck of a bottle of RC Cola. Like a wine connoisseur—a romantic one—I lifted the bottle to my nose and whiffed its fizzing fragrance, managing to sniff some of the fizz up my nose. Romantically, I wiped my nose on my sleeve.

Romantically, I tilted up the bottle and took a gulp. Romantically, I gazed at her as I chewed on the peanuts. Then, as I romantically plopped more peanuts into the bottle, I romantically popped the question: "Say, you wouldn't want to marry me, would you?" What girl could refuse an offer like that?

My idea was that we'd get married that night. It was hardly more than an hour's drive to Oklahoma, and even that late at night, I was sure that just across the Red River from Texas I could rouse some Justice of the Peace who would agree to marry us as long as I had the fee for his services. However, my new fiancé had a different idea. She wanted a more lengthy engagement, one that extended for months of anticipation instead of an hour and half of driving, one that involved tea parties, showers, and gifts of serving dishes and useful household utensils. And she wanted a wedding in a church, complete with a white dress, bridesmaids, and a flower child. She wanted to walk down an aisle, say "I do" before a real minister, and be pelted with rice.

So, after that Christmas leave and once again back in flight school, that's how I found myself engaged. And, alas, so soon we were parted. I departed Fort Wolters for further flight training at Fort Rucker, Alabama, while my beloved returned to college at Texas Tech. It was months before I saw my bride-to-be again.

I arrived at Fort Rucker in January and our wedding date was set for June, right after the projected date of my graduation from flight school. For the graduation, my betrothed came from Texas to Alabama, pinned on my wings, and following an all-night party, we got in my Mustang and drove ten hours to Texas for our wedding. The day after the wedding, we drove back east, crossed through Louisiana and Mississippi into Alabama, and dipped down for a day in Panama City, Florida, before rolling into Georgia where I was to report the next day for training at Hunter Army Airfield's Cobra Hall in Savannah.

I found what I thought to be the perfect place for a honeymoon, a motel in Savannah Beach just two blocks from the surf. Right next door to the motel was the Mousetrap Lounge where spirited persons leaving that establishment in the early morning hours after midnight took staggering shortcuts through the motel's parking lot and found great sport in knocking on every numbered door of the motel as they passed through—or until they passed out, whichever came first.

At Cobra Hall, I experienced four intensive weeks of learning the AH-1's systems and flying this fast, agile helicopter, adapting my raw skills to its sensitive handling. I was up at four each morning to make the drive to Hunter Army Airfield where for half the day I was subjected to platform instructors who felt it necessary to elaborate absolutely everything there was to know about a Cobra, including the exact number and specific purpose of all its rivets and screws as well as every last detail of not only the aircraft's armament systems but of weapons in general, including the complete unabridged history of gunpowder.

The other half of the day, I was slow baked by the Georgia sun in the enclosed double-oven canopy of a Cobra, either in the front seat while attempting to hover the aircraft with the short side cyclic—the equivalent of trying to balance a cue ball on a toothpick—or in the back seat while being berated by a zealous instructor pilot who insisted that—while flying at nearly a hundred-and-fifty knots and from a thousand yards away—I was to put a 2.75-inch folding fin aerial rocket through a target whose radius was no more than that of a bargain priced slice of baloney.

Meanwhile, during that same day, my new bride was back at Savannah Beach, leisurely lounging around the motel pool while counting the number of unconscious Mouse Trap Lounge revelers from the night before that were still lying, uncollected, in the parking lot. Or, if not that, passing the day at the beach under an umbrella, painting her toenails cute colors and clipping recipes from *Southern Living*. At the end of the day, when I dragged myself through the door of our little, rented honeymoon nest, my flight suit hanging wearily on my sagging shoulders, my new bride was there to greet me, wearing long earrings and a short miniskirt, ready for a night out in Savannah. How could I refuse? Those four weeks of concurrent honeymoon and Cobra school were among the most pleasurable, as well as most exhausting, experiences ever.

Following the end of Cobra school, I took a short leave, and after that, married barely seven weeks, I left for Vietnam, knowing I wouldn't see my lovely bride again for a year, possibly never. It was my new mother-in-law, though, who put a positive spin on this. "Look upon it as an exciting adventure," she said.

## Flying Down to Can Tho

In mid-August of 1968, I reported to the Oakland Army Base in California, and after a night there, I boarded a Flying Tigers DC-8 that carried me, via Alaska and Japan, to Vietnam. We new arrivals landed at Bien Hoa and stepped out of the air-conditioned plane into the all-natural heat of Vietnam. We were herded into blue buses, their open-air windows covered with screen wire to deflect any grenades that someone might attempt to toss into our laps. Through congested streets crowded with pedestrians and mopeds, the busses transported us to Long Binh where the 90th Replacement Battalion took custody of us. I was held there a couple of days, long enough for the Army to systematically sort through all the wanted postings it had for fresh-meat helicopter pilots and connect me with my assigned unit.

On the afternoon of the day after my arrival at the 90th, I found my name, along with two others, listed on a directive posted on a bulletin board. The three of us, who had been assigned to the 164th Combat Aviation Group, were to report at noon the next day for transportation to Can Tho, the Group's headquarters location eighty miles south of Saigon. I knew one of the other two persons on the list, George, who was in the same Cobra class as me. Since all three of our names were listed with the rank of WO-1, the beginning rank of a newly minted warrant officer, a "Wobbly One", I assumed the third person was also a pilot.

That next day, I restuffed my duffel bag, joined my comrades, and the three of us climbed into a jeep that took us back to the Bien Hoa Airport. Inside the lobby, we showed our orders to a clerk at a desk who glanced at them and put them with the bundle of others on the desk. Without looking up, busily thumbing through the sheaf of orders in his hands, he told us to wait and he would try to find a flight for us.

The pilot I had just met—sporting a freshly sprouted mustache—asked how long the wait would be. The clerk sighed, looked up, and testily explained that the military wasn't operating a scheduled airline service just for us. All kinds of aircraft, from all the military services, passed through the airport, day and night, coming from, and going to, all parts of the country, and their travels only incidentally considered would-be passengers. When he learned of something going to Can Tho, and if it had room, he'd arrange a ride for us. He added editorially that we should consider ourselves lucky that Can Tho was a fairly large base; persons trying to get to smaller or more remote parts of Vietnam might have to wait days before catching a ride. As the clerk explained how this transportation system worked, I caught on to the concept right away. In Texas, we called it hitchhiking.

The clerk told us to stay in the lobby, within earshot of his loudspeaker, and he'd call us when he found a ride. So we wandered away until we found a hard bench, and waited. Before long, the mustached pilot became interested in the young Vietnamese ladies passing through the lobby in their long, flowing *ao dais* dresses. He smoothed the bristles of his new growth and went to chat up as many of them as would stop a moment and pretend to understand English.

After a lengthy wait, we heard our names on the loudspeaker. We all returned to the clerk's desk, including Mister Moustache whose little black book was as empty as when he left us. The clerk said that a plane had just landed and, after dropping part of its load, was going farther south. It could drop us off at Can Tho, but we'd have to hurry to catch the plane because it wasn't going to wait around for us.

He gave us the tail number of the aircraft and told us we'd find it out on the ramp. We picked up our canvas bags and walked out to the tarmac where there was a bustle of activity and a multitude of aircraft, mostly airplanes of all sizes. We wandered around, sweating through our Class A khakis, looking for a plane with the matching tail number. George eventually spotted it, sitting two hundred yards away. I recognized it as a Caribou, a twin-engine cargo plane with short field capability. It had Air Force markings. Even though the Caribou had been in the Army's inventory at one time, all of them had been transferred to the Air Force after that branch of the service complained that the Army wasn't entitled to have cargo planes.

The Caribou had a loading ramp in the rear, and to make it easier to move things in and out, the airplane had a lifted tail, like a female cat in heat.

We began walking in the plane's direction. The ramp was all the way down and the plane's engines were running. The crew chief, standing at the rear of the airplane's ramp, saw us and motioned for us to hurry. We jogged the remaining way and he hustled us onboard. The cargo area was empty except for a few crates that were strapped down tightly.

As soon as we were in, the crew chief raised the rear ramp, leaving it partially open, which allowed some ventilation and a view out the back. I couldn't hear him over the engines, but I saw the crew chief's lips move as he spoke into his helmet's microphone. The engines revved louder, and the plane began rolling toward the runway. The crew chief pointed to a webbed bench seat folded against the side of the cabin. We unfolded it and sat down. He pointed to some straps just underneath it and we buckled the lap belts around us.

We rocked gently in our seats as the plane rolled onto the runway. It kept rolling, picking up speed for the takeoff. The plane climbed steeply until it reached about five thousand feet, leveled off, and continued on its way. I sat looking out the back of the plane, watching the Vietnam Delta unfold below, and settled in for the ride. At that altitude, a few thermals bumped the airplane, but otherwise it was a smooth flight.

Shortly, though, the airplane began making erratic movements. It started with the wings dipping, first on one side, then the other, as the airplane rolled from side to side like it was a canoe and someone had stood up in it. Then the nose of the plane began porpoising like it was the bow of the *Pequod* under full sail in a tempest tossed sea and in hot pursuit of Moby Dick. And soon the tail developed a nervous tic, twitching around more than a cow's tail in a swarm of flies. We flopped around in the jump seat, only our lap belts holding us to it.

I thought the plane might be receiving anti-aircraft fire and the pilots were dodging flak, but when I looked at the crew chief, he didn't seem concerned. He was hooked up on the intercom with the pilots, and surely he'd know if we were being shot at. But he looked as happy as a bullfrog at a fly-tasting convention. He nodded at something on the intercom, mouthed a "Roger", and cinched his own seat belt tighter.

Then the motions became even more erratic. The nose pitched up, hit an apex, and nosed back down. Simultaneously, the Caribou rolled way over on its side like it was a trained whale at a sea show, turning to give a wave of its flipper to people in the stands. But the worst part was the tail wiggle; the rear end of the airplane wagged from side to side like a long-tailed dog lapping up white gravy.

The aircraft tossed us up, down, and around in our seats. We Army pilots were feeling more shook up than a wet Elvis who had just plunked a short-circuited guitar.

And it got worse. The airplane jerked down into a dive, then just as suddenly, the nose lurched up and the airplane climbed. At the same time, the wings rolled almost vertical, first in one direction, then the other. And the tail of the airplane whipped around like it wanted to pass the nose and take the lead in this flight. Then the tail changed its mind and whipped back around in the other direction like a jackknifing eighteen-wheeler. Still not content, the fickle tail changed its mind again, and just as quickly, tried the other side once more.

We shot out of our seats, the seat belts caught us, and our butts smacked back down into the seats. The aircraft tried to throw us across the cargo area, then rolled the other way, slamming our backs against the fuselage wall. As the tail waggled in one direction and then the other, we Wobby Ones bobbled around like the little metal ball in a pinball machine.

I looked at George and the other pilot. The whites of their eyes were showing, as I'm sure were mine. And they were both turning green. But, as for me, I wasn't nauseous. That was because I had become hardened to the effects of erratic aircraft behavior, having experienced it so often when I was at the controls.

I was surprised, though, because I had expected better performance than this from those Air Force flyboys up front. I thought those guys were supposed to be excellent aviators. After all, what else did Air Force pilots, all of them already commissioned officers, have to do when they were in flight school? All they had to do was learn how to fly, unlike we Army warrant officer candidates, who also had to learn things like how to wax a concrete floor and to memorize the complete names, including the middle initials, of a TAC officer's dozens of cousins. Yet, apparently, these Air Force airplane drivers hadn't learned to hold a level altitude or a wings-level attitude, let alone keep an aircraft in trim. Based upon the quality of flying they were exhibiting, I began to lose some respect for Air Force pilots.

As the airplane bucked, twisted, and writhed in one violent spasm after another, I looked to the crew chief to see if he was breaking out the parachutes, but he didn't appear worried at all. In fact, he was laughing and talking on the intercom.

And that's when my opinion about those Air Force pilots changed completely. I realized they were competent alright. In fact, they were flying this airplane precisely the way they intended. They were giving us Army pilots a special newcomers' welcome to Vietnam, and the crew chief was giving them a running commentary of the effect of that welcome on us.

When I realized what they were doing, I thought it was about the most juvenile stunt I could imagine. And right then, I vowed that when I became a seasoned pilot and should I ever have an occasion to transport a new pilot in my aircraft—someone who had just gotten his wings, some innocent person who placed his trust in me, depending upon me and my flying skill to get him safely from one place to another; that is, someone who was in the same position I was at that moment—I would do exactly the same thing.

Eventually, the airplane settled down and we began descending for a landing. We touched down at an airfield, and after a rollout, the plane came to a near stop at the end of the runway, wheeled around slowly until it faced back up the runway the way it had come, then taxied up the runway and turned off at a crossway near the point on the runway where it had touched down.

The plane rolled a little farther—rattling across the airport's steel sheet clad apron—slowed to a near stop, and wheeled around to face back toward the crossway. As the airplane maneuvered, I had a panoramic view of the airfield through the partially open ramp door, and when the plane pivoted to a stop, leaving its tail pointed toward a dirty white building, I saw faded letters on the building that read "Can Tho."

The crew chief lowered the ramp all the way down and we three new warrant officer aviators unbuckled, retrieved our duffel bags, and walked out of the back of the plane. The moment we were out, the airplane revved its engines and the prop blast blew sandy grit on us. Then, like a high-tailed cat strolling away from its sand-covered litter box deposit, the airplane rolled away.

## Reporting for Duty

It was late in the afternoon when we trio of greenhorn pilots arrived at Can Tho. A jeep came to pick up us up at the open-air terminal building. The corporal driving the jeep evidently aspired to be a Grand Prix racer. I had barely plopped down in the front passenger seat when he popped the clutch, U-turned in front of another jeep, ran through the gears, snapping the floor shift with each change, and sped down a narrow street barely two lanes wide, playing chicken with opposing vehicles. He passed another jeep going the same direction as us but moving too slowly to suit him, swerved back in front of it, immediately swerved again to dodge a soldier walking on the narrow shoulder, then jerked the wheel to avoid a pothole, but instead hit it dead center. I was launched out of my seat and grabbed the dash to keep from being thrown out. George and the other pilot were saved because they were packed tightly in the back seat, stuffed among the duffel bags. Through the dirty windshield, I saw a deuce-and-half truck coming from the opposite direction, too wide for both it and us to pass on the narrow street. Our driver sped up. I braced for the collision. Suddenly, he whipped the wheel and we skidded around a corner onto another street, missing the truck by a skinny cat's whisker. The jeep zipped down the street, a whirlwind of flying dust trailing behind it. A hundred feet down the street, the driver snapped the jeep to the side of the road, stomped on the brake, and screeched to a halt beside a small building that bore a sign identifying it as the headquarters of the 235th Aerial Weapons Company, the "Delta Devils."

We got out of the jeep, dusted ourselves off, and unloaded our bags. A wood bridge, barely more than a plank with handrails, spanned a deep bar ditch that separated the building from the road. We tromped across the plank and entered the cramped building.

Apparently, we were expected. A sergeant sitting at a desk by the door immediately got up, led us a few steps to the open door of the company commander's office, and motioned for us to enter. Inside the tiny room there was barely enough space for all of us. We came to attention in front of the CO's gray metal desk and, just as we'd been taught in flight school for such occasions, saluted and announced we were reporting for duty.

From his chair behind the desk, the major returned our salutes and had us stand at ease. He asked where we were from. When it was my turn, I named Lubbock as my residence rather than my actual home of record, Climax. I felt it would avoid the possibility of a misunderstanding.

Major Manderlin proved to be a pleasant, yet no-nonsense, man. "I know you must be tired and hungry, so I'll be brief," he said. "The 235th is one of four companies of the 307th Combat Aviation Battalion. The "Phantom" Battalion, as it's called, is part of the 164th Aviation Group, which belongs to the First Aviation Brigade. The other companies in the battalion are airplane companies, two have Bird Dogs and one has Mohawks.

"The 235th is unique because it's an all-gunship company and, specifically, a company of Cobras. There's a similar unit up in Saigon, the 334th's Playboys, but the 235th was the first company to have a full complement of Cobras.

"As you're probably aware, the AH-1 is relatively new to the Army's inventory and it's destined to replace nearly all of the Huey gunships in Vietnam, but most of the new Cobras arriving in Vietnam are currently going to the Air Cavalry, and the assault helicopter companies still have Huey gunships along with their fleet of UH-1 slicks used for troop transport and utility services.

"The 235th provides additional gunship support for those assault helicopter companies that require it, and we do about everything else that calls for close air support or helicopter gunships. We support the Army's Air Cavalry, the Navy, South Vietnamese ground troops, the South Vietnamese Air Force, you name it.

"We supply aerial gun support for Navy operations inland, including a SEAL operation now and then. We're the gunships for operations employing Vietnamese Air Force helicopters.

Currently, the VNAF flies old H-34 helicopters for airlift operations and has no helicopter gunships at all.

"We support the South Vietnamese ground forces, the 'ARVNs', which include the regular Army as well as the Regional Forces-Popular Forces or 'Ruff-Puffs' as they're called. The Regional Forces are sort of like a Vietnamese national guard and the Popular Forces are village militias. The ARVN IV Corps is composed of about forty thousand men organized into three infantry divisions and supporting troops. The Corps has territorial responsibilities for the fifteen provinces that make up the IV Corps Tactical Zone.

"We provide armed escorts for medevac extractions and single-ship resupply missions. We maintain an instant-reaction fire team for search-and-destroy operations or anything else that needs us. And we're responsible for nighttime air defense of the airfield if it were ever attacked.

"You'll find yourself undertaking a wide range of missions, and the whole Delta is our Area of Operations. We cover a lot of territory, all of IV Corps from the tip of the Delta in the south and up to near Saigon in the north. We sometimes get called farther north into III Corps.

"The Mekong Delta is mostly rice paddies and mangrove swamps, but it has the U Minh forest not far south from here and the "Seven Sisters" peaks to the west near the Cambodia border, both perpetual trouble spots.

"The Delta grows about two-thirds of all the food in South Vietnam, including three-quarters of the rice. And the people are where the food is. Fifteen million people live in Vietnam, five and a half million of them in the Mekong Delta. The South Vietnamese Army and the Viet Cong both recruit and feed their forces from the Delta. Consequently, the course of the war here is critical to the rest of Vietnam."

I stared at the plaque on the wall behind Major Manderlin's desk: a head painted red, with horns and a pointed goatee.

Major Manderlin leaned back in his chair. "The 235th is named the 'Delta Devils'. In addition to maintenance units, I've got three flight platoons of pilots. Those in the first platoon are called the 'Satans'. The second platoon has the 'Death Dealers' or 'Dealers' for short, and the third platoon are the 'Vipers'.

"You'll get to fly a lot because I'm short of pilots. Of the pilots I do have, they're not all rated in the Cobra as you are. You'll start in the front seat as a copilot and gunner. As soon as you prove yourself—if you do—you'll move to the back seat as Aircraft Commander.

"I'm authorized twenty-four Cobras, but I don't have that many, and the ones I do have aren't all flyable at the same time due to different reasons: scheduled maintenance, some because of accidents, and some get shot up."

Major Manderlin leaned across the desk and stared hard at us. "Here's something I want you to understand. It's true the Army is losing a lot of pilots, either to accidents or to the enemy, but the fact is, you've got more to say about your longevity than anyone else. We've got operating procedures to reduce the chances of pilots being brought down by enemy fire or from having an accident, but ..." and he lowered his eyebrows at us "... I can't keep you from screwing up."

He brushed his hand through his crew cut. "It's hard to keep enough pilots—or enough aircraft—to meet the demand." He leaned back again and studied a chalkboard on the wall. It looked like the numbers on it had been erased and written over a lot. Then, as if he had just thought of other things he needed to be doing, he said, "Any questions?"

We all responded "No, sir." Actually, I had a bunch of questions, but "No, sir" was the most practical answer. It was the answer that would get us out of there quicker. Being a lowly WO-1, I felt the same about exposure to a commanding officer as I did atomic radiation: the less, the better.

But Major Manderlin had some questions for us individually, ones I'm sure that were intended to size us up, and he did that quickly. Even though there were three of us, he soon announced that he was only going to keep George and me. As for Mister Moustache, he was told that he would be going to Vinh Long where there was another unit of the 164th Group. Perhaps it was his fuzzy lip that had warranted him Major Manderlin's rejection. In any case, he was whisked away by the sergeant and that's the last I saw of him.

Major Manderlin informed George and me that we were being assigned to the company's third platoon but that assignment was only for temporary accounting purposes and might change. He directed us to draw our equipment from Supply and told us the sergeant would find some place for us to stay for the night. It was getting late in the day.

When we left the CO's office, the jeep driver was standing just outside the door. I learned he was the company clerk when the sergeant had a brief conversation with him before turning us over to him. I didn't hear all of it, but I gathered that the sergeant was directing him to walk, not drive, us to the Supply tent and then to our temporary quarters.

At Supply, we were issued the standard gear for pilots, including a vest with an armor plated chest protector, a six-round .38-calibre Smith and Wesson revolver, a box of bullets, and a canteen. I had hung onto the flight helmet I'd had in flight school, lugging it all the way to Vietnam.

Once we were further loaded down with this newly issued gear in addition to what was in our already stuffed duffel bags, the clerk led us along a dirty street to a block where there was a row of neatly aligned, identical wood planked buildings with a thin strip of screening under the eaves of the slanted roofs.

As daylight faded, the clerk led us inside one of the buildings, which he referred to as a "hootch." It had a hallway running the length of it with another door on the far end. On either side of the hallway were compartments enclosed by plywood, most of them with a hanging curtain at the entrance, except for one with a screen door. The clerk pointed to one compartment and said this would be my place for the night, explaining that the room's occupant was gone for a few days. He didn't explain why; he just left with George.

I pushed through the curtain and went in. When I thought to ask the clerk where I could get a meal, I stuck my head back into the hall, but he was gone. I had no idea where the mess hall was, or anything else. I didn't even know what the clerk had done with George.

The compartment was small and stifling. With a cot and metal clothes closet, it didn't have room for much else. I sat my duffel bag in a corner and leaned it against the wall. I felt no need to unpack it, but I dug into it and found the stationary on which I'd been writing a letter off and on since I left Oakland. I turned on the overhead light and sat on the cot, picking up where I'd left off.

After I finished the letter, I turned off the overhead bulb and lay down atop the camouflage patterned poncho liner that served as the cot's bedspread. I dozed off quickly but a short time later I awoke when I felt something moving on my forehead. I thought it might be some Vietnamese bug, one with a light tread, doing reconnaissance on my forehead, looking for a more tender spot to sink its teeth. Then I felt the thing slither down the side of my face and I imagined it must be some Vietnamese viper, probably one with ten-inch fangs dripping green poison as lethal as a West Texas albino rattler.

I lay motionless until I felt it slither off the side of my face. After a few moments, thinking perhaps the serpent had spared me and hoping it had crawled off the cot, I sprang up and turned on the light. I didn't see a snake, or even a bug, but I felt something else crawling on my forehead. This time, I gave the thing a hard slap. I must have squashed it, I thought, because I felt in my palm what I assumed were wet guts. I brought my hand down, expecting to see a mess of smashed innards, but all I saw in my palm was the glistening of my own sweat. That was what I had felt pooling on my forehead, overflowing, and oozing down the side of my face.

I lay back down and nodded off again until I felt more slithering, down my face, down an arm, down my leg. It was hard to stay asleep with all that slithering, but I eventually did. Then, something else woke me—the sound of thunder. At least, I thought it was thunder. After listening more carefully to the booms, I concluded it was artillery firing somewhere on the base. I lay awake thinking about that for a while. What were they shooting at? Was the base under attack? But I rationalized it was probably something routine, and so, as far as the artillery was concerned, I wasn't going to sweat it.

About 0500, I woke up. The artillery had stopped and I lay there until I heard another noise, a deep rumbling. It was my stomach growling.

I got up and walked outside, thinking it might be cooler, but it wasn't. I found the latrine down the sidewalk, a building with sinks, urinals, commodes, and shower stalls. After retrieving my shaving kit from the duffel bag, I scrapped the stubble off my face, washed away the sweat with a shower, put on a fresh uniform, and began adding a fresh layer of sweat.

I hadn't had a meal since midday the day before, and I thought my first order of business this morning would be to find the mess hall.

## The FNG

When I brushed open the curtain to step out of the compartment, I almost bumped into a tall warrant officer who was about to come in. Before I could ask him where the mess hall was, he said, "Where the hell have you been? I've been looking for you. Come on." And he turned, walking out of the hootch. I followed him—to the mess hall I expected.

Outside the hootch, he looked back at me and stopped. "Where's your chicken plate?"

I thought, chicken plate? Is that the special at the mess hall?

"Do you have a chicken plate?" he said.

I stood there, blank.

He pointed to the armor plated vest he was wearing and slowly enunciated. "Chic-ken-plate. Do-you-have-one?" He said it as if he were addressing his number one choice as candidate for the job of village idiot.

Oh, chicken plate, I thought. The clerk in Supply who gave me one of those called it a chest protector. I nodded my head.

"Then get it," he said as if he were trying to teach the dumbest mongrel in the litter to fetch.

I turned to go back to the room where I'd dumped all the stuff I'd collected at Supply the previous evening. He yelled after me, "And get all your flight gear."

I tumbled the words over in my mind. Flight gear? Then my razor sharp brain concluded, "I guess we're going flying." My stomach was a little slower in grasping the situation. "You mean we're not going to the mess hall?" it growled.

I hurried back to the compartment, found the chest protector—vest, chicken plate, whatever—that I'd been issued, pulled my flight helmet and gloves out of the duffel bag, and started from the compartment with them. Then I thought about the pistol, went back, got it and the holster it came in, and shoved the box of bullets in my pocket.

When I came back outside, the guy was gone. I trotted off down the sidewalk in the direction I had last seen him. Around the corner of a building at the end of the sidewalk, I found him. He was sitting in the back seat of a jeep, and George was sitting there too. Another warrant officer sat in the front beside the driver. I recognized the driver; he was the heavy-footed clerk.

Clutching my gear, I climbed into the jeep and wedged into the back seat between the tall stranger and George. "Hey, George," I said. George nodded slightly as if reluctant to acknowledge he knew me.

The driver had the engine running and popped the clutch. The jeep sped down the road, made a sharp turn around a corner, and raced down another road. It slowed as the driver turned onto a short, narrow drive that connected the road to the airfield's large aircraft parking ramp, which was covered with interlocked perforated steel planks. The jeep rattled across the PSP and clattered onto a crossway that connected the ramp with the airfield's runway. Just before reaching the runway, the driver turned off the crossway onto a narrow dirt strip that paralleled the PSP-clad runway. In the dawn's early light, the jeep sped along the strip between the runway and a long row of revetments in which Cobras sat facing the runway.

The revetments, a series of head high walls built of stacked sand bags standing parallel to each other and perpendicular to the runway, were open at the front and back. As the jeep zipped along in front of the revetments, I saw behind them, a few yards farther back, a body of languid water.

Toward the end of the row of the revetments, the jeep stopped in front of one. The pilot who was sitting beside the driver got out and George got out with him. The jeep sprinted ahead and, a couple of revetments farther down, stopped in front of the one at the very end of the row and which was some fifty yards from the end of the runway. My guy climbed out, and I followed him.

A crew chief was waiting in the revetment with the Cobra, which stood ready for a preflight inspection, its engine panels open, as were the panels of the armament stores behind the turret and underneath the copilot's station. The cockpit canopy hatches were open also, the one for the front seat position open on the Cobra's left side and the one for the back seat open on the right side.

When my guy took off his chicken plate to lay it in the back seat, I could read the name on his fatigue shirt: Jackson. He plugged the jack from his flight helmet into the socket of the cord from the aircraft's communications junction box and hung his helmet on a hook near the cockpit hatch. Taking my cue from him, I laid my chicken plate in the front seat and plugged my helmet into the cord there.

Jackson began a preflight inspection of the helicopter, starting with the ammo bay underneath the cockpit and checking the weapon pods mounted under the right wing stub: a rocket pod hanging underneath the outboard hard point and a minigun under the one inboard.

I stood in the revetment, trying to stay out of the way. The crew chief eyed me, judgmentally I thought, as if assessing my worthiness to fly in his aircraft.

Jackson had climbed onto the wing stub to examine the engine compartment. He looked down at me. "You know how to preflight a Cobra, don't you?"

"Yes, sir," I said. Although Jackson was a WO-1, the same rank as me, I felt the formal address was appropriate since I was what was referred to as an FNG, a F***ing New Guy.

Now, here was something I knew how to do: a preflight. I walked to the other side of the aircraft and began the inspection. I inspected with intense diligence: touching, pulling, poking and wiggling anything I could get my hands on. With each item, I frowned with thoughtful evaluation before nodding to indicate the item met my satisfaction and moving on to the next item.

I peered into the ammo bay door on the left side, confirmed the feed chutes were secure, ran my hands over the fuselage at the side of the cockpit, kicked the skids, pushed and pulled on the weapon pods under the wing stubs, blew dust off the rocket heads.

I climbed on top of the wing stub, reached inside the engine compartment, running my hand over tubes and connectors. I stepped up to inspect the rotor hub, wiggled the pitch chain links, eyeballed the Jesus nut, and thumped the anti-collision light atop the doghouse as if testing a watermelon for ripeness. After I had pondered and nodded thoroughly up there, I climbed down off the wing stub and walked the length of the tail boom, my nose practically touching every rivet on the open-for-inspection tail rotor drive shaft cover.

When I got to the tail rotor, I met Jackson coming around from the other side. I watched over his shoulder as he looked for cracks in the tail rotor blades and nicks on the leading edges of the blades. He wiggled the tail rotor linkage, testing the play before he continued up the tail boom, reinspecting the territory I'd covered. I gave the tail rotor linkage a wiggle myself, nodded my agreement with Jackson's apparent acceptance of it, and continued on around, inspecting the same side Jackson had already covered.

As we finished inspecting the tail boom and tail rotor drive shaft, the crew chief closed the shaft cover and fastened it in place. Once we had finished inspecting the engine compartment on both sides, he closed and fastened the engine panels. And when we were through looking in the ammo bay, he slid the ammo containers back into place in the bay but left the ammo bay doors open.

The panels may have been closed, but I wasn't through inspecting. I might be the FNG, but I wasn't going to accept just any aircraft that quickly. Standing back, I looked the aircraft over again, from nose to tail rotor, slowly and deliberately, as if I were a dog show judge evaluating a coon dog as a possible winner for the Best Hound division.

As I deliberated on whether or not this aircraft satisfied my inspection, I felt sure I was creating intense suspense. But I wasn't to be rushed to judgment; I took my time. I stepped up close to the fuselage and, with a sweeping flourish, wiped the surface with my forefinger. I carefully examined the dust on my finger, frowning slightly. I leaned my head against the side of the aircraft and squinted down the length of the fuselage like a carpenter examining a two-by-four for warps. I stooped to look more closely at the tip of one of the rockets in the tubes as if I thought perhaps it wasn't pointy enough. When I stood up from that, I peered thoughtfully at the aircraft, rubbing my chin as if I were wrestling with a weighty decision equal to a Supreme Court ruling. Then, kicking the skid once more, I gave the aircraft a final, conclusive nod; it was acceptable.

While I was making the inspection, it became obvious that this ship wasn't like the Cobras in flight school; this aircraft must have had some different experiences. The paint on the fuselage didn't quite match the paint on the tail boom, which didn't quite match the paint on one of the engine panels. And there were light colored splotches in several places where the skin had been patched—most likely I assumed—to cover bullet holes. But even though the aircraft might not win a beauty contest, it was evident to me that it was well maintained.

The crew chief had untied the main rotor blades for the inspection and now he began tying them down again. He reached up, slid the tie-down clamp over one of the two main rotor blades, and holding onto the tie-down lines dangling from the clamp, he pulled the blade around like leading a horse by the reins. He walked the blade around to the back of the tail boom and tied the ends of the lines to the metal stinger that stuck out from underneath the end of the tail boom. The main rotor blades were now aligned along the length of the helicopter and tied down to the stinger so they wouldn't loosely flop around and thrash against the mast if they were buffeted by the rotor wash from other helicopters that might hover by or from the prop blast of large airplanes. I was surprised, though, to see the crew chief tying down the blades. I thought we had gone to all the trouble of inspecting the helicopter because we were going to fly it.

The open ammo bay doors, lowered and extending from the fuselage, were held in place by restraining cables stretching from the fuselage to the outside corners of the doors. Jackson sat down on a door and lit a cigarette. I leaned against a wall of the revetment and lit up also.

I was curious about what we were going to do next, but Jackson didn't seem the talkative type, and I didn't want to reveal the total depth of my ignorance. As my granddad, Jesse James McDonald, might have advised me, "When you're in over your head, close your mouth."

In a few minutes, George and his pilot walked up to the revetment. George's guy didn't bother to introduce himself, but I saw the name "Taylor" on his nametag. He said to Jackson, "Everything okay?" Jackson nodded.

Neither Taylor nor George had their chicken plates or helmets with them. I supposed they had left them in their aircraft. I also noticed Taylor was wearing a black cowboy holster and belt around his waist, the holster hanging low on his hip and tied to his thigh by rawhide strings. A Smith & Wesson .38 revolver lodged in the holster—the same kind of pistol I'd been issued. Jackson had a similar holster and belt for his .38. I was curious about where they'd gotten the belts and holsters; George and I had been issued shoulder holsters with our pistols. George was wearing his. I had tossed mine in the front seat of the Cobra along with my helmet. It appeared I was the only one unarmed at the moment.

Taylor started walking away. Jackson stubbed out his cigarette on the PSP covering the floor of the revetment and fell in with him. George tagged along behind them. I grabbed my .38 out of the front seat and followed behind as I strapped on the shoulder holster.

It was just a few yards to a crossway that connected the west end of the runway with the parking ramp. Beyond the crossway squatted a small, weather battered, wooden hootch, and beyond it a couple of hundred feet, lay coiled concertina wire that marked the perimeter of the airfield, the wire stretching through the marshy growth of tall grass. Just inside the perimeter, a lookout post stood atop spindly legs.

George and I followed Taylor and Jackson to the hootch. Taylor pushed open the door and we all filed inside. Coming in from the sunlight, I couldn't see the darkened interior well, but it smelled of dust and it held an aroma akin to a gym locker, evidence of having hosted sweaty bodies.

My eyes adjusted to the dimness, and the light through the door revealed a single room twenty feet square. Some metal camp beds, unfolded, were set up on the floor with thin, bare mattresses sprawled on top of the metal springs. A couple of canvas cots sat on the floor and a couple of others leaned against a wall. A paperback book lay open, facedown on one of the beds.

A card table occupied the middle of the room, and in one of the corners near the door, a field phone sat on the floor. A wire from the phone snaked across the room and disappeared through a hole drilled in the wall. Taylor lowered himself to the phone, picked up the handset, and cranked the handle on the base. He waited and then spoke to someone on the other end of the landline. "Commo check. Ready Shack." He paused. "Right," he said, and hung up.

Taylor flipped over the mattress on one of the metal beds, allowing the loose dirt on top to spill on the floor. Dust particles swarmed in the sunlight beaming through the door. He lay down on the flip side of the mattress and pulled his cap over his eyes.

Jackson sat down on another camp bed, reached into a pocket of his fatigue pants, and pulled out a small tin can. He reached inside his fatigue shirt and pulled out his dog tag chain. On it, along with his two dog tags, was a P-38 can opener, the kind that came with C-Rations. He held the can up to his chest so that it was within reach of the opener and pinched the sharp edge of the P-38 around the inside of the can's lip until the opener had cut around the lid enough for him to pull it back. The aroma of peaches drifted my way, prompting a growl from my empty stomach.

Jackson fished a plastic fork out of the same pocket where the can had been. I watched him as he speared a peach, lifted it to his mouth, chewed it, and swallowed. I could imagine the taste of that sweet, juicy peach on my dry tongue. My mouth involuntarily chewed along with his, and I swallowed when he swallowed. Jackson ate the last peach, drank the remaining juice, and sat the empty can on the floor. I would have given three months' flight pay for a can of peaches.

The door had been left open to allow in light and to catch any breeze that might stir, but no breeze blessed us. I was sitting on one of the cots near Jackson's and the hard rail pressed against my upper leg. I occasionally shifted my weight, alternating legs to regain circulation in whichever one the rail had shut off. We sat, nobody speaking, and it grew hotter.

The phone rang and Taylor rose to answer it. He spoke into the handset. "Ready Shack." He listened, spoke a single word— "Right"—and hung up.

He was already on his way out the door when he threw over his shoulder, "We've got a scramble."  Jackson rose to follow Taylor and George fell in behind them. I jumped to fill the door behind George, accidentally kicking the empty peach can with my half numb leg.

## The Red Fire Hose

The four of us spilled out of the Ready Shack in a string and ran to the Cobras. Jackson and I broke off from the string to man our helicopter. The crew chief was no longer there. Jackson said to me, "Untie the rotor blades."

I hurried to the back of the aircraft, unwrapped the rotor tie-down lines from the stinger, then slipped off the clamp and nudged the blade. The momentum carried the blade perpendicular to the fuselage, coasting to a stop. I tossed the tie-down into the space behind the Cobra's back seat. Jackson was already strapped in and yelled "Clear!" prior to pulling the engine's starter trigger. I ran to the other side of the aircraft and stepped up to the cockpit. One foot in, I saw the chicken plate lying on the seat where I had left it. I stepped back out of the cockpit, grabbed the chicken plate from the seat, and strapped it on. The turbine engine was winding up. I put one foot on the step-up to the cockpit and pulled myself in. I squeezed into the seat, brought the seat belt around my waist, the shoulder straps over my chest, and buckled the harness pieces together at the front.

The turbine was growing louder, coming up to speed. The main rotor blade was turning, gathering speed. I squeezed the flight helmet onto my head and fastened the chinstrap. The switches on my communication panel were already on and I heard Jackson on the intercom. "You ready?" I pulled the helmet mike down in front of my lips and stepped on the intercom switch on the floor. "Ready," I said.

I glanced at the instrument panel and saw the engine and rotor tachometer needles aligning in the green arc. I heard Jackson on the radio. "Lead, Viper Three-Two's ready."

Then I heard Taylor's voice on the radio. "Can Tho tower, Viper Three-Three. Revetments one and three. On a scramble."

I heard the tower operator respond. "Viper Three-Three, cleared for immediate takeoff, runway two-five. Winds calm."

I heard Taylor's voice again. "Viper Three-Three on the go."

I saw the other Cobra lift to a hover in its revetment and ease out. Taylor hovered it directly ahead the short distance to the runway and made a pedal turn to align the aircraft with the runway. His Cobra's nose dipped, and the aircraft began moving ahead and lifting.

Jackson brought our Cobra to a hover, eased out of the revetment, and turned up the runway. Its nose dipped and the Cobra scooted down the runway, picking up speed. Before reaching the end of the runway, the Cobra began climbing, quickly reaching a thousand feet before leveling off a bit, then climbing more slowly to fifteen hundred. The lead helicopter was a half klick ahead.

As we climbed out and flew away, I tried to keep my bearings, looking for landmarks that would help me find the way back to Can Tho. But everything looked the same, a million-piece jigsaw puzzle of meandering rivers, crooked streams, crisscrossed canals, flooded rice paddies, and occasional tree lines.

After several minutes of flying, I heard from the radio "Viper Three-Two, come up two-five-five-four uniform." I heard

Jackson reply to the lead ship, "Two-five-five-four". In a moment, I heard Taylor again. "Gray Lion Six, Viper Three-Three."

"Viper Three-Three, Gray Lion Six," said another voice.

"Gray Lion, Viper Three-Three with a light fire team of Cobras is ETA five."

"Roger, Viper. Be advised I've got a ground unit in contact with Chuck. Remain on this push and contact Bronze Alpha on Fox Mike three-two-point-niner-five."

"Three-two-point-niner-five. Viper Three-Three. Roger."

"Viper Three-Two, copy the Fox Mike push?"

"Three-Two. Affirm."

After a few moments, I heard, "Bronze Alpha, this is Viper Three-Three with a pair of Cobras. ETA your position in three."

A voice answered and I heard the rattling of weapons in the background. "Viper, Bronze Alpha. We're receiving automatic weapons fire from a tree line. Can you put some ordnance on it?"

"Where are your people, Alpha?"

"I'll pop smoke when you're ready."

"Go ahead, Alpha, pop smoke."

I was trying to keep up with the conversations. I scanned the patches of rice paddies. They all looked alike to me.

"Smoke's out, Viper."

At eleven o'clock, a klick ahead, I saw a cloud of purple smoke billowing from a rice paddy. A hundred yards away, to the right, another plume of smoke—yellow—rose from the rice paddy."

"Alpha, Viper Three-Three. I have crazy grape and banana."

"Confirm that, Viper. My front extends between the two smokes."

"I understand you're receiving fire at this time, Alpha?"

"We were, but that's a negative at this moment. I think Charlie saw you coming. He's somewhere in that tree line to our immediate front, though. Can you work it over for us?"

"Roger, Alpha. Will do."

"Viper, this is Gray Lion. Confirm you have the friendlies' position?"

"Affirmative, Gray Lion, we have the friendlies."

"Gray Lion to Viper. Permission to fire."

"Roger permission to fire. Uh, Gray Lion, say altitude."

"Two-five."

"Okay, Gray Lion, we'll stay under two. Going in now."

"Viper Three-Two, go hot."

"Two's going hot."

Then, I assumed Jackson was talking to me on the intercom. "Weapons are armed."

I removed the flex sight from its mount. It controlled the turret weapons under the Cobra's chin.

"Three-Two, let's dog leg around the left side of the friendlies' line and make our run southeast to northwest, up the tree line from that direction. Break is right."

"Roger break is right."

I watched the lead Cobra ahead. It flew a quarter mile to the left of the purple smoke, and then turned right to align with the length of the tree line. Jackson followed, making a larger-radius turn, letting our Cobra slip to the left of the lead ship.

I saw the lead ship's nose angle down slightly. Its shallow dive was taking it toward the tree line directly ahead. Then, from the front of the ship, I saw red tracers streaming from the Cobra's minigun on the turret. George was shooting.

The stream of tracers hit near the edge of the tree line, kicking up water geysers in the rice paddy. George adjusted the minigun and the red stream moved into the trees. Leaves and limbs flew into the air.

The red stream stopped and I saw the flash of rockets igniting in the pods under the lead ship's wing stubs. The rockets burned briefly, barely long enough to clear the tubes. I followed the rockets' flight until their motors burned out and I lost the white bodies against the pale water in the rice paddy below. Then a burst of leaves, limbs, and other debris erupted from the trees near the edge of the rice paddy. I saw a second burst farther down, and a third even further down.

Jackson now had us in a shallow dive toward the tree line. "Ready up there?" he said.

He must be talking to me. I was already gripping the flex sight. I pulled it closer and peered through the transparent glass plate, pivoting it so that the illuminated circle, the "pipper", on the glass overlaid the position on the tree line where the last rockets from the lead ship had hit. I pushed the intercom button on the floor. "Ready."

I saw the lead Cobra turn away sharply to the right. Jackson had set us up with a clear line of fire to the tree line. "Shoot," he said.

I pressed the triggers on the flex weapons' sight. Underneath, the miniguns on the chin turret erupted in a steady clatter, each gun spitting out four thousand rounds a minute, every sixth round a tracer. Through the sighting device, I saw the red tracers streaking toward the tree line, the streaks from each gun appearing as a continuous stream of red, a familiar sight from Cobra school called a "red fire hose." The rounds landed shorter than I intended, so I tilted the handles of the flex sight slightly and the red fire hose snaked further ahead. I held the triggers and let the red fire hose run up the line of trees, matching the Cobra's speed.

The Cobra, diving at an angle, drew closer to the tree line. Above the sound of the minigun, I heard Jackson in my earphones. "Cease firing."

I released the triggers. The red fire hose was gone.

Immediately, in my peripheral vision, I saw a flash from the rocket tubes and felt a slight shake from the aircraft. The rockets, one from a pod on each side of the ship, zoomed ahead. In a few seconds, the flame from the end of the rockets burned out, but this time I could see the rockets clearly and I followed their flight. They streaked toward the tree line and impacted there, a little further up from where the lead ship's last rockets had hit. Leaves, limbs, and mud flew into the air. There was another pair of flashes from the tubes and another pair of rockets streaked down, striking the tree line twenty yards farther up. There was a third flash and another pair of rockets exploded in the trees. I heard Jackson's voice: "Shoot." And he began turning away from the tree line.

Sighting the piper, I pulled the triggers on the flex grip. As we turned, I swiveled the turret, pouring the red fire hose onto the tree line until the turret reached the limits of its travel, and then released the triggers.

I saw the lead ship had made a circle and was already nosing into another dive. Jackson tightened his turn to come around behind it and positioned our Cobra slightly off to one side. I saw the lead Cobra's rockets exploding in the tree line; then it broke away.

I concentrated on my job and got ready to shoot again. The radios had been full of chatter, but I had tuned out all the voices except for Jackson's. Like the dog in the RCA Victor ad, I was listening only to my master's voice.

Suddenly, the pace and the intensity of the chatter increased and the radio conversations swelled up and into my consciousness again. The voices were charged, the exchanges fast and intermingled. When a speaker keyed his mike, the whoosh of the radio's squelch made the voices sound as if they were pushing against the wind. The conversations were jumbled together, the voices clipped, sometimes stepping on each other.

"Whoosh. Viper, this is Alpha. Good strike. That's the spot. Now, work your way…Whoosh. Viper, This is Gray Lion Six. You flushed them; we've got troops in the open." Whoosh. "Roger, Six." Whoosh. "Three-Two, they're at my six. I can't see them. You got them?" Whoosh. "That's a negative, Lead." Whoosh. "Lion Six, Viper Lead, where are they?" Whoosh. "Lion Six, uh, this is Alpha, say again." Whoosh. "Viper, the far side of the tree line, I say again, the far side of the tree line. Whoosh. "Lion Six, this is Alpha, over." Whoosh. "Viper, they're running from the tree line." Whoosh, "Three-Two, got them?" Whoosh. "Yeah, Lead, I see them now." Whoosh. "Take them, Two." Whoosh. "I'm on them." Whoosh. "Viper, they're moving onto the dike behind the tree line. Break. Bronze Alpha, Lion Six. They're breaking contact, moving out of the far side of the tree line. Move your men directly to your right front and intercept them." Whoosh. "This is Alpha. Roger. Di Wee, get your men…." Whoosh. "Three-Two, I'm coming around behind you." Whoosh. "Yeah, come on around, Lead. There's a bunch strung out on the dike on the far side of that tree line, about where your last rockets hit." Whoosh. "Go ahead, Three-Two, sweep them up from the rear with the minis. Get what you can and I'll get the rest." Whoosh. "Three-Two, roger." Whoosh. "Lion Six, this is Alpha. I'm putting men on the dike in pursuit." Whoosh. "Roger, Alpha, close on them." Whoosh, "Lead, Three-Two. I'm going in now." Whoosh. "Roger that, Three-Two. Watch the friendlies; they're on the dike now too."

I tried to make sense of all the exchanges on the multiple radios. Who was where? What dike? There were dikes everywhere. Where were the friendlies? The smoke from the canisters had died out, but purple and yellow haze hung in the air below, mingled together.

I saw two clusters of people below. One group was near the tree line not far from where the lead Cobra's last rockets had impacted. They were strung out, some on a dike and others wading toward it in ankle-deep water. When a straggler reached the dike, he gained better footing and began running along the top of it. The other group, farther behind, was also strung out, some of them on the dike, others angling toward it.

The radios poured a constant stream of tangled voices into my earphones. "Three-Two, I've got you ... Lion Six ... break left ... this is Alpha ... We're moving ... Viper, Lion Six ... the friendlies are closing on ..."

Then, out of the jumble came Jackson's voice, "Shoot them."

Shoot who? There were two groups of people below. I sighted the pipper on one cluster. Were these the ones I was to shoot? I moved the pipper to the other group. Or were these the ones?

Jackson's voice, insistent, rose again through the jumble. "Shoot."

I had the pipper on the closest group. Then I saw they were wearing olive drab uniforms. I swung the pipper to the other group, the ones wearing black pajamas. I pulled the triggers.

The miniguns chattered. The twin streams of the red fire hose plunged down, striking the edge of the dike. The red fire hose snaked onto the top of the dike, chewing the earth into small pieces, spewing them aside. It crept toward the rearmost pajama-clad figure running on the dike. It was at his heels, gaining on him; then the red fire hose caught him and he fell in the eruption of torn earth.

The red fire hose—relentless, without pity, without joy, conscious only of its purpose—moved steadily up the length of the dike. It touched the next in the string of running figures. Then, the next. And the next. One after another, they fell when the red fire touched them.

The Cobra was closing on the dike. There were still more figures, some on the dike, some in the water near it. My master's voice spoke. "Cease firing." I released the triggers.

Jackson opened up, firing the miniguns mounted on the wing pods. Parallel streams of red tracers rained down on the dike, across it, into the rice paddy. Jackson stepped on a pedal, swinging the Cobra and the fixed-point weapons back onto the dike. Chewed dirt flew into the air, obscuring the figures, splashing into the water. It was curious, I thought; somehow the red fire was turning the water red.

Jackson made his break, turning away from the dike. I looked back. The lead Cobra was behind us. Red fire shot from the turret. Rockets exploded on the dike and in the rice paddy. Jackson continued the turn and I lost sight of the target area as we turned away. I quickly turned my head to look out of the other side of the cockpit. A cloud of dust hung over the dike, but no more pajama-clad people were on it.

"Viper, this is Lion Six. Good shooting. Standby while I take a look."

We flew off a couple of klicks to the north, making lazy circles, while the Command and Control ship inspected the area. After a time, the Air Mission Commander determined there was nothing more for us to shoot and he released us.

We flew back to Can Tho and parked the Cobras in their revetments. The crew chiefs were there and began rearming the Cobras; a tanker came to refuel the aircraft.

When we had scrambled, the backup alert team had moved into the Ready Shack and we were now the backup team to take their place if they were scrambled. As backup to the primary team, we didn't have to stay in the Ready Shack as long as we weren't too far away and Operations knew where to contact us, so we went to the mess hall for lunch.

Before, Jackson and Taylor had little to say to George and me, but as we shared the meal, they now talked with us like we were long-lost cousins at a family reunion.

## The Autocracy of Autorotations

The next morning, I was told to report to Operations for a standardization flight, a requirement to confirm that I could fly a Cobra, and also to show me how things were done in the 235th.

I hung around Operations until the company's standardization pilot, a CW2, showed up. We went to the revetment where a Cobra was parked and he looked over my shoulder as I preflighted the aircraft, asking some questions about my observations to see if I knew where things were, how they worked, and how they were supposed to look or feel. Then, I climbed into the back seat and he took the front seat. This was my first time in the back seat since Cobra school and it felt good. While I settled in, he briefed me on the Can Tho traffic pattern, radio communications with the tower, and other procedures, most of which I had picked up from the one previous flight.

We flew to an area southwest of Can Tho where he had me perform some flight maneuvers, many of them the same ones required for my final check ride at Cobra Hall, but he also showed me some other ones I hadn't been taught in the States. He was a good instructor, clearly explaining what he wanted me do to do and demonstrating the new techniques before letting me try them a time or two.

After meeting his satisfaction with all the things he asked, he had me fly to Binh Thuy, an airfield a little more than a klick west of Can Tho, to perform an autorotation, the helicopter equivalent to an airplane's "dead-stick" landing. Even though both the Air Force and the Navy had a presence at Binh Thuy, it was less busy than Can Tho.

At Binh Thuy, he pointed out a marshy area near the runway. That's where he wanted me to make the autorotation landing so that we wouldn't tie up the runway. He said he wanted me to show him a full autorotation to the ground, not one of those with a power recovery before nearly touching down. And it wasn't going to be one of those autorotations that came by surprise, one where the instructor unexpectedly cut the throttle. I could set it up to suit me and initiate it when I wanted to. Compared to flight school, I felt this was a piece of cake.

I stayed away from the runway, flew a downwind leg parallel to the marsh, rolled off the throttle, quickly lowered the collective to allow the rotor to windmill, turned a hundred and eighty degrees to put the Cobra into the slight wind, and glided toward the marsh.

The only thing that bothered me about this autorotation was the marsh. It was covered with what I estimated to be about two feet of standing water, and I didn't know what was underneath the surface. I thought there could be a small dike or a tangle of discarded concertina wire or something else that might snag the skids. Consequently, at the bottom of the autorotation, right above the surface of the water, I zeroed out the airspeed, and while raising the collective, let the Cobra settle straight down into the shallow water, essentially terminating the maneuver with a hovering autorotation.

I couldn't have been more pleased with that autorotation. However, that's not how the standardization pilot wanted it done. He wanted some ground run after touchdown. I argued my case, explaining why I thought my way was better for the circumstances. He listened patiently before explaining to me, quietly and respectfully, something he thought I ought to consider. I could either do it his way, or I could insist on doing it my way, the result of which would be that he wouldn't sign off my check ride, and I could continue my tour with the 235th as a perpetual copilot in the front seat and without the prospect of becoming an Aircraft Commander in the back seat.

I weighed the principle of my argument against the practicality of adhering to it, then I rolled on the throttle, lifted the Cobra out of the water, took off, flew a half circle, rolled off the throttle, dumped the collective, completed the circle, lined up for the marsh, and landed the Cobra in it, this time allowing the skids to scoot along under the surface a few feet before settling lightly into the mud.

"Nicely done," he said, "Someone must have taught you well."

Exactly right, I thought. It had been Mister Melette.

## Mister Melette

In flight school, every instructor pilot I had was different and I learned something from all of them, yet the one IP I remembered most was Mister Melette. He was a civilian instructor pilot in the UH-1 transition phase of flight training at Fort Rucker. That was the part of flight school where we Army helicopter student pilots were introduced to the Huey. Prior to that, all of our flight instruction had been in vintage helicopters no longer widely used outside of training or in ones used exclusively for training. The Huey, however, was a part of the Army's combat operational fleet and was the helicopter that the majority of Army aviators flew.

I entered the Huey transition phase of flight school in a state of disbelief. I couldn't believe I had made it that far. Contrary to the opinion I had about my aptitude for flying before I actually attempted to fly anything, my experience in flight school had knocked the notion from my mind that I had some natural talent for this profession. The evidence and the testimony were conclusive. In addition to the evidence of my own firsthand experience testifying to the difficulty I had in getting a helicopter to do what I wanted, several of my IPs had shared with me their opinion of my ineptness in grasping the skills of flying a helicopter. Therefore, based upon the evidence and opinions of expert witnesses, I was convicted in my mind, and beyond any reasonable doubt, that the only reason why I kept passing from one phase of flight training to the next was because each IP feared that if he flunked me, I might be recycled through that phase and he would get me again. Now, there I was, beginning the Huey transition phase and nearing the end of flight school. I wondered, how long was the Army going to let me get away with this?

Perhaps it was the luck of the draw or, more precisely, the order of the alphabet that brought me to Mister Melette. He drew three students from my class: Mathis, McComic, and McLean. Maybe it was a coincidence that Mister Melette's name also started with an "M."

Mathis was a quiet, reserved person. McLean was outgoing, and because he already had a private pilot license before starting flight school, he often volunteered to explain aeronautical things to anyone he felt needed help. He carried around a pocket notebook to jot down important information in case anyone needed to be set straight on something.

Mister Melette had flown P-47s in World War II, which may have been only slightly riskier than flying with Army student pilots trying to learn how to fly helicopters, but I learned also that he once had a crop dusting business in Munday, Texas. That fact automatically raised him several more notches on my scale of esteem. As a kid growing up on a farm in Texas and wanting to fly, among my first encounters with flying machines, other than hay balers caught up by tornadoes, were with crop dusting airplanes. Unlike a fighter or bomber I saw only in a movie, and unlike even an airliner way up in the sky too high to cast even a shadow on the field where I sweated with a hoe and a cotton sack, a crop dusting airplane had been immediate and real.

One day when I was a kid, I watched a crop dusting biplane perform its ballet, dipping into a field, skimming the rows of cotton, rearing on its tail to climb over the trees of a fencerow, circling tight, and doing it again and again. Once, as the plane's path brought it in my direction, the pilot waved down at me and I felt blessed.

Mister Melette belied the stereotype dashing aviator. He was a short, round fellow and totally without pretension. I learned that when it came to flying, Mister Melette had nothing to be pretentious about; he was thoroughly competent. And, as I have discovered to be true of most competent people in their profession, he appeared to make it easy.

And talk!? Mister Melette could carry on a continuous one-man conversation on any subject that attracted his interest, and apparently, there wasn't anything that didn't interest him. But he was especially interested in talking about anything we fledgling aviators wanted to know about flying. He always stopped to listen whenever any of us had a question and he could always ask just the right question himself to make sure we got the point of anything he wanted us to understand.

That first day of Huey flight training, Mister Melette walked us through a hands-on preflight inspection. Then, he chose Candidate Mathis to be the first one to fly the Huey. Mathis settled into the front seat with its set of controls and beside the other seat with its controls where Mister Melette sat. McLean and I climbed into the back. Mister Melette, while directing Mathis, stepped us through the start-up procedure for the aircraft. McLean and I craned our heads from the back. I watched every step as if I were trying to learn the intricacies of brain surgery. McLean took notes and repeated to me some of the steps that he thought I might have missed.

After the engine was running, the rotor was turning, and Mister Melette had explained all the proper readings for the instruments, I was surprised that he simply said to Mathis, "Okay, let's go." Because this was the first time for any of us in a Huey, I expected he would at least hover it himself out of the crowded tie-down area.

Mathis took the controls and brought the aircraft up to a hover with barely a bobble. He hovered it through the tie-down area and up to the runway with hardly any fishtailing at all, and he held it pretty close to three feet off the ground all the way. I was glad Mathis was doing this and not me.

With Mister Melette directing the way, Mathis flew the helicopter out to the stage field. On the way there, Mister Melette pointed out key landmarks, including the distant Dothan radio tower and the pasture with the lone hollowed-out pine tree where, he assured us, an owl roosted during the daytime.

All the way there, Mister Melette talked about a variety of subjects, including the full spectrum of significant airspeeds: those for normal flight, best rate-of-climb, best glide ratio, not-to-exceed, and others. He talked about engine-out procedures and explained at length a personal theory he had developed about how to determine the health of an engine by smelling the exhaust.

We soon arrived at the stage field, a piece of pasture with an asphalt runway, a small building, and a windsock, all surrounded by a barbed wire fence. Mister Melette had Mathis land the helicopter on the grass beside the runway. When the aircraft came to a rest, he asked Mathis to roll the throttle to flight idle. Then Mister Melette turned to the back seat, looked at my nametag, and said, "McComic, it's your turn."

I said, "Yes, sir," and nodded my head, but my knees were shaking "no."

I thought, this was it; this is where it all comes to an end. Oh sure, I had survived all of preliminary flight training at Fort Wolters by the grace of some benevolence. And thus far at Ft. Rucker, I had even managed to fly a TH-13 on cockpit instruments alone without totally inverting it, even though I was hooded like some dray horse. But this was different. This was a real helicopter—a Huey—just like the ones that real helicopter pilots flew, not some farm boy like me.

But, having no other recourse other than immediately agreeing to spend the rest of my Army career as an infantryman, I climbed into the front where Mathis had been and strapped myself into the pilot's seat.

I sat there, fumbling with the seat adjustment, trying to delay my last moments in flight school. Mister Melette filled those moments by reviewing the green zone of every instrument on the panel that had one, then moved to an analysis of why the ash tray in the aircraft was located where it was, and concluded with an opinion regarding the misplacement of the stage field's runway in relation to the prevailing wind.

Eventually, seeing as how I could no longer delay the inevitable, I shifted in my seat like a bronc rider in the chute settling onto "Ol' Thunder and Lightning" and I rolled on the throttle, watching the engine and rotor tach needles marry; that is, align with one another on the combined tachometer.

Just as he did with Mathis, Mister Melette said to me, "Okay, let's go."

I pulled up on the collective and wiggled the cyclic and foot pedals but with little expectation of holding the Huey in one spot as it came off the ground. Why wasn't Mister Melette on the controls with me? Didn't he know that, by myself, I wouldn't be able to hover a real helicopter and keep it within the confines of the state of Alabama, let alone within the perimeter of a stage field? Mister Melette, unconcerned, was caught up in an explanation of why windsocks were shaped the way they were.

When I eased the Huey off the ground, to my surprise, it only drifted a few inches before I was able to catch it and hold it on that spot. Mister Melette said, "Give me a normal take off." I pulled up some more on the collective, nudged the cyclic forward, and up we went, climbing away from the stage field. I kept waiting for Mister Melette to show me how I really ought to be doing a takeoff with a Huey, but he simply said, "Stay in the pattern." That meant I was supposed to climb to only 500 feet above the ground and stay in a flight path close to the stage field, a pattern that was an approximate rectangle and where part of one of the long sides of the rectangle was the runway. It was the standard flight path used for landings.

On the climb out from the stage field and as I turned the crosswind leg of the traffic pattern, Mister Melette pointed out a pond that he felt had promising fishing potential. As Mister Melette continued talking about fishing the pond, I turned to the downwind leg of the pattern, paralleling the runway. I handled the controls gently so as not to disturb whoever, or whatever, was actually flying this Huey. It couldn't be me. Maybe the Army had installed some kind of autopilot on a Huey that no one had mentioned.

About halfway along the downwind leg, Mister Melette was speculating on the best bait to use for fishing the pond. That's when he reached down and rolled off the helicopter's throttle. He interrupted his bait discussion briefly to interject for my benefit, "Simulated engine failure", before continuing the discourse.

Cutting the throttle was such a surprise, I didn't have time to think; I just reacted. I automatically shoved down the collective in my left hand to reduce the lifting pitch of the rotor blades so the rotor could continue to turn without a disastrous degree of coning. With no power from the engine, the Huey began to sink. Only the up rushing air was keeping the rotor blades spinning.

This maneuver with a helicopter, called autorotation, was similar to a dead-stick landing with an airplane. In the event of an engine failure, it allowed the rotor blades to freewheel, providing some gliding capacity to reach a landing spot and preserving enough spin in the rotors so the pilot could use the lifting inertia in the spinning blades to cushion the helicopter at touchdown. However, "gliding" wasn't the most accurate term for describing a helicopter in autorotation. A more accurate description was "controlled free fall." There was an ongoing debate between members of helicopter academe about whether a helicopter in autorotation flew like a falling rock or fell like a flying rock.

Although I was in the pattern and set up for a landing on the stage field's runway, surely Mister Melette wasn't expecting me to make an autorotation landing, was he? Sure, I had practiced this maneuver in other helicopters, but this was different. This was a Huey, a helicopter made for real pilots. Mister Melette needed to be on the controls with me.

No longer under the delusion that anything or anyone other than me was flying the aircraft, I gripped the controls, holding the helicopter straight ahead on the downwind leg of the landing pattern. I waited for Mister Melette to tell me when I should turn the base leg back toward the runway but he apparently wasn't paying attention to those details. He was half turned toward the back seat, elaborating for Mathis and McLean the proper aging of stink bait. With a quick glance to the back seat, I saw that McLean was taking notes on this.

The helicopter continued losing altitude, its rotor windmilling. Out of the corner of my eye, I watched the runway slipping away behind me. When it seemed to me that I was about to get too far away from the runway, I decided to go ahead and make the turn. I wasn't sure that it was the right time to do that, yet when I started the turn, Mister Melette simply asked me, "Where do you plan to touch down?"

I replied tentatively, "On the runway?"

"That's good," he said, "but where exactly on the runway?"

It seemed to me that Mister Melette had misplaced priorities. Here we were, in a helicopter falling out of the sky, with some farm boy he had met only that day at the controls, and he was asking this boy to be precise about where the impact would occur. Why wasn't he on the controls with me?

I hastily picked a spot. "Uh, I guess there beside the stage field building," I stabbed. I had no more confidence in predicting where I would touch down than I did in picking a winner when I went to the weekend dog races in Panama City.

I was wide-eyed, rounding out the turn to line up with the runway while riding the collective, adjusting it up and down, adding and subtracting pitch on the rotor blades to keep the rotor tachometer in the green zone.

As we plummeted toward the ground, Mister Melette studied the building alongside the runway, a wooden building some fifty feet long with two small windows facing the runway. "Tell you what," he said, "if you can touch down right across from the second window, I'll buy you a coke."

McLean thought it was a wager. "I'll raise you two cokes," he said, and he wrote it down. I took a grim satisfaction in knowing that McLean would never collect those cokes since I felt certain, with me at the controls, none of us would even survive the fundamental basis of the bet.

I sweated with the controls, puzzled about why it was that Mister Melette had me confused with someone else. He was expecting this person, sitting in the seat where I was, to not only somehow land this autorotating helicopter on the runway, but to touch down on a precise spot no longer than the length of a few windowpanes. When was he going to get on the controls with me?

As the runway approached, Mister Melette held forth on the subject of transformations: trading airspeed for altitude and converting the potential lifting energy in autorotating rotor blades into practical kinetic energy for touchdown. And I was sure it was for my benefit that he added a footnote on the relationship between excessive nose-up flare angles and bumping the tail boom stinger.

He only stopped that discussion because something else caught his interest. "Look over there," he said to Mathis and McLean. Pointing out the window, he said, "See that deer in the trees." He stuck his head out of the open window to see it more clearly. "I think it's a white tail," he said.

I despaired. More interested in wildlife than even his own self-preservation, I no longer had any hope that Mister Melette was going to save us. Obviously, Mister Melette wasn't a judge of flying ability, and his mistake in judgment by letting me attempt this autorotation landing all by myself was going to prove disastrous.

So, realizing that it was all up to me, I decided I had to perform at least well enough to convince the accident investigating board—when it studied the resulting wreckage—that the flight training dollars the Army had spent on me hadn't been totally wasted.

The hurtling Huey was fifty feet above the runway. I pulled back on the cyclic to flare the aircraft, attempting to slow its forward momentum and its descent. I held the cyclic back, trying to be careful and not flare the aircraft so much that it ballooned up into the air. I felt the pressure on the seat of my pants as the plunging Huey began slowing its rate of descent. I continued holding backpressure on the cyclic. Nose up, the Huey was now skimming above the runway and sinking toward it at a more sedate rate. Then, as the Huey's forward speed slowed, I eased the cyclic forward to level the aircraft and bring the skids parallel with the runway. As the nose came down, the aircraft began to fall again. I pulled up on the collective in an attempt to cushion the impact with the runway. I braced myself, squinted my eyes, and held on. The Huey touched the runway as gently as a puffy snowflake on an outstretched mitten, scooted forward on its skids a few feet, and stopped.

Mister Melette pulled his head from the window. "Yep, definitely a white tail," he said.

McLean was jubilant. Looking back at the stage field window Mister Melette had picked, he said, "Hah, you missed it over ten feet. You owe me ...", and he paused to refer to his notes, "... three cokes."

I sat there, in disbelief. I had done it. I had made that autorotation landing all by myself. But how was that possible?

Then, a possible explanation came to me. Maybe I actually was becoming a real helicopter pilot. Maybe all those other IPs had, in their own way, actually prepared me to become one. And maybe, between the two of us, only Mister Melette had been the one that believed that.

This was an invigorating thought and from that moment on, even though it was still challenging, autorotations were fun.

I asked him, "Mister Melette, can I do that again?"

"Sure," he said, "you can do it again tomorrow, but right now ...", and he turned to the back seat, "... it's McLean's turn."

## Chickenman

After the standardization ride, the company clerk told me that the CO wanted me to finish inprocessing so he could keep his morning report straight. If I was needed, Operations would find me and bring me to the flight line. I spent the rest of the day completing forms so that the Army could account for me in its jungle of paperwork. I felt it was time well spent since I didn't want the Army to lose me and forget to tell me when I could go home.

Toward the end of the day, the clerk found me. He informed me that I had been assigned to be the Assistant Officer-in-Charge for perimeter guard duty that night.

Before sunset, I reported to the perimeter command post allocated for my appointed office, a flimsy stack of ragged sand bags with a tin roof. When I had been assigned the duty of Assistant OIC, I had envisioned something more substantial for a command post, something like the storm cellar back home in Texas that was made of sturdy railroad cross ties and packed dirt. I had spent the greater part of my youth in that cellar, along with family and neighbors, weathering out tornadoes, hail, and lightning. I expected something of at least an equivalent defensive structure for a command post. But, I rationalized, I was new; perhaps my expectations were too high.

In fact, I was so new to Vietnam that my just-issued jungle boots still had the manufacturer's original shine on them, and the discovery was still fresh to me that this was a place where people I didn't even know were trying to shoot me. This revelation was somewhat of a culture shock to me since, from where I came, folks had the courtesy to get to know someone before they shot at him.

At the command post, I chatted briefly with the few other persons with whom I would be spending the night. I was handed an M-16 rifle and a heavy, loose-fitting metal combat helmet, a "steel pot." The radio in the command post, essential for communications with the other posts along the perimeter, was issued to the Sergeant-of-the-Guard, someone who the Army apparently felt could be better trusted with such a piece of gear as that.

I checked to make sure the M-16's safety was on since I didn't want to accidentally shoot any important piece of government property, especially myself. Then I assumed my duty of Assistant OIC by placing my steel pot in a corner of the command post, the rounded side up, and sitting on it.

The sun set and darkness prevailed. With the darkness, came suspicion. I began to suspect there were Viet Cong lurking about. What sounded like the splash of a frog in the swamp could be the footstep of a careless Viet Cong. A sneeze in the dark could be a signal that, according to their prearranged plan, the wire had been cut. As my suspicions grew, I donned my steel pot and clutched the M-16 closer to me. From behind the sand bags, I often raised my head to peer into the darkness. Each time, the steel pot on my head slid down and banged the bridge of my nose.

In the command post, it was too dark to see each other and no one spoke. Only once an hour, the radio came alive briefly as each of the stations around the perimeter checked in with a brief and solemn radio check. As the hours passed, I became more convinced that there were hordes of Viet Cong gathering just outside the perimeter, ready to slither through the wire and pounce on us.

The night stretched eternally. Man-eater Delta mosquitoes, ones that could guzzle a quart a minute, sampled me at their leisure. Throughout the long night, I expected the Viet Cong—"Charlie" as they were called—to throw themselves upon us at any minute.

As it neared dawn and Charlie hadn't come yet, I became even more convinced we were about to be overrun. I knew what those Viet Cong were up to. By waiting this long, they were trying to lull me into thinking they weren't even out there at all.

I didn't know from where exactly along the perimeter the attack would come, but it occurred to me that Charlie might take a special pride in hitting the command post first. Being new, I was uncertain as to the proper protocol for attacks of this nature.

I hunkered down inside the sand bag walls and nervously fingered the trigger of the M-16 to assure myself I could actually find it when I needed it. Suddenly, the radio in the command post crackled to life. Voices were shouting, "He's everywhere! He's everywhere!"

This is it, I thought, the call to arms. I sprang up to the wall, pointing the M-16 into the darkness. Quickly pushing back the steel pot that had slid down over my eyes, I was ready.

As I waited for the oncoming assault, I had a moment to reflect. I reflected on the fact that my Army recruiter had specifically promised me as a condition of my enlistment that, if I became a helicopter pilot, I wouldn't experience situations such as this.

I wasn't in a hurry for it, but it seemed to me the attack was taking a long time to get underway. There was no gunfire, no exploding grenades, no other sounds other than the croaking of frogs and the buzz of mosquitoes. After a while, I began to think about what I had actually heard from the radio. Then I recognized what had happened. Somewhere in one of the bunkers along the perimeter, someone had been listening on his transistor radio to the Chickenman program from AFVN, the Armed Forces radio station in Saigon, and had keyed open the mike of the bunker's radio transmitter just in time to pick up the program's tag line.

Before I went to Vietnam, I sometimes listened to "The Adventures of Chickenman, the Winged Warrior", this spoof of a crime fighter hero who donned a chicken suit to fight "crime and or evil." Of course, every radio program involving a hero requires a trademark phrase. For example, near the end of every Lone Ranger program, someone would ask, "Who was that masked man?" and when his identity was revealed to this clueless person of the old West, the program ended with the Lone Ranger's hearty "Hi yo, Silver, away!" And at the beginning of the Superman program, people on the street debated what they were seeing. "Look, up in the sky," someone would say, "it's a bird." "No," someone else would argue, "it's a plane." Finally, a third party would put an end to the debate by declaring, "It's Superman!" In similar fashion, at the beginning and end of the Chickenman program, a chorus of shrill, dissonant voices would declare the omnipresence of Chickenman. "He's everywhere! He's everywhere!" they'd shout. And that's what I had heard from the command bunker's receiver.

Although relieved to realize there was no attack, I knew that by springing to the wall, I had confirmed my status as an FNG. As fortune would have it however, it was so dark that no one had seen me do it. So, saved from both destruction and embarrassment, I gratefully relaxed to wait for the dawn. Taking off my steel pot and placing it in the corner, I sat on it—like a chicken on an egg.

## Anatomy of a Cobra

The Cobra was a product of Bell Helicopter, the same company that produced the Huey. Although the Cobra inherited some of the same components and concepts proven with the earlier Huey models, it was unique because it was specifically designed to be a gunship. Combining a streamlined fuselage and a higher performance engine, the Cobra was more agile and faster than Hueys.

It was easy to distinguish a Cobra (an AH-1) from a Huey (a UH-1). The most obvious difference was the AH-1's narrow fuselage. Whereas a Huey was designed for a crew of four and was wide enough for two pilots to sit side-by-side, a Cobra's fuselage provided for a crew of only two, one pilot sitting behind the other.

Our Cobras were all G-models, the first production models of the gunship. The AH-1G had a single turboshaft engine, a Lycoming T-53L-13. The engine could produce more than fourteen hundred horsepower, but the output shaft to the rotor couldn't handle that much, and a pilot had to be careful not to overstress the drive train by pulling too much power.

The expression "pulling power" came from the way the pilot adjusted the power from the engine to the rotor. Power was controlled by an up-down handle called a "collective", which also adjusted the amount of concurrent pitch for both rotor blades. Power and pitch were correlated with the collective. Pulling up on the collective increased the pitch of the rotor, increasing the blades' "bite" into the air, and that action also sent more power to the rotor to accommodate that increased bite. A torque meter on the pilot's panel measured how much stress was being placed on the drive train and a pilot had to be careful not to exceed that redline limit by pulling too much power.

It was important that a gunship be faster than the typical aircraft it protected. An Army helicopter gunship not only needed to keep up with a flight of Hueys, it needed to be able to dash ahead of it; for example, when escorting a flight of Hueys toward an LZ, it needed to be able to speed ahead and put in a preparatory strike at the LZ before the Hueys arrived. Whereas a loaded Huey typically cruised at less than a hundred knots, a loaded Cobra's typical cruise speed was about a hundred and forty knots (about a hundred and sixty miles per hour). Its redline speed was a hundred and ninety knots (two hundred and sixteen miles per hour), which it could reach in a dive. A Cobra could literally fly circles around a Huey or a flight of them.

The Cobra was not only fast; it was smooth. It was equipped with a Stability and Control Augmentation System that was designed to help smooth out aircraft motions that weren't due to pilot inputs; wind gusts, for example. The SCAS was important to the Cobra's role as a gunship; it aided its stability, improving the accuracy of its weapons.

Because it was designed to be a gunship, the Cobra's armament system was integral to the aircraft. It had movable weapons and fixed weapons. The turret, at the front and just underneath the nose, held the movable weapons. The aircraft's two wing stubs, one on each side of the fuselage and aerodynamically shaped to reduce drag, held the fixed weapons.

The early turrets on the AH-1 held a single minigun; the Cobras I flew at Cobra Hall had that TAT-102A turret. The 235th's Cobras had a newer chin turret that accommodated two weapons, and although it could be configured with a variety of combinations and arrangements of weapons, the 235th's Cobras employed only two: either two miniguns or a minigun paired with a grenade launcher.

A minigun was a six-barreled Gatling-style machine gun whose barrels were rotated by an electric motor. It fired 7.62-millimeter rounds at a rate of either two- or four-thousand-rounds-per-minute. In our unit, all the miniguns were set at the four-thousand-rounds-per-minute rate. A chain of linked rounds was fed to a turret's minigun from a metal ammo box in the bay behind the turret and underneath the cockpit's front seat position. A box held four thousand rounds, thus each minigun had a maximum of one minute's worth of ammo. A grenade launcher, a "chunker", fired forty-millimeter projectiles at a maximum rate of four-hundred-rounds-per-minute. Its ammo drum, also located in the ammo bay, held up to four hundred rounds.

The weapons on the chin turret were movable and could be pointed at targets by rotating the turret and flexing the weapons up or down. The turret could rotate horizontally a hundred-and-ten degrees either left or right, a total of two-hundred-and-twenty degrees, and the weapons could be flexed up twenty degrees and down fifty degrees.

A handheld targeting device in the front part of the cockpit, the gunner's station, controlled the movement of the turret weapons. The system was designed so that when the gunner in the front seat moved the targeting device up or down or rotated it from side to side, the turret weapons followed the motion.

To sight a target, the gunner looked through a transparent piece of glass on the targeting device and aligned a lighted "pipper" displayed on the glass with the target on the ground. To fire a weapon, he pressed a trigger on the handgrip of the targeting device associated with the weapon he chose.

The gunner, who was in the front seat, normally used the pipper initially to aim the weapon at the target and then adjusted the fire by observing the tracer rounds and where the rounds actually impacted. Rounds were fed to the minigun in metal clips linked together in a chain. Typically every sixth round had a tracer that made a red streak when it was fired. At four-thousand-rounds-per-minute, the tracers looked like one continuous colored stream from the gun, a stream referred to as a "red fire hose." Once the rounds came pouring out, the gunner could direct the rounds by observing the tracer stream, similar to aiming a water stream from a hose.

The gunner usually operated the turret weapons, but a switch allowed them to be fired from the pilot's station in the back. In that case, the turret weapons were stowed in a fixed position straight ahead and couldn't be rotated or flexed.

The weapons on the chin turret were movable. The ones on the wing stubs weren't. The pilot aimed those fixed weapons by aiming the aircraft toward a target, and fired them from his position in the back seat. The pilot's station had a fixed sighting device mounted atop the back seat instrument panel that helped to align the aircraft, and consequently the wing stub weapons, on a target. The sighting device was called a "rocket sight" although the fixed weapons on the wing stubs could be something other than rockets. In our unit, the wing stubs carried either rockets or miniguns, depending upon how an aircraft was configured.

Our Cobras had two configurations: "scout" and "hog." A Cobra configured as a scout had a minigun and a rocket pod on each of the wing stubs. In our unit, the minigun was on the inboard hard point and the outboard hard point held a nineteen-tube rocket pod. Also, in a scout configuration, the turret was rigged with two miniguns.

A Cobra hog had rocket pods on all four hard points, nineteen-tube pods on the inboard hard points and seven-tube pods on the outboard hard points. A hog's turret was rigged with both a minigun and a grenade launcher. In our unit, the minigun was on the right and the grenade launcher on the left

The rocket pods were designed to hold 2.75-inch-diameter, folding fin aerial rockets (FFAR) in their tubes. An assembled rocket consisted of a "motor" with fins at the rear, and on the front, a screw-on warhead with a fuse. The motors held a material that, when ignited, propelled the rockets from the tubes. When loaded into a tube, the rocket's four fins were folded back and in line with the length of the cylindrical rocket assembly. When fired and clear of the tube, the metal fins sprang out and, like the feathers on an arrow, served to stabilize the rocket's flight.

A complete rocket with the more common so-called "ten-pound" warhead was about four-and-a-half feet long. "Seventeen pounder" rockets with a longer warhead packed more punch and were about ten inches longer.

Rocket warheads were packed with different payloads. The most common were high explosive (HE) warheads packed with pieces of cast iron shrapnel. We also used warheads filled with white phosphorous. Phosphorous is highly ignitable; it's the material on match heads. "Willie Pete" warheads were especially effective for igniting targets because phosphorous burned upon contact with almost anything, and because they produced lots of smoke, these warheads also served to mark targets or locations.

Occasionally we ran across a stockpile of flechette warheads, which were packed with hundreds of metallic, finned darts. When these warheads exploded, they released a cloud of red powder to mark the impact area and showered the target area with the lethal missiles. Victims of rockets with these darts, called "nails", could be found literally nailed to a tree. Flechette warheads were effective anti-personnel weapons, but their large bursting radius could endanger friendlies if they were too close.

Warheads were primarily fitted with point detonating fuses, which exploded upon impact. Occasionally, warheads were fitted with proximity fuses, which produced an airburst near the ground.

The rocket pods on our Cobras had either nineteen tubes or seven tubes. Each tube of a rocket pod had an igniter arm at the back that was designed to carry an electrical impulse to a metal contact on the rear of a rocket motor. In the Cobra, the electrical pulse to fire rockets was triggered by a depressing a red button on the left side of the cyclic grip, the same button that fired the miniguns mounted on the wing stubs.

The wing stub weapons were fired in pairs. A selector panel inside the cockpit allowed the pilot to select either the outboard or inboard weapons and, for rockets, the number of pairs to fire: one, two, four, seven, or nineteen. Most often, we shot rockets in single pairs and sometimes two pair at a time.

Part of the rocket armament system was an intervalometer, a device that timed the release of rockets when more than one pair was selected, automatically ripple firing them, which delayed by a fraction of a second the firing of rockets after the first pair so that the blasts from rockets leaving the tubes wouldn't disturb subsequently fired rockets. I liked the name of this device so much, I anticipated some day naming one of my children after it; I thought "Intervalometer McComic" had a certain ring to it.

The rockets were fired in a fixed order based upon their positions in the tubes. For a seven-tube pod, it was relatively easy to remember the order. The nineteen-tube pod also had a set sequence but it was more complex. Theoretically, that level of knowledge could enable arranging rockets in the tubes to ideally suit a mission, but experience taught me I couldn't predict the needs of a mission to that detail. I concluded that the only practical application of knowledge about the firing sequence of rockets was knowing that the first rockets came from the center tubes. Those tubes were sometimes specifically loaded with a Willie Pete warhead with the expectation that its white smoke could serve as a highly visible initial marker round.

Practically speaking, we often didn't have much of a variety of warheads to choose from. Flechettes were rare and when I ran across them, I would load some, mostly for their novelty. Can Tho and some of the larger airfields had white phosphorous warheads, but at the smaller, remote airfields in the Delta where we often rearmed, the stockpiles there usually offered only plain vanilla HE warheads. Even though our choice of warheads was usually restricted to HE, which weren't ideal for some targets, they were usually adequate enough for most targets. Even if we couldn't burn it or nail it, we could usually blow it up.

Although there might be a choice of either ten-pound or seventeen-pound HE heads, I didn't favor seventeen-pounders. In my opinion, the extra oomph wasn't worth the weight. In our unit, we were cautioned to not fully load a nineteen-tube pod with seventeen-pounders because of weight restrictions. Compared to a smaller number of seventeen-pounders, I preferred a larger number of ten-pounders.

When loading rockets into the tubes, it was important to make sure the igniter arms were in contact with the rockets' contact points. With the rocket pods on our Cobras, the rockets were pushed tailfirst into the front of the tubes. It was important that the rockets were shoved far enough back to make contact with the igniter arms. If they didn't, the rockets wouldn't fire. And although the igniter arms had a heavy spring designed to push the arms against the buttons, sometimes a rusty arm, or one that had otherwise become too stiff, got pushed back when a rocket was loaded and didn't spring back to make contact with the rocket. After loading rockets into the tubes, we usually tapped the backs of the igniter arms against the back of the rockets to ensure they had good contact. The Cobra's break out knife, intended to smash open the Plexiglass canopy in case we needed a fast exit, was a convenient tool for tapping the arms.

Sometimes rockets didn't fire. It could be a problem with the rocket but was more often a problem with the igniter arm, the electrical connection between the cockpit and the arm, or the tube. As a rocket tube aged, the lining within its tubes sometimes split or curled. Sometimes, we'd discover tubes were no longer working and it wasn't obvious why. It wasn't practical to replace an entire rocket pod when just one or a few tubes were inoperative; we'd have to wait until enough of them quit working before getting a new pod. Until that time, we marked inoperative tubes with a grease pencil, an indication to not load those tubes when rearming. There was no use in loading a rocket if it was only going along for the ride; an empty pod saved weight.

Sometimes a rocket wouldn't ignite at all, but a potentially worse case was when a rocket did ignite but failed to launch and remained in the tube. When that happened, the rocket could simply burn itself out, but it was possible that the fire from a hung rocket could spread to the entire pod, and from the pod to the aircraft. Although a switch in the cockpit allowed jettisoning a pod by firing the explosive bolts holding the pod to the hard point, I heard of cases where the bolts failed to fire or where one would and the other wouldn't, leaving a burning pod dangling from the wing stub.

As a safety precaution, all weapons were locked out until a toggle switch on the instrument panel, protected by a red flip-up cover, was enabled. This switch was officially named the "master arm switch", but more commonly was called the "hot switch."

The Cobra had a maximum takeoff weight of 9,500 pounds, which just about equaled the collective weight of a Cobra with a crew of two, full ordnance, and a full load of fuel. But that weight was a book number based upon "standard day" conditions that included a sea level altitude, a mild temperature, and moderate humidity. Higher altitudes, temperatures, and humidity reduced that limit. High altitude wasn't a problem in the Delta—much lower and we would have been underwater—but it was hot and humid. Nobody carried around a slide rule to calculate the maximum takeoff weight on a mission-by-mission basis, though. Company policy simplified the matter. Taking the typical Delta climate into consideration, we used 9,300 pounds as a maximum takeoff weight. And assuming we loaded up with full ammunition, which was nearly always the case, we made up the two hundred pound difference with less fuel.

The engine burned JP-4 and we measured it in pounds. Even though the Cobra could hold 1,600 pounds of fuel, we typically topped off at 1,400 pounds. Conveniently, the fourteen-hundred-pound number made it relatively easy to figure our duration; that is, how long we could fly without refueling. The aircraft's rate of fuel consumption varied based upon a number of factors, but for planning purposes, we used a rate of ten pounds per minute. Based upon that rate, the aircraft would burn 1,200 pounds of fuel in 120 minutes; that is, in two hours, leaving a reserve of 200 pounds. The two-hundred-pound reserve coincided closely with the fuel quantity caution light, which we called the "twenty-minute fuel light", meaning that when the light illuminated, we had an estimated twenty minutes of fuel left, which was termed "bingo fuel." The actual time we could fly on that remaining fuel, however, might be more or less, and because it might be significantly less, a lit fuel light was something to worry about. We planned on two hours duration between refuels, but kept an eye on the fuel gauge. Fuel, including where to find it when we needed it, was a consistent consideration in all our operations.

## Cobra Avionics

A Cobra's avionics included its navigation and communication equipment. The latter was as essential as the aircraft's armament.

Since nearly all of the navigation I did in the Delta was by pilotage; that is, using visual landmarks and a map, I normally didn't use several of the aircraft's electronic navigation instruments. And that was just as well since there were few corresponding ground navigational aids in Vietnam upon which those instruments depended.

If I needed to determine a heading, the magnetic fluid filled "wet" compass, easily visible to both the pilot and copilot, was sufficient. It was a type of compass that had been used for decades in aircraft and didn't require electrical power; however, the Cobra's Radio Magnetic Indicator was more easily readable and more precise. There were two RMIs, one on the pilot's panel and one on the copilot's. A quick glance at the RMI told me the aircraft's current heading, and in rough air, it didn't bounce around like the wet compass, nor did its heading indicator lead or lag direction in turns, dives, and climbs as did the wet compass.

In addition to serving as a heading indicator, the RMI had two needles intended for use with ground-based navigational aids. The thinner needle pointed toward a selected VHF Omni Directional Radio Range navigational aid, but I wasn't aware of any VORs in the Delta. The RMI's wider needle worked in conjunction with an Automatic Direction Finder (ADF) receiver and pointed to a different kind of navigational aid that was more primitive than a VOR but had a greater range. As with VORs, I wasn't aware of any navigational aid in the Delta specifically intended for the ADF; however, the ADF receiver was useful for a purpose other than navigation. It had the ability to receive audio, which allowed a pilot to hear the Morse code letters identifying the specific navigational beacon to which it was tuned, but it could also tune AM broadcast radio stations, and by tuning the ADF receiver to AFVN, the Armed Forces Vietnam Network radio station in Saigon, we could listen to its programs. It was like listening to an AM car radio. When tuned to AFVN, the ADF needle pointed toward the station's transmitter; that is, toward Saigon.

Our Cobras were equipped with a transponder, a device that worked in conjunction with a ground-based radar facility. When the facility's radar sent an interrogation signal, the transponder could return a coded signal, essentially a number, that specifically identified the aircraft on the facility's radar screen. For the radar controller to know what aircraft was associated with a code, it required coordination between the controller and the aircraft's pilot. The controller verbally told the pilot the code to "squawk" and the pilot dialed that number into the transponder's panel. The transponder had an "Ident" momentary contact switch that, when activated, caused the squawked code to be enhanced on the operator's screen for a short time so the radar operator could more easily spot it among others he may have on his screen.

The aircraft was equipped with three two-way communication radios: a UHF (Ultra High Frequency) band radio, a VHF (Very High Frequency) band radio— both AM radios—and an FM (Frequency Modulation) radio. The "Fox Mike" radio was used to communicate with ground units. Universally, ground units carried the battery-powered, portable PRC-25 ("Prick Twenty-Five") FM transceiver, which shared a common band of frequencies with a Cobra's FM radio.

Generally speaking, the VHF ("Victor") radio was employed for communications between individual aircraft that were part of the same unit; for example, conversations between the individual helicopters in a flight of slicks. In our case, the VHF radio was used for conversations between the individual Cobras in a fire team.

The UHF ("Uniform") radio was generally used for more global communications. For example, an airfield with a control tower had a UHF frequency used by any aircraft that wanted to talk with the tower. It was a frequency that rarely changed and it was unique to that airfield's range of communication. The UHF band was used also for communication with an area's radar facility. In addition, the UHF radio was used for a common communication channel with airmobile operations that employed air assets from different units. An airmobile operation coordinated by a Command and Control ship was given a temporary, designated UHF frequency for that operation and all its air assets communicated on that frequency. Those air assets included the Air Mission Commander and, for example, an assault company's lift ships, the assault company's gunships, and one of our fire teams assigned to the operation. An airmobile operation that warranted an AMC typically had at least twenty, usually more, aircraft. If each aircraft tried to talk on that one frequency, it would be pandemonium; so typically only the spokesperson for a particular air asset used that channel; for example, the flight leader for a group of Hueys or the fire team leader for gunships.

Sometimes, though, it was still pandemonium. When things got hot, the radios came alive. People were talking on all the radios simultaneously: gunship fire team leaders, slick flight leaders, Air Mission Commanders, sometimes other assets, and people on the ground talking with people in the air. Especially in those situations, persons would sometimes try to transmit at the same time; for example, a fire team leader might key his mike to talk with the AMC on the UHF channel at the same time as a slick flight leader keyed his mike for that channel. Usually when that happened, nobody could hear any conversation on that radio, only static or a loud squeal as the radio signals collided with each other.

Both the UHF and VHF radios had the capability of receiving a "guard channel", a frequency set aside for emergencies. The UHF guard frequency was 243.0 megahertz; for the VHF radio, the guard channel was 121.5 megahertz. These radios could receive communications on the guard frequency concurrent with any other frequency to which they were tuned. Virtually every aircraft in Vietnam monitored those guard channels so they could respond immediately to an emergency call if they were in a position to do so. The UHF and VHF radios had a selector switch that a pilot could set to transmit on a guard channel in case of an emergency. And no pilot gained greater disdain than one who—even accidentally—transmitted "on guard" when it wasn't an emergency.

Besides the radios, there was the intercom. It was used for two-way communications between persons in an aircraft. In a helicopter, an intercom was essential; it was otherwise too loud for a conversation with normal volume. In a Huey, the intercom allowed all the aircrew members to talk with one another. In a Cobra, it allowed the pilot and gunner to talk with one another.

There were a lot of things to listen to: the intercom, three two-way radios, and perhaps the ADF. I listened to all the radios when I needed to, and sometimes when I didn't. During the daylight hours, there was usually constant radio chatter of some sort, and when en route somewhere, I would sometimes randomly turn up a frequency on the UHF or FM radio to see if I could catch something of interest. And, while cruising, I'd often listen to AFVN on the ADF receiver, especially if there was music rather than a program about foot hygiene. On one occasion, when our fire team was out alone, putting in strikes on preselected targets, I enjoyed an especially memorable rocket run while listening to Jackie DeShannon sing "Put a Little Love in Your Heart."

A signal distribution box, one on the pilot's panel and one on the copilot's panel, allowed selecting which radios to listen to. The box had a row of switches, each switch associated with a specific radio. To listen to that radio, the switch had to been turned up. Turning off a switch silenced the radio connected to it. The intent of turning off switches was to allow a pilot or copilot to individually disable audio from one or more radios, perhaps allowing him to concentrate more on specific conversations, but I thought it better to listen to as many things as I could.

The box also had a rotary switch with numbers where each number was associated with a specific two-way radio or the intercom. To transmit on a radio, a pilot had to first select it with the rotary switch; then to transmit, the pilot activated a switch on the cyclic grip. Although the Cobra had the same cyclic grip as a Huey, it used a different switch to activate the mike.

With a Huey, the pilot squeezed a switch on the front of the cyclic grip to key his mike. The switch had two indents. Pressing the switch to the first indent turned on his mike to speak on the intercom. Pressing it further, to the second indent, keyed his mike so he could transmit on a selected radio. Especially when things got hot, it wasn't uncommon for a Huey pilot to tighten his grip on the cyclic and press the transmit switch to the second indent, thus broadcasting to the world, when he intended to only key the intercom.

A Cobra pilot was no less immune to a cyclic-grip reflex, but was less likely to accidentally broadcast to the world. That was because the Cobra used a different switch on the cyclic grip. The Cobra's radio transmit switch was located at the top of the cyclic grip and facing the pilot. It was a cone shaped switch that resembled a Chinese hat. In fact, it was called a "Chinese hat switch." A Cobra pilot usually operated the switch with his thumb. By pushing down the hat, it keyed the mike to speak on the intercom. Pushing up the hat keyed the mike to transmit on the radio selected by the rotary switch.

In the Cobra, both the back seat cyclic grip and front seat cyclic grip had this Chinese hat switch, but the gunner, who normally wasn't the one doing the flying and consequently didn't have his hand on the cyclic grip in front, more often used the foot switch on the floor of the cockpit to key his mike. And in most cases, the gunner kept his mike selector switch set to "Intercom".

With all the different units, ground and air, in Vietnam and with all the different operations, I knew there had to be some coordinated way of assigning frequencies to different units and for different operations, but I didn't know who did that. As far as I was concerned, what I needed to know was in the SOI.

On the first mission of a day, each pilot was issued a booklet called the "Signal Operations Instructions" or the "codebook" as we more commonly called the SOI. It was the phone directory for contacting someone when we needed to. It had the frequencies of all the towered airfields in the Delta, as well as the call signs and assigned frequencies for most of the units that had a permanent location. The permanency of units was relative, however, and because frequencies sometimes changed, there was a new edition of the codebook about every month.

Other frequencies, especially those needed for only a short time—for instance, only for that day or for a particular short-term operation—were assigned when needed. Each fire team, concurrent with its first mission of the day, was assigned a specific VHF frequency to use between the aircraft in that team. When we were assigned a mission, we were given the necessary call signs and frequencies for the units involved in that operation, or at least the principal unit.

The codebook was about the size of a pocket note pad and had strings attached to it so we could wear it around our neck. I normally put the string around my neck and tucked the codebook in the front pouch of my chicken plate. At the end of a day of flying, in addition to completing the aircraft's logbook and writing up an after-action report of our activities, we had to turn in our SOIs.

## Front Seat Bullet Catcher

New pilots with the 235th started off as a gunner in the Cobra's front seat. Some of them stayed there because, even though they were qualified Army pilots, they hadn't undergone the specific training to permit them to be Aircraft Commander of a Cobra. Pilots who were Cobra qualified wanted to move to the back seat pilot's position as soon as possible; that's where nearly all of the flying was done. It was also a bit safer. One pilot referred to his gunner as "his second chicken plate". This did not endear him to the gunner.

The more common nickname for a gunner was "the front seat bullet catcher." The gunner sat at the nose end of the aircraft with Plexiglas at the front, overhead, and on both sides. Although he had the best seat in the house for seeing things, a gunner was also more exposed. In the event of a front-on shot, the gunner was more at risk than the back seat pilot. Although taking ground fire from the front was rare, it did happen. One of our Cobras took a near head-on shot through the left front of the canopy. The round flew past the gunner and hit the rocket sight on the top of the back-seat panel. Fragments from the shattered sight cut up the pilot's face under his helmet's visor. At the club that night, the gunner fell under some criticism from the bandaged pilot who accused the gunner of ducking.

Like all new pilots, I was first a front seat bullet catcher and manned the turret weapons. I came to prefer the turrets on the scout-configured Cobras because they had a second minigun rather than a grenade launcher, which was characteristic of a hog Cobra. In my experience, the grenade launcher on a hog was a last-resort weapon, used when the turret's minigun was out of ammunition or inoperative.

A grenade launcher was called a "chunker", perhaps because "launching" was too generous a word for how the grenades exited the barrel. When I thought of launching something, I pictured a space ship or a missile that was boosted on its way with a burst of power and propelled to great speed. But the grenades from a turret were sent on their way more like the ceremonial launching of an ocean ship where, after being smacked with a bottle, it's pulled by gravity and slides slowly down and into the water. A forty-millimeter grenade, when launched, had less sustained momentum than a badminton bird. With about as much aerodynamic shape as a Dairy Queen twist cone, it popped out of the barrel with some initial enthusiasm, but when it hit the wind resistance, it quickly lost its zeal, gave up, and let gravity have its will. Rather than launching a grenade, trying to put one on a target was more like playing drop-the-hankie. My prejudice against grenade launchers was also due to their frequent jamming.

Miniguns jammed also, but less often. Some of the minigun jams were due to the barrels warping. The company's armament officer had to constantly scrounge to get enough replacement barrels for the miniguns, often resorting to offcast barrels from Air Force "Spooky" airplanes, AC-47s armed with a bank of miniguns on the side that could pour a torrent of fire on a target. The Air Force policy was to replace its minigun barrels, discarding the used ones, after less time of operation than was the Army's policy, and we often ended up with hand-me-down barrels on our miniguns.

Since we were dispatched all over the Delta, roaming from place to place and often with little advance notice, we rarely saw our crew chiefs after we left them at Can Tho. To transport our crew chiefs, we had to rely on other units.

Occasionally, when our first operation of the day was scheduled far enough ahead; for example, when we were to cover an assault company whose Hueys were making a troop insertion, the company would agree to send a slick to pick up our crew chiefs and take them to join us at the staging area, but even then, the crew chiefs sometimes failed to appear because they were stood up like a prom date who had suddenly sprouted a huge nose wart. Also, because we were such nomads, dispatched around the Delta at the whim of the fortunes of war, even when the crew chiefs were carried to our initial staging point, they often arrived only to discover we had been sent somewhere else. There were days when our team's crew chiefs caught rides, chasing us from one place to another around the Delta, but never caught up with us. And on missions like IV Corps Standby when we were scrambled on short notice to some location, our crew chiefs had no practical way to rendezvous with us. Consequently, the pilots handled nearly all of their own rearming and refueling when away from Can Tho.

As we roamed around the Delta from one assignment to another, we could usually find stockpiles of rockets. They were strategically placed at several airfields, even the smaller ones. However, it was rare to find linked 7.62 ammo for the miniguns or chains of 40-mm grenades at the smaller airfields. Whenever we shot up all the ammo for the miniguns or grenade launchers, those weapons often stayed empty until we could get back to Can Tho or to some other, larger airfield. We had to be judicious about how we used this ammo since it might have to last us all day.

It took far more time to load and rearm the miniguns and grenade launchers than it did to load rockets. In situations where ground troops were in sustained contact and we had shot out our armament, we would hustle to the nearest place that had a stockpile of rockets, and even if there were belts of 7.62 rounds and chains of 40-mm grenades there, we would usually reload only the rocket pods to save time on the turnaround back on station. Because of their greater availability and faster time to reload, we predominantly relied upon rockets for most of our firepower.

When we were away from Can Tho and without crew chiefs, it was my job as a gunner to clear jams and, when the situation allowed it, to rearm the turret weapons. When we were on a fast turnaround, it was my job to reload the rocket pods while the pilot stayed in the running aircraft. And as copilot it was my position to pump the gas and generally to cater to any whims my Aircraft Commander might have.

A veteran Warrant Officer, one of those aviators who wasn't qualified in the Cobra and was a perpetual gunner, taught me how to clear minigun jams. I was supposed to have learned how to do that in Cobra school, but I was on my honeymoon during the school and sometimes had other things on my mind.

When the minigun jammed, it could be cleared by breaking the ammo link where it fed into the minigun and rotating the barrels by hand. With a jam, there was nearly always at least one live round somewhere near the exit end of the system. Rotating the barrels allowed any live rounds to fire off. Since it was uncertain exactly how many live rounds there might be, we would rotate all six barrels, firing off any rounds, until they were all cleared.

In flight, the minigun barrels were rotated by power from the aircraft, but on the ground with the aircraft shut down, they were hard to rotate by hand. It helped to have some leverage. My tutor used a foot-and-a-half-long metal bar that he stuck between two barrels and it gave him the leverage to rotate the whole barrel assembly. Apparently he thought the source of this bar was some militarily classified information for which I didn't have clearance because he never told me where I could get one like it. So, left to my own ingenuity, I tried to use the rocket pusher, the long rod that we carried in the ammo bay and which was intended to be used for seating the rockets in the tubes of the rocket pods. The rocket pusher had a shaft about three feet long and I tried to use it between the barrels to turn them, but the aluminum shaft just bent; the barrels didn't budge. So, I wrote home and asked my dad to send me the biggest screwdriver he could find at the tractor store. He mailed me a heavy-duty one with a shaft a foot-and-a-half long and a quarter-inch in diameter. It did the job.

I heard about people and things being hit by stray rounds while miniguns were being cleared. We didn't have them at first, but later we were required to use bullet catchers when unjamming or rearming the miniguns. These were heavy iron cylinders that could be bolted onto the ends of the minigun barrels and had an end plate thick enough to stop any rounds fired off when rotating the barrels. Incidentally, based upon personal experience, I would suggest to anyone that he never drop a bullet catcher on his foot.

The policy and tactics in the unit changed during the time I was with the 235th. When I first came to the unit, the tactics emphasized the idea that a Cobra was a kind of airborne artillery piece, and like artillery, a Cobra was to be used to shoot at targets from a distance. For example, the company policy initially was that rocket runs were to originate from twenty-five hundred feet above ground level, all of them were to be made at a shallow dive angle, and the runs were to be broken off above fifteen hundred feet and well away from the target. In fact, we were never to fly below fifteen hundred feet at all except for takeoffs and landings. Perhaps this cautious approach was due to the fact that Cobras were still relatively uncommon in Vietnam at that time and the Army was still gaining experience with them in actual combat situations.

The policy also was to lead off all rocket runs by firing the minigun on the front turret of the Cobra at the target, using it for suppressive fire before firing the rockets and to use the turret minigun again for suppressive fire on the break from the target. Using the minigun for the warmup act and encore for a rocket show was a sensible policy, but because we were to stay so far away from the target, the minigun wasn't very effective except as a noisemaker. Consequently, the pilots often chose not to use the minigun because its limited effectiveness at that range wasn't worth the work of having to reload it, though this was more often the case when the pilots had to perform the reloading themselves.

A few months after I came to the unit, the policy and tactics changed. Our Cobras were freed to be used more like the Huey gunships with which the Army had more experience. Low altitude restrictions were lifted and we found ourselves performing a wider range of traditional gunship tasks, including more close-up work on targets. Universally, the pilots liked this policy change. Also, our armament officer was caught by surprise when the demand for minigun ordnance rose remarkably.

## A Man with No Name

During my first days with the 235th, a newbie and still relatively unproven, I hadn't adhered to a team. I was a drifter, bouncing around among the flight platoons and filling in with different fire teams. And because I wasn't yet an Aircraft Commander, I was a proverbial "man with no name" or more specifically, I had no call sign.

Only pilots who had Aircraft Commander status, or who had other leadership positions, had a call sign. Among the 235th's flight platoons, an AC's call sign consisted of a name and a number. The name designated his platoon and the number was his unique identifier within that platoon. For example, an AC in the second platoon, the "Death Dealers", might have the call sign "Dealer Two-Seven" where the "Two" signified the second platoon, as did "Dealer" but more obtusely. An AC in the first platoon "Satans" might have the call sign "Satan One-Four". A "Six" as the second digit in a pilot's call sign indicated he was the platoon leader. For example, the platoon leader of the third platoon "Vipers" had the call sign "Viper Three-Six." Pilots who served as company-wide officers bore the call sign "Devil" followed by a single digit. For example, the company CO was "Devil Six" and the company Operations Officer was "Devil Three."

For Cobras, Army aviators logged flight time as "Aircraft Commander", "Pilot" or "Copilot". To become an Aircraft Commander in a Cobra, an aviator had to be Cobra qualified;

that is, he had to have completed a specific training course to learn the intricacies of the Cobra. In addition, he had to satisfy the unit's criteria of experience and competence. When flying as an Aircraft Commander, the pilot logged "AC" time. If an aviator was Cobra qualified but not an Aircraft Commander or if he was an AC but not flying in the capacity of Aircraft Commander, he logged time as "Pilot." If an aviator wasn't Cobra qualified, he flew only in the front-seat position and logged time as "Copilot." To simplify the references, the aviator in the back seat was usually referred to as the "pilot" and the front seat aviator was referred to as the "gunner."

Beyond the designation of Aircraft Commander, there were tactical assignments as Fire Team Leader and sometimes Section Leader. Most Army helicopter aviators were warrant officers rather than commissioned officers, and because of that greater number, most fire team leaders were warrant officers. Sections leaders, a less common position, were sometimes warrant officers. Platoon leaders and positions above, which held a greater degree of personnel command responsibility, were nearly always held by commissioned officers who, in contrast to warrant officers, were referred to as "real live officers."

As a newbie, I served as a gunner with any fire team that had an empty slot to fill for that position. Consequently, I flew with many of the pilots in the company, and from all of the flight platoons. I didn't especially like floating around so much, yet I benefited from that early experience of flying with a variety of pilots. I learned something from all of them, including things I thought I could use, which I adopted, and things I thought I should avoid. And there was a lot to learn.

Each Cobra at work required a crew of two: a back seat pilot and a front seat gunner. Sometimes, there were more persons available to fly them than there were aircraft available. Although the company was authorized an inventory of twenty-four Cobras, eight for each flight platoon, that full number was hardly ever in service at one time. Aircraft often weren't available because they were undergoing routinely scheduled maintenance. Sometimes aircraft were destroyed by enemy action or by accident and it might take months to get a replacement for it. Even if an aircraft was only damaged, it might take several days or weeks to repair it and put it back in service.

Although sometimes there was a surplus of pilots for the number of aircraft, it was more often the case that there was a shortage of pilots. The company typically didn't have a full complement of pilots available at one time, and for conceptually the same reasons as for a shortage of aircraft. Some pilots might be undergoing routine maintenance; that is, they were given a "down" day or perhaps were on a more extended Rest and Recuperation leave. Occasionally, some pilots became ill, although most pilots rarely went on sick call even when they qualified. Some pilots were damaged by enemy actions or accidents; that is, injured. Also, some pilots were destroyed, killed by enemy actions or accidents.

The more common case of an excess number of aircraft for the number of pilots could be credited to the maintenance personnel who made an extraordinary effort to keep aircraft operationally ready. Yet, there was cause to sometimes list an aircraft as available for service when that status was dubious. Maintenance officers' efficiency reports were at least partially based upon the number of aircraft kept in service. Company commanders were evaluated upon their unit's readiness, which for an aviation unit included the number of aircraft available for assignment. No one wanted an unsafe aircraft in operation, but there was incentive to list as many aircraft as possible as service ready. On the other hand, an Aircraft Commander had the prerogative to "red X" an aircraft; that is, ground the aircraft, if he found something that he felt made it unsafe to fly, and sometimes a pilot might red-X an aircraft over a marginal issue because he wanted to be reassigned a different aircraft, one he preferred more.

Overall, there was more demand for Cobras and Cobra pilots than could be produced and sustained.

## A Back Seat Driver

Although I was initially assigned to the third platoon, I was soon permanently reassigned to the first platoon "Satans", and with my very next flight after that, I was allowed to fly in the back seat of a Cobra, at the controls of a light fire team's wing ship. The entire fire team was composed of members from the first platoon. The fire team leader was Malcolm Emerick and the Aircraft Commander of the wing ship was Ken Englund, a fresh looking lad with dusty hair and an equally light colored mustache. Although Englund was an experienced AC, he took the gunner's position in the front seat.

After a preflight of the scout-configured Cobra, I climbed into the back seat and Englund got in the front. In flight school, we had used a printed checklist for just about every procedure, including starting the aircraft to shutting it down, but in Vietnam, helicopter pilots typically didn't use printed checklists. Other than the check ride, this would be the first time for me to start a Cobra without a checklist and I didn't want to screw up, especially on my first flight after being adopted by my new platoon. Englund didn't ask it, but I felt the need to explain to him everything I was doing as I did it. By announcing the individual steps I was taking, using a conventional checklist call-and-response, I thought Englund could correct me before I did something to damage this perfectly good Cobra entrusted to me for the day.

I eased into the back seat, buckled up, and began a recitation of the starting checklist from memory, each step an implied question about the state of an item followed by a statement of its condition.

"Canopy? Open.

"Loose equipment? Stowed.

"Seat and pedals? Adjusted.

"Safety belt and shoulder harness? Fastened.

"Shoulder harness lock? Checked.

"Canopy jettison lock? Secured and safetied.

"Cyclic? Centered.

"Collective? Down.

"Throttle fiction? Off.

"Searchlight switch? Off.

"Landing light switch? Off.

"AC circuit breakers? In. Weapon Sight out.

"Battery? Off.
"Generator? Off.
"Inverter? Off.
"Non-essential bus? Normal.
"Engine air? Screen.
"Force trim? On.
"Fuel switch? Off.
"Engine oil bypass? Set.
"Governor? Set to Auto.
"Free air temperature? Check.
"SCAS power? Off.
"Signal distribution panel? Set.
"Instruments? Static indication and markings checked.
"Altimeter? Set.
"VSI? Zero, no deflection.
"RMI? ADF position.
"Emergency collective hydraulic? Off.
"Wing stores jettison switch? Off and covered.
"Compasss slaving switch? Set.
"Clock? Set.
"Weapons select switch? Set.
"Master armament switch? Off.
"Gunner/pilot control switch? Set to Gunner.
"Point/area switch? Set to Point.
"Wing stores jettison select? Both.
"Rocket pair select? Single.
"Wing stores armament switch? Off.
"Radios? Set and off.
"Pitot heat switch? Off.
"Rain removal and heat switch? Off.
"Vent control? Set.
"Navigation aids? Set and off.
"Transponder? Set and off.
"Instrument and console lights? Off.
"Anti-collision light? Off.
"Position lights? Off.
"DC circuit breakers? In.
"Cockpit light? Secured and off."

At this point, I put on my helmet and Englund his. I noticed his helmet had dozens of nicks, one that I imagined could be a possible bullet graze. My helmet had a couple of spots with chipped paint, the evidence of having been dropped and banged a few times.

I continued my one-way conversation of call-and-response.

"Battery? On.

"RPM audio? Off.

"Chip Detector? Test.

"Governor RPM Decrease?" I held the switch for ten seconds before announcing, "Decreased."

"Throttle? Full travel; flight idle; engine idle stop; full closed; set below idle stop.

"Fuel switch? On.

"Master caution and RPM warning panel? Check.

"Caution panel? Tested and checked.

"Fireguard?" I looked outside and saw the crew chief standing nearby. "Check."

"Main rotor?" I confirmed the rotor blades had been turned perpendicular to the length of the fuselage and thus were untied. "Check.

"Voltmeter? Twenty-two volts."

Here we go, I thought, as I prepared to engage the starter. I yelled out the open canopy, "Clear!" before continuing my recitation.

"Starter?" I pressed the starter switch underneath the collective handle. "Engaged."

"Clock?" I punched the clock starting its timer hand. "Started."

"EGT and gas producer? Coming up."

I closely watched the EGT and the N1 gauge. Things were happening faster now and my callouts became statements.

"N1: Forty percent.

"Starter: released.

"Collective: confirm full down.

"Generator: on.

"Inverter: main.

"Engine oil pressure: rising.

"Transmission oil pressure: rising.

"Fuel pressure: normal.

"Throttle: Set to flight idle, stop checked.

"Gas producer: seventy percent.

"Engine oil pressure: in the green.

"Transmission oil pressure: in the green.

"Master caution light: off.

"SCAS power: on.

"Fuel quantity test: two hundred pound drop; return to normal.

"Radios and nav aids: on.

"Transponder: standby.

"Force trim: release and check; off and check.

"Hydraulic system one: test and check.

"Hydraulic system two: test and check.

"Hydraulic test switch: both; lights out.

"Force trim: on."

I rolled on the throttle.

"Throttle: six thousand rpm."

I beeped the governor switch up.

"Governor increase: sixty-seven hundred."

I beeped the governor switch back down a bit.

"Governor decrease: sixty-six hundred.

"Throttle friction: set.

"Instruments: normal and in the green.

"Voltmeter: check.

"Generator: off; master caution light and warning lights on.

"Non-essential bus: manual.

"Aft fuel boost light: out.

"Non-essential bus: normal.

"Generator: on; lights out.

"Main inverter circuit breaker: pulled; auto switchover.

"Standby inverter circuit breaker: pulled; pressure gauge drop and caution light on.

"Main inverter circuit breaker: in; gauges normal; lights out.

"Standby circuit breaker: in.

"Engine air switch: set to bypass position; confirm screens open; set to de-ice position; EGT rise; set to screen position; confirm screens closed.

"SCAS channels: disengaged and checked.

"SCAS gunner: disengaged and checked.

"SCAS gunner: reengaged.

"SCAS: reengaged.

"Front fuel boost pump: check.

"Aft fuel boost pump: check.

"Radios: on.

"Magnetic compass: heading correct.

"RMI: Heading correct.

"Attitude indicator: Appears normal."

"Fuel boost circuit breakers: in.

"Forward fuel boost pump: check.

"Force trim: set.

I reached up, pulled down the canopy hatch and locked it in place. In the front, Englund did the same with his canopy.

"Canopy hatches: pilot's station secured."

Englund signaled a thumbs-up that his latch was in place.

"Anti-collision light: on."

The Cobra sat in the revetment, its turbine engine a steady whine, its rotors spinning, ready to go. The crew chief had moved toward the front of the revetment and to the side, making doubly sure nothing had caught on fire during the startup or come loose.

The UHF radio was dialed to the Can Tho tower frequency and the VHF radio set to our fire team's assigned air-to-air frequency for that day.

Emerick's Cobra was in a nearby revetment, its rotor already spinning and its anti-collision light on. Immediately after I switched on my anti-collision light, I heard him in my headset. "Ready, One-Seven?"

I sat there a moment until Englund prompted me, "Talk to him." Englund was letting me use his call sign for the day. I clicked up the Chinese hat switch at the top of the cyclic grip and spoke into my helmet's microphone. "Uh, yeah, we're ready."

I heard Emerick on the tower frequency. "Can Tho Tower, Satan One-Four. Flight of two, revetments eight and eleven. Ready for takeoff."

The tower operator came back. "Satan One-Four, Can Tho Tower. Winds calm. Direction of takeoff at your discretion."

"We'll take east," I heard Emerick say.

"Satan One-Four, cleared for takeoff. Runway zero-seven."

"One-Four," Emerick acknowledged.

I watched Emerick pick up his Cobra to a hover. He slid the aircraft straight ahead out of the revetment and onto the runway. He pedal turned the nose, aligning the helicopter with the runway. The nose dipped and the Cobra went skimming along the surface of the runway. It picked up speed and then ballooned into the air.

In preparation for a take off, I began announcing a pre-hover checklist on the intercom to Englund, but he interrupted me. "Just do it."

When I had flown the Cobra on the check ride with the unit IP a few days before, we had lifted off from the airfield's large, open ramp. Now, I had to bring the aircraft to a hover while it was in the revetment. Before, when I had been sitting in the front seat and not handling the aircraft, I hadn't noticed how confining the revetment walls were. Now, they seemed as close as the sides of a coffin and I worried that, as I lifted the aircraft to a hover, I might let the tail boom twitch too much, possibly slamming the tail rotor into the side of the revetment. I ever so gently pulled up the collective until I felt the aircraft become light on the skids; then I eased the collective up some more, my feet tense on the pedals, ready to catch the tail's slightest wayward yaw.

The Cobra slowly lifted a few feet and I paused, getting a feel for the hovering aircraft in the revetment. Its rotor beat the air, the downwash splaying torrents of frenzied air against the walls. Cascading gales rebounded from the walls, flogging the aircraft. The gusts buffeted the fuselage and roiled underneath it. The aircraft jerked and bobbed in the swirled violence.

The Cobra felt like a nervous racehorse in the starting gate. I held a tight rein, checking its flinches. Then, gently, I eased the cyclic forward, letting the Cobra slowly slip out of the revetment.

I concentrated on keeping the tail centered, my feet gingerly on the pedals as if I were tiptoeing on ice.

Moving at glacier speed, I cleared the revetment and crept ahead onto the runway, holding a textbook three-foot hover. I slowly pressed one pedal while easing the pressure on the other one, forcing the aircraft to nose around and align with the runway. I paused a moment more, feeling the aircraft straining at the reins. I nudged the cyclic forward, giving the Cobra its head. The nose dipped and the Cobra sprinted down the runway, skimming above it, picking up speed. I felt it roll off the cushion of ground effect air, dipping slightly before it hit translational lift and the increased flow of air through the rotor produced more aerodynamic lift for flight.

In seconds, the aircraft reached eighty knots. I pulled up on the collective to add more power while easing back on the cyclic and allowed the Cobra to soar into the air as I had seen Emerick do. The altimeter's dial spun like an over wound clock. As the Cobra gained altitude, the airspeed bled off. When it approached zero, I pushed the cyclic forward, allowing the aircraft to level off and regain speed. I soon caught up with the lead ship and adjusted the power setting to match Emerick's altitude and speed, holding a loose echelon left formation.

Emerick led us to Tra Vinh, sixty klicks east of Can Tho and near where the Mekong River and its Bassac branch emptied into the South China Sea. It was 0700 when we landed at the airfield. A dozen Hueys from an assault helicopter company were already there, parked nose to tail along one side of the runway. Behind the line of slicks was a pair of the company's Huey gunships.

After a briefing for this troop insertion, the ARVNs boarded the slicks. The Hueys took off and formed up for the flight to the Landing Zone, ten klicks further east. A Huey gunship flew on each flank of the slicks' formation; our fire team followed behind and a hundred feet above the formation. Another five hundred feet higher was the Command and Control ship, the Huey that carried the operation's Air Mission Commander.

In a few minutes, the slicks reached the Initial Point and made a slow turn toward the LZ, letting down from their cruising altitude. Still in formation, they landed in the shallow water of a rice paddy and the troops got out, wading away as the slicks lifted off.

On the approach to the LZ, the Huey gunships kept close to the flight, but shortly before the slicks landed, the gunships broke off to form a daisy chain pattern around the flight until it lifted off, and then followed it as it flew away. During the insertion, as we were directed, we remained overhead, ready to spring into action if the insertion was challenged, but it was uneventful.

After putting the troops into the LZ, the slicks and their gunships departed for their home base, and we returned to the nearby airfield, ordered to wait and see what developed with this search-and-destroy operation.

## Cooking Up Trouble

At the airfield, we parked beside the runway and tied down the rotor blades. There were no other aircraft and there was no telling how long we might have to wait. We had left Can Tho long before the mess hall opened, and Emerick's gunner, Chub, decided he would have breakfast.

Chub was one of the first persons from the first platoon that I had met. I learned right away that he had a ravenous appetite and I thought perhaps he had earned his nickname from that, even though he appeared to be about average weight for his height. I learned, though, that someone had dubbed him Chub because of his round face, which someone had thought resembled one of the pair of cherubs in Raphael's painting, *Sistine Madonna*. Whoever did this naming obviously had a greater knowledge of art than I did.

Chub retrieved a box of C-Rations from behind the back seat of the lead Cobra, a meal that featured a can of chopped ham and eggs. And since it appeared we would have plenty of waiting time, he commented that he was going to heat his meal. I was curious about how he intended to do that, so I asked him. He said he would make a stove. I thought that was even more curious and when I asked him how he intended to do that, he said he would show me.

He began with an empty C-Ration can, making several diagonal slits near the top for ventilation. He filled the can half full with dirt and crawled under the belly of a Cobra, soaking the dirt with JP-4 from the aircraft's fuel drain. Away from the helicopters, he set the container on the ground, dropped a lit match into it, and was rewarded with a can of flames. He pulled from his pocket a couple of thin wires, the booster shorting clips used as a safety device for stored rocket motors, and laid the wires atop the can to serve as a grill. Apparently he carried around several of these discarded wires for occasions such as this.

With the stove going, he opened the can of ham and eggs with the P-38 opener on the dog tag chain around his neck, the same device he had used to make the slits in the stove, and he left the can's lid partially attached so he could bend it back and make a handle for the can. He sat the can of ham and eggs on the stove and hunkered beside it, humming a tune while his meal heated, occasionally stirring it with a metal spoon he pulled from the same pocket where he carried the wires. The spoon, I learned, was one he had stolen from the mess hall, a crime he readily confessed. It was a companion of the knife and fork he also carried in his pocket. After the ham and eggs were warmed, he removed the can from the stove and dug into the breakfast, a smile on his face.

Between bites, Chub said there were plenty of C-Rations and suggested I heat one on the stove since it still had flame. I declined the meal but said I could use some coffee, although I added wistfully I knew it couldn't be had. But just like that, Chub pulled from his pocket a packet of instant coffee. He volunteered that he had plenty; he had hoarded them from C-Rations accessory packs, and I was welcome to one.

He went back to the Cobra, rummaged in the back, and returned with another empty C-Rations can. He filled it with water from his canteen and sat the can on the stove. As soon as the water was steaming, he dumped the instant coffee into the can of water and stirred the contents with another spare safety wire. Then he beckoned me to try it. I sipped the brew, and although it wasn't as strong as I preferred, I nodded my satisfaction.

While Chub was building the stove, Englund had sought shade underneath his Cobra. He had crawled under it, stretched his long, lanky frame lengthwise under the aircraft, pulled his cap over his face, and was soon asleep, blowing small bubbles through his wispy moustache. Emerick was already napping on an ammo bay door in a thin line of shade on the side of the Cobra away from the sun.

After Chub finished his breakfast, he went to the lead Cobra and sprawled into the front seat. He was soon asleep, the canopy open, his head rolled back, one leg dangling outside the cockpit, and unmindful of the direct sunlight beaming on him.

I was too keyed up to sleep, so I opened an ammo bay door, sat on it, propped up a knee as a writing table, and began scribbling a letter.

A half hour later, I jotted a close to the letter and tucked the paper into my pocket. Shortly, Emerick rose and stretched. Chub climbed out of the front seat, smacking and scratching as he walked a few yards away to relieve himself. And eventually Englund crawled out from his resting place underneath the aircraft.

Beside the runway a short distance from where our Cobras were parked was a rearming point. Englund strolled down to the cache of rockets and came back carrying three rocket motors, ones without a warhead. He announced a plan to build a homemade rocket. I assumed building homemade rockets was a common pastime of his, but I learned later he had never before attempted to make a homemade rocket. Nevertheless, he seemed confident and appeared happy about the expected outcome.

Emerick, appearing dubious and yet curious, watched this project unfold. England, the glad scientist, set Chub and me the task of cracking apart the tubes of the rocket motors while he went back to the arsenal to gather other materials. With the help of the Cobra's breakout knives, we cracked open the rocket tubes, and when Englund returned, he had us scoop out all of the propellant from the tubes we had just mutilated and pack it into the open end of a creosote coated cardboard tube, a shipping container for individual rockets, that he had brought back.

Among the materials that Englund had found was a block of C-4 explosive, something I knew about but hadn't seen before. I thought this soft, pliable material resembled Sterno and I tested a small sliver of it by holding a cigarette lighter to it. It readily caught fire and burned evenly in the open air.

Englund stuffed most of the C-4 into the bottom of the cardboard tube and had us pack all the propellant from the three rockets on top of it. After we did that, Englund punched holes in the closed end of the tube for thrust exhausts, and squeezed the open end of a used C-Ration can around the upper, open end of the cardboard tube to seal it. The rocket was almost complete.

We didn't know how high or how far the rocket might soar, so instead of pointing it straight into the air, we laid it on its side and rested it on a rock, which propped it up at a slight angle, before carefully sighting the projectile down the runway.

Englund had me mold a piece of the remaining C-4 into a thin roll and directed me to stick one end of the roll into an exhaust hole of the tube and leave the rest of the roll sticking out to serve as a fuse. Then, apparently struck by inventive inspiration, Englund decided to lengthen this fuse. With Chub and me aiding the labor for this endeavor, he extracted gunpowder from several .38 rounds he was carrying in his gunslinger's belt. Chub and I contributed some more rounds and Emerick even donated a few from his. Beginning at the end of the roll of C-4 extending form the homemade rocket, Englund sprinkled a trail of gunpowder along the ground for about a foot or so. Apparently that was long enough according to his, no doubt scientific, calculation, and because he had some left, he poured the remaining gunpowder into the exhaust hole from which the rolled C-4 fuse extended.

All of this preparation had taken more than an hour, but the rocket was ready. All that awaited was to set fire to the trail of gunpowder, which would burn its way to the roll of C-4, which would burn its way to the C-4 and propellant packed inside the tube, and which would send the rocket with its triple load of propellant shooting down the length of the runway, just above it, and how far beyond that we couldn't predict. Our only concern was that, instead of zooming away, it might explode first.

It was time to light the fuse. I was as eager as anyone else to see the spectacular, perhaps even explosive, result of this experiment, but I lost a considerable amount of my enthusiasm when Englund appointed me as the one to light the fuse.

The other three backed far, far away, leaving me alone with the rocket. I looked back at them, longing to be where they were, but I gathered my courage and stooped down near the back end of this untested missile, a Zippo lighter in my hand. I flicked the lighter into flame. Poised for a quick getaway and as far away as I could get, I stretched my arm to touch the flame to the end of the gunpowder trail. It immediately caught the flame and I sprinted as fast as I could, hoping to save my skin in case this device exploded. As I neared the distant point where the others crouched, I dove for cover, hurling myself face down to the ground.

I didn't hear an explosion or any other noise, so I cautiously picked myself up and joined the others in a crouch. We watched intently as the flame sparkled along the gunpowder trail to the fuse of thinly rolled C-4. From there, the flame slowly burned toward the tube, creeping toward the explosive concoction within.

We felt our position was far enough away to be out of danger of the exhaust when the rocket blasted off, yet we didn't know with absolute confidence where this possibly misguided missile might go. At the last minute, I thought about getting my helmet out of the aircraft and putting it on, but it was too late; the flame had almost reached the tube. I hoped there was nothing downrange in the rocket's path; at supersonic speed, nothing would be able to dodge it.

When the flame touched the bottom of the tube, we stuck our fingers in our ears, and although not a word was spoken in agreement, we all inched a little farther back. There was a moment of suspenseful silence, then sparks spangled from the tube as the gunpowder inside ignited; flames shot out the rear of the tube; then the rocket fell off the rock, lay on the ground, and burned to ashes. As it burned, we slowly rose, watching it. It was as spectacular as watching a birthday candle melt.

## Practice and Puttering

A few hours later, the ARVNs hadn't made any contact, but we were called out to destroy a suspicious hootch on the edge of a canal.

I didn't see what was suspicious about the hootch, but making rocket runs on it provided me my first direct combat experience for firing the wing store weapons. Englund had me blow the old dilapidated hootch to smithereens, again and again, while he critiqued my technique. He found my use of the wing pod's miniguns acceptable, but insisted on more finesse in keeping the aircraft in trim when shooting rockets. Good trim helped to better streamline the rockets as they came out of the tubes, making them run straighter. He also admonished me to make tighter turns when getting in position to cover the lead ship. He wanted me to perform the maneuvers I had been taught in Cobra school quicker and with greater precision. And he taught me other maneuvers I hadn't learned there, including a version of a wingover, pulling the Cobra into a sharp climb, bleeding off the airspeed to near zero, then kicking the pedal to make a sharp, slipping turn and nosing down at a steep angle, a technique for putting plunging fire onto a target, such as combatants in foxholes.

Englund also reinforced to me the importance of mutual support and position. Fly close, he said, but not too close to the lead ship and don't fly right behind it; move off to the side. There might be some bad guys on the ground who missed the lead ship but were just waiting for another shot.

After the target practice, we returned to the airfield to reload the rocket pods. While we were doing that, a jeep came down the runway to the arsenal. The Vietnamese driver, in broken English and using hand signals, informed us we had been released from that mission.

After rearming, we headed back to Can Tho. En route, Emerick checked in with Devil Ops to report our position and the aircraft's status. Operations acknowledged the report and assigned us another mission. We were to rendezvous with a slick making an ash and trash run. Operations gave us the map coordinates and other information, including the call sign of the Huey, which was coming from Soc Trang, and its contact frequency as well as the ground unit's call sign and contact frequency.

We arrived at the ground unit's location before the slick. Emerick contacted the radio operator, asking about any threat. The radioman reported they had been mortared during the night, but it had been quiet so far that day. When the Huey showed up twenty minutes later, Emerick coordinated with it over the radio and we flew a loose formation behind the slick, one Cobra on each side, as it approached and landed. We circled overhead while things were unloaded from the slick and other things put on it. As the Huey took off, the lead Cobra and mine took up positions behind and either side of it, and we stayed close to the slick until it reached cruising altitude.

We had burned so much fuel getting to the location of the ground unit, circling overhead while waiting for the slick, and escorting it, we were close to bingo fuel. Since we were closer to Soc Trang than Can Tho, Emerick took us there to refuel. We quickly passed the Huey on its way to the same place. At Soc Trang, we landed and refueled the Cobras from the fuel bladders along the side of the runway. Normally, the job of refueling fell to the Cobra's front seater, and this refueling stop presented a delicate situation. Although Englund was flying in the front seat, he was officially the Aircraft Commander and I was the mere pilot. Yet Englund didn't stand on protocol; he allowed me the luxury of lounging in the back seat, the engine running, while he handled the hose.

Now past midafternoon, we were back in the air and once again headed toward Can Tho. When we were within radio range, Emerick contacted Devil Ops and gave them our fuel and armament status and our ETA. Operations acknowledged all that but assigned us another mission. This time we were to provide cover for a medevac pickup. The Operations clerk identified the position as near Ca Mau. I didn't know where Ca Mau was; I simply followed Emerick as he turned toward the southwest.

We arrived before the medevac ship and Emerick made contact with the ground unit. A half hour later, the medevac arrived and took away a Ruff-Puff with a toothache. After the medevac departed, we turned once again toward Can Tho. On the way, Emerick reported in. Sure enough, we were assigned another mission. The troops that we had helped insert earlier that morning wouldn't be spending the night in the field. They were being extracted and a pickup had been hastily arranged. We arrived in the vicinity of the PZ, the same place that had been the LZ that morning, and circled some distance away while we awaited the arrival of the slicks. A half hour later they arrived, this time without their own gunships, and we flew overhead cover for the extraction of the troops from the same location where they had been deposited that morning.

By the time the troops had been extracted, it was late afternoon and we had burned more fuel. As a precaution before flying back to Can Tho, Emerick decided to refuel at Tra Vinh, the little airfield from which we had staged that morning; it was only a five-minute flight. He led us there, but when we landed, we discovered the fuel pumps for the bladders were inoperative. Apparently, when the troops were extracted, someone had decided the fuel was no longer needed and had shut down the pumps.

Emerick and Englund discussed the situation. They thought the nearest place there was sure to be fuel was Soc Trang, which was closer to where we were than Can Tho but in a different direction. They estimated we could probably reach Can Tho without refueling but the flight would put us well into the aircrafts' twenty-minute reserve, so to be on the cautious side, they decided we would fly to Soc Trang and refuel before returning to Can Tho.

After filling the Cobras' tanks, we flew to Can Tho, landing in twilight after a full day of puttering around the Delta. By the time we shut down the aircraft, the ACs made their entries in the aircraft logbooks, and Emerick wrote a report at Operations of our activities during that day, the mess hall had closed. The Operations jeep and its truck were otherwise occupied, so we walked back to the hootches.

I had finished my first full day as a Cobra back seat driver. I threw my chicken plate and flight helmet on the cot in my new

domicile in the first platoon hootch, stashed my revolver, and
went to the O-Club. Chub was already there, sitting at the bar
with a beer and eating a pickled pig's foot.

## The Banana Tree

Each of the 235th's three flight platoons had its own hootch.
The rectangular buildings, aligned lengthwise beside each other
and twenty feet apart, each had doors on the narrow sides and all
the doors on one end faced a common sidewalk that led past the
platoon hootches to the mess hall, the PX, the tailor shop, group
headquarters, and other of the airfield's buildings. The Satans'
hootch was first in the line of platoon hootches. Next to it,
toward the mess hall, was the second platoon Dealers' hootch,
and next in line after it, was the third platoon Vipers' hootch.
Immediately beyond the platoon hootches was one occupied by
the three platoon leaders and the company commander.

The Vipers had planted a banana tree beside its hootch,
between it and the Dealers' hootch. Maybe it was an award in
recognition of some achievement, like the palm tree in the movie
*Mister Roberts*. In any case, it was a runt of a tree, barely three feet
tall, and it suffered abuse. People in a hurry and taking a shortcut
to the Officers' Club were always running over it or, more often,
stumbling across it when returning from the club.

One evening shortly after I had been assigned to the first
platoon, we Satans, including our platoon leader, Captain Keys,
were sitting around in our hootch swigging beer. We had been
swigging for quite a while when I stood up, announcing I was
going to the latrine. But Captain Keys stopped me. He said,
"Mac, you need to learn that the first platoon does things
together." Turning to the others, he said, "We're not going to let
him undertake this mission alone, are we?" The other Satans
answered unanimously and in unison. "Most definitely not."

Captain Keys sat down his beer can and stood up.
"Everybody on your feet," he said. The others stood up. Captain
Keys bellowed out, "Platoooon, attenhut!" We all snapped to.

Captain Keys commanded, "Single filllle, march!" and
started stepping down the narrow hall through the middle of the

hootch. The rest of us followed him, trailing behind like baby ducks.

At the end of the hall, he pushed open the door and we marched outside to the sidewalk. When he commanded, "Column lefffft, March!", we all followed along in a single file, me in the rear. I was confused, though, because the latrine was in the other direction.

In the darkness, Captain Keys marched us down the sidewalk, past the second platoon's hootch, the rest of us still following, more or less in step.

As we neared the third platoon's hootch, he commanded again, "Column lefffft, March!" We stomped along beside the third platoon hootch for a few feet until he commanded, "Platoooon, halt!" We had come to the banana tree.

I don't remember the exact command Captain Keys issued next, but it was something on the order of "Circlllle, tree!"

When we were all in position, he commanded, "Presennnnt, arms." Everybody complied with the spirit of the command except me—who still hadn't gotten it yet. I snapped my best flight school salute, until I saw what everyone else was doing, then dropped my salute and adapted.

When we all had our situations in hand, Captain Keys' next command was a dramatic, "Readdddy, Aimmmm, Fire!"

Ah, sweet relief.

It's not uncommon for men to either whistle or sing during this activity, and someone began singing the opening words to *Stagger Lee.* "Oh, the night was cleeear and the moon was yellooow ...." Then someone else ad-libbed, "And so was the Vipers banana tree." We all thought that was hilarious, and started laughing so hard that we were soon not only soaking the banana tree, but also putting a wet shine on our own boots, as well as that of our neighbor's.

It was then, in the darkness, that we heard the voice of the company CO. "Gentlemen, what's going on?"

We immediately came to attention, chest out, chin in, arms at our sides. We were a perfect textbook model of the military attention position—except for one item, which was still out of place.

And there we stood in silence, except for a sound like running faucets.

Eventually, Captain Keys answered. "Sir, we're paying our respects to the third platoon's banana tree."

Then again the silence returned, except for the sound of the running faucets, which, after a time, slowly subsided, becoming the sound of dripping faucets, and then eventually petered out to complete silence.

Being a Wobbly One, there were several questions in my mind at that moment. Was this banana tree considered government property? What penalty might there be for what we were doing? In view of the fact that I was now in the presence of a senior officer, and under these circumstances, was I expected to salute? Also, could it be considered—even from a strictly legal viewpoint—that I was, at the moment, out of uniform? I tried to remember everything I had been taught about the military's Uniform Code of Justice, but I couldn't recall anything addressing this particular situation.

We all stood there silently around the banana tree, its leaves drooping, their wetness glistening in the faint light. I was afraid to move, even to reholster my weapon.

After what seemed an eternity, the Old Man sighed a deep, deep sigh. "You're dismissed," he said.

## A Demanding Mentor

Even after being assigned to the first platoon, I was still farmed out occasionally to other platoons, always as a gunner. I didn't like those itinerant assignments because I was increasingly identifying myself as a member of the first platoon, and when I flew with my own platoon, I was more often flying as the pilot.

On one of those assignments, I flew as gunner for a first lieutenant from the second platoon. He was the fire team leader for a mission providing extra gunship cover for a troop insertion. During the preflight, I got a taste of what my day would be like with this lieutenant, a straight laced, career minded professional. He supervised the inspection, quizzing me thoroughly about what I was looking for and having me explain why those items were important. I hadn't been quizzed that thoroughly on my standardization ride.

After the preflight, we flew a short distance north to the Vinh Long airfield where the air assets for this operation would stage. We were on time for the scheduled briefing, but other parts of the operation were running late. While we waited, we enjoyed a rare luxury on a flying day: a real breakfast in a mess hall, even if the eggs were a shade of green that Dr. Seuss could never have imagined.

As soon as I sat down with my tray at the table where the others were sitting, I was ready to dig in, but before I could get my fork in the chartreuse eggs, the lieutenant asked me if I had any questions about anything. I quickly sized up the situation. I knew what would happen if I didn't have any questions; the lieutenant would start snapping questions at me. Since I thought I'd fare better on the shooting end of questions than the receiving end, I took the offensive. I said that I had so many questions I hardly knew where to begin—and that was the truth. In any case, because I got to ask the questions and he had to do the explaining, the immediate benefit was that he did most of the talking and I got to do most of the eating. However, the longer-term benefit was greater; I learned a lot. I especially gained valuable insight into how operations were coordinated with air assets from different sources and the essential logistics of who did what and why. It would have taken me months, maybe an entire tour, to discover on my own what I learned from the lieutenant in that half hour.

Eventually, we assembled for a briefing. Some of the details about the coordination of assets were still confusing to me, but I discovered I could grasp most of the briefing because I had gained from the lieutenant the big picture, and from that perspective, I could see how our fire team fit within the operation, and I could better understand what our role was and what was expected of us.

After the briefing, we took off in the Cobras. The lieutenant handed me the section of a tactical map he had been given for the operation and gave me an assignment: "Tell me how to get to the LZ."

During the briefing, I had jotted down the map coordinates for the Initial Point, the place where the slicks would go before turning on their direct approach toward the LZ. I had written the coordinates on the back of my hand, a convenient place to note things that might have immediate usefulness. I studied the map to find the location of the coordinates, and when I found them, I gave the lieutenant a heading. I thought he must have agreed with it because he turned in that direction. As we flew toward the IP, I lined up features on the ground that correlated with ones depicted on the map. Before, without a map, everything below me had been an endless maze of checkered rice paddies and a tangle of canals, rivers, and streams. Now, I could see the larger picture, how the paddies and waterways fit together, and with the map, I could not only find where I was in the picture, I could see where I was going. It was an epiphany. Having that map was like having a geographic crystal ball; it allowed me to see what lay ahead.

We arrived before the slicks and the slower Huey gunships that stuck close to them. Our job was to prep the LZ, putting in strikes along the tree lines on the three sides of it, and saving some of our ordnance for the arrival of the flight, in case it came under fire.

Throughout the prep, the lieutenant peppered me with questions. Where was I going to place my fire? Why there? What would I do if we started receiving fire? What would I do if he was hit right then and I had to fly the ship? What if the engine quit? If I were the pilot making a rocket run, in what direction would I make it? Why that direction? In what direction would I break? Why?

Eventually, the slicks arrived and the insertion was uneventful. Because I was allowed to focus my attention on watching for threats, those were the only moments of respite I had from the lieutenant's relentless interrogation.

For the remainder of the day, the lieutenant bombarded me with questions. What was the rate of fire of the minigun? What's its effective range? What's the range of a rocket? What are the best uses for a white phosphorous rocket head compared to one with flechettes? What would I do if a rocket hung in the tube?

What would I do if one caught on fire in a pod? And it went on and on.

At the end of the day, when the Air Mission Commander finally released us, the lieutenant wasn't yet through with me. "You've got the aircraft," he said. "Take us home."

I took the short handled controls in the front seat. Okay, I thought, where is Can Tho? I knew it was somewhere south, so I turned in that general direction, but as far as I could see, nothing looked familiar. Then I remembered something simple: Can Tho wasn't far from Vinh Long. I could probably see it if I had a little more altitude. I added some power and climbed another five hundred feet. From that loftier view, I saw a river in the distance at ten o'clock that resembled the stretch of the Bassac just north of Can Tho, and sure enough, there was a sizable town just on the other side of that river, and placed right where Can Tho ought to be. Since I thought the town stood a good chance of actually being Can Tho, I pointed the Cobra in that direction. Soon, I saw the Can Tho airfield, and as it turned out, I had turned to a direction that put me in a perfect position for a straight-in approach.

I knew from the beginning that I had a lot to learn, but after flying with the lieutenant, I became more intense about learning as much as I could. I kept the tactical map section from that operation, and it became the starting piece of an effort to stitch together a collection of such maps with the aim of composing a composite map of the entire Delta, a project that I would never entirely complete.

I never saw the lieutenant after that and I didn't know what became of him. My regret was that I didn't take the opportunity then, and I never had the opportunity later, to thank him.

## The Only Entirely Independent Person in the World

Before long, nearly all the fire teams in which I flew were with members of my own platoon, and I mostly flew in the back seat as a wingman, although with a more experienced pilot who was an Aircraft Commander in the front seat. The platoon, like the company, was short of pilots, and I flew nearly every day, sometimes with different ACs during a day.

In a few weeks, and after taking another check ride, I was made an Aircraft Commander. I was given my own call sign, "Satan One-Three", and I was assigned my "own" aircraft, one with my name stenciled on the side of the fuselage right above the name of the crew chief. I called the aircraft mine although the Army technically owned the aircraft and despite a more reasonable case that could be made that it belonged to the crew chief. I was fortunate that my aircraft came with a crew chief who I felt was the best in the company, and I came to consider my Cobra the best and most reliable one in the entire company, due largely to his efforts.

Cobras, like other Army aircraft, each had a unique number assigned to it when it entered the Army's inventory. For helicopters, this "tail number" was painted on the tail boom or tail fin and sometimes in shorthand on the nose. The number had several digits, but usually only the last three were used as shorthand when referring to an aircraft. My Cobra, a hog, was "Six-One-Four." From the time Six-One-Four took my name and until the end of my tour, I was the one who flew it nearly all the time. I sometimes flew other aircraft when it wasn't available and sometimes Operations assigned it to someone else, but whenever it was flyable, I was the one to whom it was nearly always assigned.

I flew Six-One-Four so much that I knew intimately its special feel and responsiveness, and I felt somehow it was attuned to me. It was like a good cutting horse; all I had to do was suggest what I wanted, and it did the rest. Six-One-Four would perform with ease things I had to wring out of other Cobras.

As a new Aircraft Commander, I recalled Mark Twain's claim that a riverboat pilot was the only entirely independent person in the world, and I felt much the same way about being a warrant officer AC. As a warrant officer, I felt as unfettered as a Duke or an Earl. Royal figures of such titles rarely did anything other than what they pleased. Likewise, as an Army warrant officer aviator, I was allowed to fly and expected to do little else, which pleased me perfectly because that's all I wanted to do. I considered myself carefree when compared to a commissioned officer. Commissioned officers who, along with their other responsibilities, were burdened with the less prestigious cares of their command authority, which might include administering morning reports, the enforcement of hair lengths, and the hiring of hootch maids. An aviation warrant officer was largely free of those burdens since his responsibility and authority typically extended only as far as the dominion of his lordship's specialty, and as a warrant officer, my realm was my aircraft.

Furthermore I might have been only a lowly WO-1, but when it came to responsibility for operating the aircraft, there was no greater authority than an Aircraft Commander, despite his rank. During my tour, I had occasions to fly with an assortment of persons in the front seat—my crew chief, a chaplain, a TV cameraman, a nurse, a Filipino go-go dancer, pilots of other kinds of aircraft who coveted a flight in a Cobra, and several higher ranking officers, including a bird colonel—and none of them questioned or tried to override my authority, except the chaplain. He appealed to his boss for divine intervention that would save him from the lunatic at the controls.

I had one occasion when an officer from Group headquarters, who happened to be Cobra rated, was riding in the front seat and insisted he wanted to show me something. I let him take the controls, but apparently the only thing he wanted to demonstrate was that he could make the aircraft go faster, something that wasn't required for that mission and that burned up more fuel unnecessarily, reducing our available time on station. What he didn't know was that during this demonstration I had my hand on the collective to keep him from over torquing Six-One-Four.

After becoming an AC, I was flooded with a variety of new experiences. I flew missions day and night, early morning, late evening, and every time in between. Each one was filled with things to learn: learning the nuances of being an effective and dependable wingman, learning the AO, learning the people, learning radio procedures, and learning how to balance pushing

my aircraft's performance in relation to the demands of the
mission.

I was learning to find my way around the Delta; at first, to
places where we went most often, places such as Vinh Long, Soc
Trang, Rach Gia, and Ca Mau; then to lesser frequented places
such as Go Cong, Bac Lieu, Chi Lang, and Long Xyuen. I
learned to recognize the subtle bends and sandbars that
distinguished each of the several major rivers that ran diagonally
across the Delta; then I learned to recognize many of the smaller
rivers and tributaries. I learned the names and call signs of the
different units we worked with. I learned the locations of the
numerous uncontrolled airfields, which ones could be depended
upon for fuel and armament, which ones were not so dependable.
I was forming in my head an encyclopedia of locations all
connected by headings, distances, and flight times. I was
following the advice of one veteran fire team leader who put it
like this: "You've got to know the Delta better than the freckles
on your best girl's butt."

Before I had become an AC, on that very first mission I flew,
I had learned the importance of keeping up with the radio
chatter. I paid attention to the conversations on all of them. The
radios were an important supplement to the map of the Delta I
was piecing together. Tidbits of information I might hear from
miles away helped me understand what was happening in the
Delta. The map was a visual representation of the Delta; the
radios were an audible representation.

As a gunner, I had humped a lot of rockets, loading them in
the pods, tightening heads onto the bodies, removing safety
wires, pushing the projectiles into the tubes with the long rocket
pusher or more often by hand, and tapping the hooks on the
backs of the tubes, but now I was trying to make more educated
choices in selecting particular warheads for a mission: high-
explosive, white phosphorus, or fleschette. I compared ten-pound
warheads with seventeen pounders, and I experimented with the
rare warheads that had proximity fuses. I made the choices when
I could, but the ordnance wasn't always available to support
those choices.

It wasn't long also before I heard the sound of ground fire hitting Six-One-Four, and since this was now my aircraft, I felt Charlie was getting personal. Hits from small arms ground fire reminded me of hail on the tin roof of the barn back home. More often, though, I didn't hear the hits. In a Cobra, with its enclosed cockpit, the constant high-pitched whine of the engine directly behind me, the occasional low-pitched whop of the rotor overhead, and the frequent chatter of the radios, I most often didn't hear those rounds and only discovered the hits after I landed and found the holes. Nearly all of those hits peppered the tail boom, evidence of VC who failed to lead their aim enough.

Even more often, I didn't know when I was being shot at, but not hit. About the only way I knew I was taking fire was if I happened to see the muzzle blasts, which wasn't often since Charlie rarely engaged a Cobra head on, or when a ground unit or a Huey in an operation informed me I was taking ground fire. In a Huey, with its open windows and side doors and with a four-man crew, there was better opportunity to both see and hear ground fire.

After becoming an AC, I was even more aware of what might happen if I screwed up, and perhaps even if I didn't. Just after landing at Ca Mau and sitting in Six-One-Four, letting the engine cool down, I was watching a flight of Vietnamese Air Force H-34s on a downwind for landing when I saw a blade fly off the tail rotor of the lead helicopter, and I watched it plunge nose-down into a rice paddy, killing the pilots, the other crewmembers, and all the troops on board. Then there was the Huey that took a round through the transmission, but because the transmission oil pressure and temperature appeared normal, the pilot, rather than landing immediately, elected to fly to Can Tho where Maintenance could take a look at the possible damage. Five klicks short of the airfield, the transmission froze and slung a rotor blade. On the ground, the spot marking where the Huey fell and burned remained blackened for months until the monsoon rains eventually washed the mark away. In contrast, the nearly intact remains of the Air America Porter were removed quickly after it pitched over from a climb too steep for even an STOL airplane of its kind.

The VNAF pilots earned my respect. The ones who flew the A-1 Skyraider attack airplanes were fearless, and the South Vietnamese helicopter pilots at that time had to make do with ancient H-34s, which required constant maintenance that was often beyond the knowledge and skill levels of their mechanics.

The biggest problem for me with the VNAF pilots was communication. At airfields, when VNAF pilots were around, they often neglected to use the radio so we would know what they were intending to do, although that wasn't uncommon for US pilots either, but when a VNAF pilot did check in, sometimes the only clue about what he was up to was a brief "I land now." With anything lengthier, though, I struggled to understand what they were saying. That probably worked both ways; even if they understood English perfectly, they may have had trouble trying to decipher my Texas talk.

I had hung onto the small-scale map of the entire IV Corps area that I had acquired at Long Bien as part of an introductory overview of Vietnam. It was somewhat useful for a wide view of the Delta, but its scale lacked the detail for precisely pinpointing locations to the degree necessary for our typical operations. Sometimes, during mission briefings at remote locations, the Air Mission Commander would hand out sections of a large-scale map for the area of that mission. Maps, especially the large-scale ones that showed a smaller area but in greater detail, were so precious that it wasn't a common practice to give them out at briefings, and when they were, often the fire team leader was the only one in our team who got one. When the mission was over, I would ask the fire team leader for that scrap of a map so I could add that patch to the map of the Delta I was quilting.

After gaining more experience as an AC, I sometimes flew in the front seat, but those occasions were when I was mentoring a new arrival, not yet an AC, who was in the back seat. It was a milestone for me when the company got two new pilots, one of them assigned to the first platoon. It meant I was no longer the junior officer in the platoon, and more importantly, there were now some pilots in the company—poor devils—with more time left to complete a tour than me.

Other pilots eventually joined the company, all of them Cobra rated. One of the pilots that joined the first platoon was on his very first mission when the aircraft in which he was flying was shot down. Another first platoon pilot, flying his first mission as gunner with a fire team leader from another platoon, gained immediate notoriety as a result of mistakenly shooting at friendlies. I thought of my first mission and reflected how easily that could have been me. Fortunately, none of the friendlies were hit, but the mistake prompted one joker to suggest circulating a petition asking Uncle Ho, our sardonic reference for North Vietnam's Ho Chi Minh, to please place bullseyes on all his troops to help this FNG with target discrimination.

One of the new pilots who joined the first platoon was named Jim. I snapped a photo one time of several pilots huddled around a map. I had asked them to pose for the photo, pretending they were studying the map. Everyone cooperated, pretending this map was more interesting than a Playboy centerfold; that is, everyone except Jim. He was looking directly at the camera, a possum grin on his face, and the bill of his cap turned up like one of the Bowery Boys. Some of the most fun I had was when Jim was around, and maybe not coincidentally, Jim was often involved whenever something bizarre happened. For instance, there was the time Jim's aircraft had a tail rotor failure and the time he almost shot down a Command and Control ship. And then there was the time when he did shoot down our platoon leader.

## The Birthing of a Fire Team Leader

The day I flew with the lieutenant was when I gained the first solid insight into what a fire team leader did. From that point on, I observed and analyzed that role. I picked the brains of the veteran fire team leaders, trying to understand their thinking, what choices they evaluated, and why they made the choices they did. I came to see the degree of difference between the role of a wingman and a fire team leader. A fire team leader thought more about logistics, how to marshal the team's resources, how to balance the demands of the mission while protecting the team.

He was constantly measuring, estimating, and calculating, factoring units of time, distance, angles, headings, and fuel endurance. He calculated the odds of what to expect next. It wasn't that a wingman didn't do those things; it was rather that the fire team leader had the primary responsibility for them.

The company was not only short of pilots and Aircraft Commanders; it was critically short of fire team leaders. Within a few weeks after being made an Aircraft Commander, I was informed that I had been selected to become a fire team leader. My training would start the next day.

Becoming a fire team leader was an entirely on-the-job training experience. There were no formal classroom sessions. My professors were the few experienced fire team leaders in the company; my classroom was the Delta; my textbooks were whatever notes I jotted down and my far-from-complete map of the AO; the syllabus was dictated by whatever situations arose.

The first day of my training, I flew with the most experienced fire team leader in the first platoon, the young man from Georgia named Malcolm Emerick, but who everybody simply called "M". I had flown wingman for him several times before, including that first time flying in the back seat of the wing ship with Ken Englund. M couldn't be rattled; whatever the situation, he remained calmly in charge.

M was short; not only short in terms of the remaining days of his tour, he was also a couple of inches shorter than the average height for helicopter pilots. I was about average height, and when I sat in the back seat of a Cobra, I raised the seat as high as I could. I preferred that my perch in a Cobra be as high as possible so that I could see things better. Those few extra inches allowed me a better angle to see what was below me on the sides and gave me a less obstructed view of what was in front. M, though, had a different preference. Even though he was a few inches shorter, he put his seat as low as it would go. His reason was simple: he was less likely to get shot if he was down in the cockpit as far as he could get and his head wasn't sticking up like a gobbler at a turkey shoot.

My first mission as a supervised fire team leader was providing gun cover for a Chinook from the 271st "Innkeepers" that was relocating an artillery piece and its rounds. I didn't have experience with this specific kind of operation, but the mission appeared benign. Both the pickup location and the new position for the artillery were close to Vinh Long, which had little reported enemy activity recently. The mission had the convenience of being close by, just thirty klicks from Can Tho, and it had the luxury of not beginning until midmorning.

With M in the front seat, I departed Can Tho, leading the wing ship, for the brief flight to Vinh Long where we parked in the revetments that paralleled the runway. The revetments at Vinh Long were arranged differently that the ones at Can Tho. At our home airfield, the two-sided revetments for our Cobras faced the runway. At Vinh Long, the revetments for transient helicopters were three-sided affairs aligned parallel to the runway. At Can Tho, the parking was head-on; at Vinh Long, it was more like parallel parking. It required hovering close to the revetment, positioning the aircraft parallel to the length of the revetment, and then hovering sideways into the three-sided container.

After tying down the Cobras' rotors, we waited in the revetments with the helicopters; the Innkeeper Chinook had been delayed. About a half hour later, a jeep appeared at the revetment and the driver informed us the Chinook had departed Can Tho and would be at the pickup site shortly. We cranked and took off, arriving at the artillery site a few minutes before the CH-47. When it arrived, I called on the radio and introduced myself.

We stayed overhead while the artillery piece, which was already strapped, was hooked underneath the Chinook. When the Innkeeper lifted off with the artillery piece dangling under it, we stayed with the aircraft until it reached its cruising altitude, then I attempted to race ahead to scout out the location where the artillery piece was being relocated, but the Chinook beat me there. Even carrying the artillery piece, the powerful twin-engine, twin-rotor Chinook was a racehorse.

The new firebase was about a hundred yards off a busy road and screened by a line of trees along that side of the road. The Chinook simply flew straight to the site over the road and tree line, came to a hover, and slowly descended with its load until the artillery piece touched the ground, eased down a few more feet to put some slack in the straps, and released the straps from its hook. With the artillery piece delivered, the Chinook flew away to the original location to begin several round-robin trips of moving pads of artillery rounds to the new site.

With the artillery piece on the ground, I stayed there, watching over it and the artillery crew. Before long, the Chinook returned with a load of shells, deposited them, and left to transport another load. I watched the artillery crew position the gun more precisely and move the shells in place. I also kept an eye on the road and its traffic, mostly civilian vehicles, especially mopeds. Everything was going well and there wasn't anything for me to do other than fly circles overhead, yet the thought occurred to me that I was a fire team leader, and by doggie, I needed to do something. I applied my imagination and concluded that the road and tree line along it constituted a possible threat. Some daring Charlie on a moped could pull off the road, and using the tree line as cover, take some shots at the Chinook the next time it returned to deliver a load.

When the Chinook reported that it was inbound with another load, I directed it to change its approach. Rather than flying a straight-in approach, a path that placed it over the road at only a few hundred feet high, I told the pilot I felt it would be safer to stay at a higher altitude crossing the road, go past the drop-off site, turn, and approach it from the opposite direction.

The CH-47 pilot followed my directions, dropped off the load, and departed once again. I felt pretty good about my creative assessment of the situation, patting myself on the back for being a proactive fire team leader.

After a while, the Chinook pilot reported he was returning with another load and added that he was going to resume the same straight-in approach he had used before. I was about to object, until he explained that the directions I had given him forced him to approach the site downwind, which made the approach less safe, a factor I hadn't considered.

The following several weeks were an intensive learning experience; the company couldn't offer the luxury of developing me more slowly. And way before I thought I was ready, the apron strings were cut; I was officially designated a fire team leader.

About that same time, a new company policy required fire team leaders to wear epaulets on their uniforms. My fatigues and Nomex flight suits didn't have epaulets, so I had to have them sewn on by the base's Vietnamese tailor. Even though I was officially a fire team leader—after all, the epaulets proved it—the position was a continual learning experience. Any time I felt I was getting good at the job, that's usually when I was about to learn another, humbling lesson.

## Thanksgiving Day in Vietnam

I stood just inside the open doorway of the Ready Shack. Through the curtain of water cascading from the roof, I watched sheets of rain, blown by the wind, sweep across the airfield, the gusts obscuring all but the two Cobras in the revetments closest to the shack.

I was still a wet-behind-the-ears fire team leader and my team had been on IV Corps Standby all day, on ready alert in case someone in the Delta urgently needed gunships. That morning, after preflighting the aircraft in the rain, we had stayed in the Ready Shack near the end of the runway, waiting for a call, but none came. Throughout the day, the rain had increased steadily from the thickening clouds. A few aircraft had landed and taken off that morning, but as the rain increased and the clouds lowered, air traffic tapered off. The last aircraft in and out of Can Tho had been a C-130 that appeared out of the clouds, landed, quickly unloaded, and departed, disappearing back into the gray clouds. That had been before noon. It was now late afternoon and the rain was pelting harder on the roof of the ramshackle Ready Shack. Inside, we had set cans on the floor to catch the drips from the leaky roof, the drips pinging into the empty cans until enough water accumulated in them that the sound of the drops had became plops.

A typhoon off the coast had brought a chill, gale force winds, heavy rain, and low ceilings to the entire Delta, and the next day was supposed to be worse. As far as I was concerned, the prediction couldn't have been better. Tomorrow was Thanksgiving Day, and with this kind of weather, I had no doubt we'd be grounded. That meant we could all enjoy a traditional Thanksgiving meal at the mess hall, complete with turkey, dressing, cranberry sauce, and pumpkin pie. Chub, the platoon glutton, stayed informed on all things gastronomical and had personally confirmed the menu with the mess sergeant.

As the dim light under the thick clouds diminished even further at the end of the day, we were officially relieved of our standby duty. The Operations truck pulled up in front of the Ready Shack and we all dashed into the canvas-covered bed of the truck. Its tires splashed across the parking ramp to the Operations building where we piled out of the truck and ran through the rain to the building. We turned in our SOI books and I filled out an after-action report for the day with a short note: "No flying. Nothing to report."

We boarded the truck again and the driver dropped us off as close as he could to our hootch before we ran through the rain to get inside. After an evening meal at the mess hall, which we all considered simply a rehearsal for the Thanksgiving spread scheduled for the next day, we went directly to the Officers' Club for liquid refreshments. No one kept track of his alcohol intake since there would no flying on the morrow. We'd all be sleeping in, rousing only early enough for the Thanksgiving feast at the mess hall.

The assignments for the missions for the following day usually came down from Operations sometime after 2200, and the assignments were normally delivered personally by the Operations Officer who handed each fire team leader a slip of paper with basic information about his team's assignment: the names of the team's pilots, a report time at Operations, and sometimes a brief description of the assignment. We would learn our specific aircraft assignments and more details about our assigned jobs when we reported to Operations at the designated time. Happy was the pilot whose slip read "No duty assignment."

The Operations Officer usually had no trouble finding us. At that time of the evening, we were either in our hootches or in the club. It was such a small community, it was almost impossible for someone not to know where a person could be found.

This evening, the Operations Officer was early and he didn't have far to search; we were all in the club. He simply went from table to table, handing out slips of paper. The other fire team leaders there glanced at their slips and shouted their joy at the confirmation of a down day. I took mine and set it on the table while I studied the cards I'd just been dealt.

After a deliberate, hopeful consideration, I concluded I had a hopeless hand. I laid my cards on the table, took a sip of beer as consolation, and picked up my slip. I stared at it, unbelieving; I had an assignment with a 0700 report time at Operations.

Surely this was a mistake—or a joke. I showed my slip to the other pilots at the table and they all agreed with me; I was the butt of the Operations Officer's attempted joke—although an unusual one since we all knew the Operations Officer had no sense of humor. I looked up to question him, but he had already left.

It was a nuisance, but I'd get this cleared up right away. I left the club, ran through the rain to the first platoon hootch and rang up Operations on the field phone. The Operations Captain hadn't had time to get back to the Operations building and I'd be speaking to the night clerk who I felt certain wouldn't carry a joke far enough to lie to an officer, especially a warrant officer who could finagle a way to get the clerk a ride in a Cobra sometime.

The clerk answered, and to show I was a good sport about being the foil of this joke, I laughed when I told him what was on the assignment slip. He excused himself for a moment before he came back on the line. "Well, sir, it does have you listed on the assignment board for tomorrow."

"What?" I said. "That can't be."

The clerk agreed. "Yes, sir." Then he added, "But you're on the board."

"Have the Operations Officer call me as soon as he gets back there," I demanded and hung up.

I waited by the phone and several minutes later it rang. It was the Operations Officer. Tactfully, choosing only the politest four-letter words, I questioned the assignment. He explained that this mission had been requested three days before, but there hadn't been the aircraft or crews available to fill the request, until now.

"If it's been pending for three days," I reasoned, "then it can't be that urgent."

Apparently not, he agreed, since the request for a fire team was noted as "when available."

"Well, then, that's easy," I said. "Just ring those %*$&!^# idiots who assigned the mission and tell them I'm not available."

I had some insight about how mission assignments were handled at our company's level, but as for how mission requests from around the Delta reached our unit, I didn't know how they were shuffled and doled out, or who did it. I simply referred to these dolers as the MAFOH, "Mission Assigners From On High." Only an anointed priest, like an Operations Officer, was permitted to communicate with this august body, and not some profane layman like a mere fire team leader.

I waited by the phone another twenty minutes, disgruntled because I was loosing valuable drinking time. When the phone rang again, I picked it up. The Operations Officer reported the assignment was still active; my team and I were to report at Operations at 0700. I was so astonished all I could get out was "Why me?"

The Operations Officer, an epitome of rationality, explained clearly the reasoning behind his selection of me to fulfill this mission; he had chosen me because I was the most junior fire team leader. As for the other team members, they were simply chosen at random, victims who happened to be in the same platoon with me.

After I hung up the phone, I sloshed back to the club. I found the random victims and broke the news to them. They all agreed this was the poorest joke I'd ever attempted. Eventually, my grim countenance and, more importantly, my refusal to drink the fresh beer offered me, convinced them it wasn't a joke. When the realization of their ill fortune fell fully upon them, they all expressed their unhappiness in the foulest language imaginable.

The next morning I awoke to the alarm I had set and pulled on my flight suit. It was cool enough that I dug out my flight jacket, which I had thought I would never need in the balmy Delta. I disliked the cold; I wasn't accustomed to it. Back in Climax, when the temperature dropped below sixty, we brought the livestock into the house with us to share their body heat, and I thrived in West Texas when it sometimes got hot enough for the devil to consider converting to Christianity.

I considered it unfortunate that the day before hadn't been cold enough, and I hadn't gotten soaked enough, to catch pneumonia. It would have relieved me of this assignment.

I gathered up the rest of the team, whose disgruntlement from the night before had not abated. I rang Operations, which agreed it wouldn't terribly inconvenience them to come pick us up, seeing as how there weren't any other crews flying that day.

When we arrived at Operations, I was hoping that overnight the MAFOH would have realized it was all a mistake and had cancelled the mission, but I saw we were still on the board. The adjutant Operations Officer was on duty and was sympathetic enough of our plight to make another inquiry, but his call only confirmed that the mission was still on. I could only speculate that the mysterious MAFOH members must all reside in some haven where the sun always shined or else in some windowless dungeon that prevented them from observing the current weather outside.

The mission details were vague, indicating some kind of come-and-shoot-em-up operation with unspecified targets, and apparently not urgent ones if the request had been dangling around, unfilled, for three days. And it was odd that the location where we were to report was at the extreme of our AO, an airfield I had never heard of, more than a hundred and twenty klicks northeast of Can Tho, almost midway between Saigon and Vung Tau. From the coordinates that came with the mission assignment, I found the location on the wall map at Operations, but with weather conditions like this, that didn't mean I could find the actual airfield itself.

We trudged back out to the truck and the driver took us to our Cobras parked in the revetments. We preflighted in the rain, our crew chiefs standing aside, covered with their hooded ponchos. At least, they'd be able to enjoy Thanksgiving lunch after we left.

I tried hard to find something that would ground my aircraft, but my crew chief took too good care of it. Besides, if I grounded it, there were plenty of other aircraft that could be assigned to me. Nobody else in the 235th was flying.

We climbed into our Cobras and quickly closed the canopy doors to keep the blowing rain from getting the radios wet. Before cranking, I turned on the UHF radio long enough to call Operations and inquire, hopefully, if we'd been given a last-minute reprieve. We hadn't.

After cranking, I called the tower operator for takeoff. He sounded incredulous: we were really taking off in this? He read us the current conditions as if trying to pound some sense into us: ceiling, barely a thousand feet; winds zero-two-five at three-zero knots, gusting to four-five. The wind was strong and gusty, but at least it was straight down the runway.

After taking off, I tried to keep five hundred feet between us and the thick clouds and winged toward our destination. Visibility was less than half a mile. The wingman stayed close so he wouldn't lose sight of me in the heavy rain.

The canopy cover for the back seat was leaking along the seam where the top of the canopy door hinged. It was the worst possible place for a leak because several of the radios were aligned right under the seam, just below seat level. I had the copilot fly while I rigged a cover for the radios using cardboard from the C-Rations boxes behind the back seat. It worked well enough to protect the radios, but the diverted drips spilled onto my leg, wetting it as thoroughly as if a big-bladdered Saint Bernard had lifted its leg on mine.

Winging north, I recognized the *Co Chien* as we crossed it. The river branched off from the Mekong about ten klicks upstream of Vinh Long, flowed past the town and, further downstream, returned to the mighty Mekong. Although I couldn't see the town in this heavy rain, the river, which ran roughly east and west, served as a latitude indicator, yet it wasn't very precise for longitude because I didn't know how far from Vinh Long we were when we crossed the river.

The course I had planned took us north-northeast from Can Tho, passing close to My Tho. Early in the flight, I was familiar with the area and recognized enough landmarks to confirm we were on course. Eventually, though, I entered territory where I hadn't been before, and my navigation switched from pilotage to dead reckoning. Using my estimated ground speed based upon past landmarks and holding the heading that had worked thus far, I worked out in my head a time-and-distance estimate for the destination. We flew on, a tail wind pushing us, and when I estimated we should be in radio range at our low altitude, I made a call on the contact frequency I had been given, which I assumed was the tower frequency for this airfield. I transmitted several times but no one answered.

We flew several more minutes before my copilot glimpsed through the rain, off to the right, what he thought might be a camp. I informed the wing ship of the sighting and made a sweeping turn back in that direction. Sure enough, there were several tents, some larger than others, and what appeared to be a landing strip under construction. Near the strip scrapped out of the dirt, I saw a stilted structure that I assumed was a control tower. I keyed the radio again using the frequency I had tried before, but there was still no answer.

I turned to align with the presumed runway for a landing approach. When we were on short final, the noise must have alerted someone in the tower. A voice called on the radio asking who we were. The voice had an accusatory tone as if that person had been expecting not to have to handle any traffic that day.

I was too busy to answer him right away; we were at a hover, bobbing in the wind gusts. I maneuvered the Cobra to the side of the scrapped-dirt strip, and avoiding the water filled drainage ditch along that side of the runway, I hovered to the other side of it and eased the Cobra down until it was planted in the mud.

I radioed the tower, told him who we were, and asked about the planned operation that day. The guy didn't know about any operation. I asked him to rouse somebody who did know something and get back to me on the radio. I didn't want to get out in the rain. Apparently, neither did he. He said he didn't have radio contact with the field's Operations center but told me where I could find the tent that housed it.

On the radio channel between our Cobras, I told the wing ship crew to sit tight and I'd venture out to the Operations tent. I opened the canopy hatch, placed a foot on the step-up on the fuselage and made a long step with the other foot to the ground, which sank angle-deep into mud. I waded across the water filled ditch to the runway and slogged across the muddy strip to the other side where I found a plank walkway, portions of it submerged in water. I followed the planks to a tent with a screen door, which I assumed was the Operations center for this makeshift post and barged through the door. A surprised Spec Four lay stretched atop a counter reading a paperback. When I inquired, this Supply clerk informed me I had missed the Operations tent and he gave me better directions than I'd gotten from the guy in the tower.

I splashed back into the rain and followed the waterlogged planks to another tent where I barged through that door. There I found another Spec Four, this one leaning on a counter and doodling on a pad. He blinked at me from behind thick glasses, as startled as if The Creature from the Black Lagoon had lurched in on him.

When I asked him if this was Operations, he confirmed it was. And when I asked him what he knew about a mission today, he looked over my shoulder to confirm that cats and dogs were still falling head over paws outside, then looked at me as if I were loony. He said he didn't know anything about a mission.

I asked him who was in charge, and he gave me the name of the Operations duty officer, adding that he was in his tent. I thought about asking the clerk to go get him, but there was no need for him to get wet when I already was. He gave me directions to the tent. I plunged back into the rain, stepped into a water filled hole, and got lost. Fortunately, I stumbled upon a private sitting in a top-down jeep, wearing a poncho, his head ducked over a cigarette. Why he was sitting in a jeep out in the rain, I didn't know and didn't ask. This miserable looking soul directed me to the correct tent.

I found it and when I pulled back the tent flap, there was a captain sitting on a canvas cot, wearing horned rim glasses, reading a thick book. He kept reading for a moment, so as not to lose his place in this tome entitled *The Anatomy of Amphibians*. When he finally looked up, he was seemingly unsurprised to see a dripping stranger at his flap.

I told him who I was and asked about the mission that had brought me to this mud hole. He studied me placidly as if I were some new species of frog that had just hopped into his tent, then casually remarked, "Oh, that." He informed me there was no mission, and returned to the book. I persisted, telling him that no one had informed me of that. He shrugged and said he had told the clerk to cancel it last night. In any case, he added, with weather like this, who wouldn't assume the mission had been cancelled?

Just out of curiosity, I asked with strained patience, what was the mission? He said he didn't know. He had only been directed by the major, who was the CO of the company, to request the assets. Did I want to talk with him? At that point, I had no interest in talking with anybody else. However, I was interested—extremely interested—in having the pleasure of kicking somebody's butt.

I stood there, allowing myself to cool off some. Although I thought a good butt-kicking was in order, I wasn't sure who would be an appropriate target, and kicking the butt of a Captain or a Major wasn't likely to improve my prospects with a Promotion Board. I turned and left, ducking through the tent flap.

There was no longer a dry patch on me and water was squishing in my boots. I took the most direct path to the Cobras, cutting between two larger tents, one of which I assumed was the mess tent because it had a smoke stack sticking out of the top.

Tromping across the muddy strip, I caught the attention of the wingman and his gunner sitting in their aircraft. I pointed to my ears, signaling that I would talk with them over the radio. I climbed into the back of my Cobra, trying to avoid dripping on the radios. I plopped my helmet on my wet head, flipped on the battery switch, and called the wing ship. Chub, in my front seat, put on his helmet to listen in. I informed them the mission had been scrubbed.

The rain hadn't let up and the ceiling was lower than when we had landed. I offered my opinion that we should wait to see if the conditions might improve. They agreed, but none of us was eager to sit in the aircraft while we waited. Chub was the one who suggested it would be a good use of our time to have a meal, even if it was only C-Rations. That suggestion prompted me to remember the mess tent I had passed on the way back and I mentioned it as a possible alternative.

Chub was all for it, even though it would mean getting out of the helicopters and getting soaked. Chub argued that a hearty Thanksgiving meal in the mess hall would be worth the soaking. We didn't need much persuasion; the thought of roasted Turkey with all the trimmings and the temptation of pumpkin pie were persuasive enough.

We climbed out of the Cobras and waded into the downpour, me leading the way to the smoke-stacked tent. We pushed through the tent's screen door and stopped to savor the expected aroma. We stood there and the few dozen diners at the wooden tables turned to gape at us.

We walked up to the serving counter where an aproned cook gawked at we strangers who had just burst through the door. I explained our plight to him: we had flown through the typhoon all the way from Can Tho and now we were stuck waiting for the weather to improve. Could we possibly partake of a meal, here among our fellow soldier brethren, on this day of thanksgiving?

The cook, a sympathetic soul, took pity on us and agreed to share their collective bounty. He pointed to the small collection of trays and we each took one. Behind the counter, he prepared our meal as we waited expectantly. Shortly, he slid a plate to each of us; each plate held a bare baloney sandwich. He pointed to a stack of cups and a water bag on a tripod in the corner. "There's some grape drink in the bag," he said. "Help yourself."

Chub was the one who voiced our collective disappointment. What about the turkey? the dressing? the cranberry sauce? the pumpkin pie? Is this how you treat strangers in a strange land?

"Take a look," the cook said, pointing to the other diners. We turned to look. They were all having the same thing, baloney sandwiches. "We haven't been supplied in more than four days," he explained. "This is all we've got."

I took the plate, mumbled our thanks to the cook, and carried my tray and cup to an empty table. The rest of the team sat down with me. We ate the sandwiches while the other diners munched on theirs. When we finished, we returned our trays and plates to the counter. "Much obliged," I said to the cook.

We walked to the screen door. The rain hadn't let up, but we stepped out of the door and into the heavy rain. It was better than remaining in the mess tent where disappointment had heavied our hearts.

We made our way back to the helicopters. Chub and I climbed into Six-One-Four and the wingman and his gunner took refuge in their Cobra parked behind.

We waited in the helicopters, watching the rain come steadily down. In a while, I turned on the VHF radio and the red, rotating beacon atop the Cobra's doghouse. Hopefully, the beacon would signal the wingman that I wanted to talk with him. In a moment, I heard him call on the radio.

We talked over the situation. The rain hadn't let up since we left Can Tho, but it hadn't increased either. Although the ceiling had dropped since we first arrived, it hadn't dropped any more since we had been at the mess tent. It was after midafternoon and we'd start losing daylight soon. Did we want to try to get back to Can Tho or remain here, at least overnight, and possibly longer if the weather worsened? It wasn't a lengthy discussion; we all had the same opinion: we didn't want to stay there. It probably wasn't a smart decision, but it was unanimous.

We took off in the blowing rain, climbing toward the wind whipped wisps of clouds roiling underneath the more compacted layer of gray and black clouds overshadowing the wisps. To stay below the clouds, we flew at four hundred feet and with the same half-mile visibility we had on our flight to the remote airfield. Immediately after taking off, I saw a landmark or two that I recognized from our inbound flight to the airfield, but then everything became a washed-out landscape where it all looked the same. I concentrated on holding a heading, one that I thought would take us toward Can Tho. But without any distinguishable landmarks, it was impossible to determine how close we were to that course, nor our ground speed. From what I could tell from the ripples in the paddies below, we had mostly a headwind with some right crosswind. At this altitude and distance, we were too low and too far for Paddy Control, the radar facility at Binh Thuy, to get a ping on us. Although there was likely a similar facility near Saigon, I didn't know how to contact it. Besides, we were flying in a direction away from Saigon and I didn't expect that radar facility would have any better luck in locating us on a scope that the one in Binh Thuy. The only navigation aide was the ADF radio. It was tuned to AFVN in Saigon, and its needle pointed toward the radio station, but it only indicated our direction from Saigon and was far from a precise indicator of our position in relation to Can Tho.

One thing was for certain, though: as we pushed farther south, the ceiling was getting lower. To stay out of the clouds, we were down to three hundred feet over the paddies. After another twenty minutes, we had been pushed down another hundred feet. If we were forced much lower, we'd have to land in a rice paddy, not a happy prospect to think about.

We kept going, the ceiling continuing to lower. I concentrated on holding the heading and keeping the airspeed steady. I watched the clock, running the numbers in my head, factoring the elapsed time since we left the airfield, the indicated airspeed, and the estimated wind speed and direction, calculating an estimate of how far we had flown. I thought that if my numbers were correct and we were on course, we should be somewhere near Vinh Long, but I didn't see any landmarks that looked familiar; as far as I could see it was all one big watery world.

Another five minutes and the clouds had driven us down to a hundred feet. Our rotors were whirling through ragged pieces of the lower hanging clouds. I began looking for a rice paddy that would accommodate two Cobras.

Ahead, things were looking more ominous. We were approaching what appeared to be a sheet of even heavier rain.

This is it, I thought; we would have to put down right where we were. The sheet was coming toward us fast. I would have only a moment to warn the wing ship. But when I looked closer. I saw the watery sheet wasn't rain; it was a river. And I realized it had to be the *Co Chien*. That meant that if we were near to being on course, somewhere on that river—hopefully not far—sat Vinh Long. I turned up the river, hoping I had turned the correct direction, and the wing ship followed.

I dialed in the frequency of the Vinh Long tower and gave it a call. After a few seconds of suspense, it answered. I explained I had a flight of two Cobras somewhere over the river and, I thought, headed in that direction. The tower operator reported the winds, which favored an approach to the airfield's westerly runway, a good thing because that would allow us a nearly straight-in approach. The operator added there was no traffic and we were cleared for landing. That was fine, I thought, if we were flying in the right direction and, even if so, we could see the airfield.

The ceiling had pushed us further down so that our skids were almost in the river's water. As much as I disliked the notion of landing in a rice paddy, even more I didn't want to have to put down in the water.

Chub keyed the intercom. "I see hootches at ten o'clock." When I looked, I saw them also. They meant we were somewhere on the outskirts of the town of Vinh Long. I edged closer to the south bank of the river but stayed over the water; we were low enough that we could put our skids into a tall hootch.

We flew, skimming over the river's surface. In a moment, I thought I recognized a bend in the river. If I was correct, the airfield should be off to the left and I turned in that direction. I hoped the wing ship still had me in sight. I keyed the radio. "You still there?" The wingman came back. "I'm on you."

A half minute later, I sighted the runway as I was about to cross it. I had missed seeing the approach end and was intercepting the runway at an angle. I turned to align with it, hauled back on the cyclic to quickly slow the helicopter, and pushed down the collective to keep from ballooning into the clouds. I managed to bring the helicopter to a hover at the far end of the runway and I eased the aircraft down onto the surface in the gusty wind. My wingman announced he was down also, on the runway behind me. As soon as we were down, a rainsquall swept over the airfield, knocking visibility down to zero. I couldn't see the tower nor could it see us. I keyed the mike. "Vinh Long, Satan One-Three. Be advised we're down on the runway, but I can't see s&%#."

The operator was reassuring. "That's okay. Just stay where you are. You're not in anybody's way."

We throttled down to flight idle and waited. The squall eventually spent itself, and with its passing, the ceiling lifted a few hundred feet. And it appeared the visibility was improving further south. My wingman and I talked it over. Can Tho was only seven minutes away; we'd go for it.

I thanked the Vinh Long tower operator and we lifted off. Finding our way to Can Tho wasn't hard. Even down low, I had enough familiar landmarks to know where I was. And since Can Tho Airfield's runway heading was almost the same as Vinh Long's, I could make a straight-in approach. Even before I could see the airfield through the rain, I called the Can Tho tower and was cleared for landing.

The runway materialized through the watery veil and we shot our approach nearly straight into the blustery wind, coming to a hover over the strip of swamp behind the revetments. The only remaining problem was putting the Cobras in the revetments. The problem was we'd have to make a left pedal turn to align the aircraft with the length of the revetments. Applying left pedal, asking the helicopter to turn its nose in that direction, opposite the way the main rotor's torque was trying to push the nose, sucked power from the engine. Plus, nosing the aircraft in any direction meant asking it to overcome its natural tendency to weathercock into the wind. I pushed in as much left pedal as I had and the aircraft slowly, reluctantly swung its nose in that direction, but not far enough. It was still cocked at an angle toward the wind and with each gust, it swung more into the wind and away from the revetment. The nose swung left and right like a wayward compass. Holding left pedal, I edged up close to the back of the revetment and waited. Eventually, the wind lulled enough momentarily that the aircraft could turn the full ninety degrees to align with the revetment and I was able to slip the Cobra into its berth. The wingman took advantage of the same lull to park his Cobra.

It was approaching dark when we finished the paperwork at Operations, but the mess hall was open for the evening meal. We changed into dry uniforms and enjoyed Thanksgiving Day leftovers, thankful to be have been delivered from the storm.

## A Simple Matter: Hot is Cold and Cold is Hot

As a new fire team leader, one of my early learning experiences was a lesson in vocabulary.

Our fire team was dispatched to provide cover for a medevac extraction from within the U Minh forest, a VC sanctuary south of Can Tho. The medevac Huey had been dispatched from the Binh Thuy air base near Can Tho and was already on the way. We were to rendezvous with it at the PZ.

Our Cobras arrived on site before the medevac ship. I contacted the ground unit and learned it had one "Whiskey" (wounded) for pickup. I was informed the PZ was cold; nevertheless, I thought gunship coverage was a good precaution since the U Minh was Indian territory, a thousand square miles of thick mangroves that harbored a horde of the Delta's most tenacious VC.

Shortly, the medevac ship arrived and I told the pilot what I had learned from the ground unit; then all three of us—the ground unit, the medevac, and me—got on the FM radio to coordinate how we would handle this extraction.

The PZ was a small clearing in the heavy forest. Shaped like the Greek letter omega, the PZ had a narrow inlet of clear space between two forested fingers, the inlet leading into the broader, circular opening about a hundred yards in diameter.

The medevac would come in low-level over the narrow inlet and into the more expansive opening, landing in the middle of it. The ground unit was positioned within the cover of the trees near the outer, left edge of the opening. When the medevac ship was on the ground, the troops would carry the littered patient to it.

After coordinating our plan, the medevac dropped down to near treetop level, and made for the PZ. Our Cobras dropped down and picked up the medevac as it was coming in, one on each side. I was in the lead and placed my Cobra beside the medevac on the right; the wing ship took the left side, following a little farther back.

The medevac zoomed over the inlet and into the PZ, flared, and sat down. As it slowed for the landing, the wingman and I set up a racetrack pattern around the ship at low level.

Two soldiers emerged from the trees carrying a litter. When they were half way to the ship, as I came around for another lap, automatic weapons fire erupted from the trees to the front of the medevac. I immediately straightened my Cobra toward the fire and had time to send a pair of rockets in that direction before making a sharp bank, turning left. The turn was designed to screen the medevac ship but I had turned so sharply my gunner couldn't put minigun fire on the spot from where the fire was coming. Fortunately for me, though, the wingman was in a position to place suppressive fire, which probably saved the belly of my Cobra from getting stitched.

The eruption of the ground fire had put the litter bearers into a run. They quickly raced to the medevac and slid the litter onto the Huey, which was already light on the skids. As soon as the litter was onboard, the medevac pilot lifted to a hover, pedal turned a hundred and eighty degrees, and flew out the way he had come.

After the fire erupted and during the short time the medevac waited for the litter bearers, we had continued our racetrack pattern, putting ordnance into the trees, which suppressed the fire but didn't completely eliminate it. When the medevac took off, we shot another volley into the trees before turning to escort the Huey.

When the medevac was well away and had reached a safe altitude, we went back to the PZ and worked it over some more. There wasn't any return fire; Charlie was willing enough to pick on the medevac even while we were present, but was smart enough not to engage us when we weren't encumbered with having to protect it.

We all escaped without taking hits; however, I was surprised we had taken ground fire from this "cold" PZ. I learned later from a veteran medevac pilot that I shouldn't have been surprised. He explained that medevac units had a policy that they wouldn't make an extraction from a PZ designated as "hot" unless the medevac ship had gun cover. And ground commanders understood that policy; consequently, since hot PZs were usually where the most critical casualties were, it was common practice to call a hot PZ "cold". From a ground commander's viewpoint, he wanted his critically wounded to be extracted immediately, and the necessity of arranging gunship cover for the medevac was a possible delay in getting those wounded picked up.

Also, I learned from this veteran that cold PZs were often designated as "hot". The reasoning was that if the wounded weren't in serious condition, they could afford to wait while gunships were coordinated to cover the medevac, and the medevac ship might as well have added insurance. So, you see, he explained, it was simple: "hot" PZs were cold, and "cold" PZs were hot. The medevac pilots all knew that and acted accordingly.

In this case, our gunships happened to be readily available to cover the extraction and the medevac pilot, with us there, likely went in knowing this "cold" PZ was actually hot. Perhaps he thought I had known the real difference between a hot and cold PZ for medevac extractions. Actually I hadn't, but once the veteran medevac pilot explained it to me, it all made perfect sense.

## The Maturing of a Fire Team Leader

When I was under the tutelage of other fire team leaders, I learned they had a great deal of independence in making decisions, often ones of life or death. But it was only after I was fully designated a fire team leader and trusted to the job on my own that I felt the full weight of that responsibility.

A fire team leader was depended upon to use good judgment, to balance aggressiveness and restraint. Being too constrained, not acting when he should, could allow people to get hurt that he was supposed to protect. On the other hand, being too aggressive could get people hurt. If he tried to shave an air strike too close to friendlies, he might hit them with errant fire. And taking unnecessary risks could needlessly endanger his team; targets sometimes shot back. If I screwed up, people could get hurt. And I still had a lot to learn, plenty of possibilities to screw up, and even more opportunities to embarrass myself.

One time I led a fire team providing extra firepower for an Air Cavalry operation near Vinh Long. During the operation, a cluster of VC was discovered in a dense growth of nipa palm and my team was called upon to help eliminate the combatants. The Air Cavalry had dealt with most of the VC, but one of them in particular was proving tenacious. The Air Cavalry had chased him from one hiding place to another until he came to an especially big tree. Their gunships hadn't been able to eliminate him because he kept hiding behind that tree, circling around it as they tried to target him.

A scout pilot in an LOH pointed out the tree that shielded the VC and I made a couple of passes at the target, letting the gunners use the turret miniguns. Each time we pulled away from a gun run, I looked back and saw the elusive VC was still there, holding onto his rifle, peeking around that fat tree. After yet another pass and I saw him still there, this time aiming his rifle at us, I decided that since a precision approach wasn't working, I'd go for volume. When I came around again, I put the tree in my sight and salvoed the load of rockets from the inboard pods— over thirty rockets counting inoperative tubes— at that one, lone tree. The spectacle of that carnage brought a hoot from the Air Cavalry gunship drivers, claiming it was a first-prize winner in the category of "Most Overkill." I didn't know absolutely if I got that dodger or not, but no one reported seeing him again.

Early on, I developed a habit of carrying my gun runs extremely close to the targets, so close that I would fly through the debris and shrapnel of my own rockets, sometimes putting nicks and holes in the fuselage and rotor. My crew chief got so tired of patching them that he offered to teach me how to do it, suggesting that if I continued the habit, I would indeed have to do the patching myself. Yet, I still didn't learn better until I was "shot down", even though that was only in a technical sense. I took a rocket run in so close that I overflew the target and that gave a VC too good of a good shot at me to miss. The round severed a hydraulic line. Although I had an emergency hydraulic reserve, I had to return to the remote airfield from which we were staging and make a running landing as a precaution. Maintenance came to fix the line and I was flying again within a few hours, but those folks weren't happy with me. And I wasn't happy with myself either; I had let Six-One-Four get shot.

Sometimes I got to share the embarrassment. For example, the 235th's new company commander may have been an able administrator, but he inserted himself into tactical situations where his presence was more detrimental than helpful. He had a propensity for rushing to where the action was, which by itself may have been commendable, but he would try to take over the operation, which created confusion and delay, and sometimes put assets at greater risk.

On one occasion, our company sent two gun teams to support the Air Cavalry after its scouts had flushed a group of VC who began a protracted withdrawal under the cover of natural terrain, moving toward safety that lay across the border in Cambodia. When the CO learned about the chase, he left the comfort of his air-conditioned office and raced to the operations area.

When he arrived, he swarmed in, among the other air assets, seeking an opportunity to bag some VC trophies. He pressed his search, flittering from one location to another, all at breakneck speed, on one false trail after another, until eventually he found himself nearly out of fuel and out of reach of a fuel source. He had to set down in a rice paddy; then he demanded to be picked up immediately, which required diverting resources to cover his downed ship and to extract him from the mess he had put himself in. Not only had he put his Cobra out of action, he wanted to commandeer another one for himself, taking a gunship out of the hands of someone else. When folks from the Air Cavalry asked me who this monkey in the wrench was, I was embarrassed to inform them it was the 235th's company commander

The assignments for the next day came down to the fire team leaders at night, usually between ten and midnight, and almost always, whatever the assignment might be, it involved an early morning get-up just a few hours later.

Operations tried to get the assignments to us as soon as they could, but it took time to coordinate all the necessary elements to allocate fire teams. There were more requests for our gunships than there were resources to fill them, and the requests had to been sorted out by priorities. The Operations staff had to wait on a report from maintenance to see how many aircraft were likely to be available the next day, and which ones. They looked at the pilots' flight times and tried to balance the time between all of them. In addition, Operations had to consider a team's makeup. Some pilots were Cobra qualified and some were not. Some were qualified as Aircraft Commanders and some were not. Some were qualified as fire team leaders; some were not. There were also more subtle considerations involving an individual pilot's experience. It was desirable to maintain team unity by keeping the members of a team as consistent as possible, yet it was also desirable to have a balance of experienced pilots and newer pilots on a team so that the newer pilots could learn from the more experienced ones.

Most of the time, the fire team leader and the wing ship AC were assigned to the same team, but the copilots were often wild cards. I preferred that the copilots on my team be from my own platoon; but often they were from another one. Operations would sometimes give me an assignment for the next day with an incomplete team list, usually an unnamed gunner. The staff hadn't yet figured out who would fill that slot. When I was a new guy myself, I remember being that "player to be named" on a team roster. Those first weeks when I was a roving gunner, I felt like the last kid picked for a schoolyard game, the one that no one wanted. And later I discovered that wasn't too far from the truth. As I gained experience and eventually became an AC flying wing and then a fire team leader, I wanted persons on my team who I knew and could trust. The game we were playing was sometimes deadly serious.

Altogether, it was a juggling act for Operations to put together assignments and sometimes, just when the staff would have the assignments made up, some last-minute urgent mission would come from the Mission Assigners From On High that made it necessary to rearrange things to accommodate that.

After receiving my assignment, I went to the other members of the team, informed them of the assignment and gave them a time for a morning rendezvous to leave for the flight line. Since I was a night person rather than a morning person, I'd shower and shave late at night rather than in the morning, and I was sure it must have shocked some commissioned officers to discover that a warrant officer actually did shower occasionally.

During the latter part of my tour we got an influx of veteran gunship pilots, ones who had flown Huey gunships with other units and had subsequently been trained in the Cobra. This was also a learning experience for me; its principle lesson was that I was glad I was flying a Cobra. Yet some of those pilots who had flown Huey gunships as well as flying Cobras expressed a preference for the Hueys. Even though the Huey gunships were slower, generally less maneuverable, and could carry less armament, these pilots liked having the Huey's extra crewmembers, the crew chief and a gunner, who manned the M-60s at the side doors and covered the ship's flanks. Also, the two additional crewmembers were extra eyes to spot ground fire and be in a position to return fire. I benefited from having these former Huey gunship pilots on a team; I learned new techniques of the trade from them.

I usually led a "light" fire team of two aircraft, but occasionally a mission would warrant a "heavy" team with three Cobras. I was gaining experience, refining my skills, sharpening maneuvers, adding new ones, and learning better how to finesse the aircraft. I continued learning my way around the entire Delta, flying into even more obscure outposts, continuing to add pieces to my growing map, not only the one I carried beside me in the aircraft but also the one in my head, so that I could find my way from place to place as easily as a trail boss on a cattle drive.

I wanted to learn how to do my job better, and the most consistent lesson I learned was that the making of a fire team leader was never complete.

## A Day in the Delta

We flew nearly every day. Down days, those days when we were relieved from flying, came irregularly, averaging about once a week. Most days that we flew began early, before sunrise, and ended at dark. During those days, we typically logged three to six hours of flight time, but sometimes less, days where we departed Can Tho before sunrise, flew to some airfield, only to wait there all day until we were released and could fly back to Can Tho. The days were not only long, but each of them was different. If there was such a thing as a typical day, it was filled with so much individual variety that I could never predict entirely what missions would come our way during a day, or where we would go.

Often, our first mission was to provide firepower for a first-light insertion of troops initiating a search-and-destroy operation. The Landing Zone was usually a rice paddy where Huey slicks would carry in a company, sometimes more, of Vietnamese troops, usually with an American advisor. We would fly to the designated LZ, arriving a few minutes prior to the slicks. Sometimes, we would only scout the area, looking for signs of any enemy threat. Sometimes, we would either perform a recon-by-fire; that is, shoot into places of concealment around the LZ in an attempt to discover, by drawing return fire, any enemy forces there, or if the Air Mission Commander preferred, we would preemptively strafe possible hiding places near the LZ where Viet Cong might be waiting in ambush. In any case, we would save some of our ordnance until the slicks arrived in the event we needed to suppress enemy fire. Most often, there weren't any enemy forces waiting at the LZ. That's as it should be for a search-and-destroy operation; good operations planners didn't pick an LZ that they knew was right in the middle of a large nest of VC.

If we found evidence of an enemy presence, especially if we were able to entice any VC to shoot at us, the AMC could choose to abort the insertion, depending upon the strength of the enemy forces. Even when we drew fire, the AMC might choose to proceed with the insertion, depending upon how he judged the relative strength of our assets and those of the enemy.

A company of slicks usually came with their own Huey gunships, ones from their own company. Their gunships flew in with the slicks, usually a pair on each side of the formation, and as the slicks touched down in the LZ to offload the troops, the gunships would set up a race track pattern, flying low level and placing themselves between the slicks and any places of concealment around the LZ. We'd usually provide high cover for the insertion, flying above the slicks and their gunships, and circling the perimeter of the LZ.

If the slicks didn't have other gunships, we'd usually escort them into the LZ. If we prepped the LZ with fire, we'd race to intercept the slicks as they crossed the Initial Point to begin their approach.

The slicks were rarely on the ground more than a few seconds, just long enough for the troops to jump out. Sometimes the slicks didn't land at all, especially in a flooded rice paddy; they'd simply come to a hover and let the troops splash into the water. If a slick spent more than a few seconds in the LZ, it was usually because some troops were reluctant to get out and had to be coaxed to do so, sometimes forcibly; helicopter pilots didn't like being stationary targets. As the flight of Hueys lifted off, we'd position ourselves to the sides, toward the rear of the flight, and a little below it so we would have a clear shot at threats from the front and be able to maneuver easily toward threats from the sides.

Sometimes, an insertion required multiple flights of slicks. This might be the case if there were an especially large number of troops or if the LZ was too small to accommodate all of the slicks at one time. In those cases, we'd escort one flight until it was clear of the LZ, then race back and intercept another flight coming off the IP.

Our presence, even if it were just flying around and making noise, could make any VC have second thoughts about taking on the flight when there were Cobras around. Intelligence had reported finding leaflets on captured VC advising them it was okay to shoot at "fat" helicopters", but to keep their heads down when there were "skinny" ones around.

After all the troops had been inserted, we'd usually hang around the LZ for a while, keeping a watch over the troops until they'd had time to regroup and reach some relative safety beyond the open area necessary for the slicks to land.

After an insertion, we served at the discretion of the AMC. Sometimes he would have us fly to the closest airfield and wait to see if the troops ran into any trouble. Sometimes we'd hang around an airfield all day and never get called. More often, though, after an insertion, we gunship drivers were dispatched elsewhere by impetus of the Mission Assigners From On High. As soon as we were refueled and rearmed after an insertion, we were often sent off to other places around the Delta as if we were on a large-scale aerial scavenger hunt. We'd go shoot up alleged Viet Cong headquarters at one place, shoot rockets at suspicious sampans at another place, accompany a Huey ash and trash mission, or escort a Medevac helicopter. Sometimes we would race to places where troops on the ground had made contact with the VC; sometimes those were the same troops we had helped insert earlier.

A regular assignment was IV Corps Standby, during which we'd usually spend part of the day lounging in the Ready Shack, or "Hero Hootch" as it was called. There were rare days on IV Corps Standby duty when we weren't scrambled at all. Other days, though, it was one scramble after another.

A call to scramble gunships was similar to a call to a firehouse that sent fireman and fire trucks speeding to a scene. For us, when we arrived at the scene of a call, it was sometimes a blazing firefight with troops in heavy contact. At other times, the scene was more like a cat in a tree. The latter scene was especially more likely if the call came from the Ruff-Puffs, and experience taught me that if they were in the field somewhere, we could expect one of those calls about lunchtime. That time of day, they nearly always seemed to have an urgent need for gunships to come out where they were and shoot something. No doubt, gunship exhibitions were dining entertainment for their midday repast.

The Delta Devils were hired guns. We answered calls for a variety of operations that needed close air support or additional firepower. We performed reconnaissance missions similar to an Air Cavalry hunter-killer team, which employed a light observation helicopter (LOH) as a low-level scout and with gunships as overhead cover. In our case, we used another Cobra as a scout, although not nearly as effectively as an LOH. We also took the role of air artillery, employed to take out selected targets. And because of the Cobra's speed, we were often the first ones called out when someone suddenly ran into trouble.

It was a nomadic life, covering a lot of territory. We refueled anywhere there were fuel bladders available and rearmed at ammunition caches scattered around the Delta. We carried canteens of water and boxes of C-Rations with us; "Cs" were our most common meal. At some airstrips, Vietnamese women would approach us offering food for sale, much of it unidentifiable. I was leery of those offerings, but a person might eat anything if he were hungry enough. Sometimes, women or children vendors would come around offering bottles of Coca-Cola. I thought these bottles were safe to drink; yet I always examined the lids for evidence they may have been opened and resealed. These bottles were never iced, and after a while I developed a taste for warm Coke.

Just as we'd catch a meal when we could, we'd also catch sleep. Because our assignments usually came late in the evening and nearly always required a predawn wakeup, we got little sleep at night. We would try to make up for that loss with naps during the day when we found opportunities. My preferred place for napping was on the ammo bay door of a Cobra. I could prop my chicken plate against one of the cables supporting the let-down ammo bay door, and the concave shape of the chicken plate, designed to fit around a chest, made a suitable head rest, although not a soft one. After laying my head on a chicken plate and pulling my cap over my face, I could drop off in an instant.

Two of the most valuable skills I learned in Vietnam were the abilities to eat anything and to sleep anywhere.

Our Area of Operations was all of IV Corps and more, roughly anywhere in the Delta south of Saigon, which was within III Corps. Sometimes we roamed farther north. The capital city wasn't part of our regular beat. The Pink Panthers, another all-Cobra unit, had that. I thought of the Pink Panthers as city cops, serving metropolitan Saigon and its surrounding suburbs, and the Delta Devils as more like a county sheriff's deputies serving more rural areas.

With such a large area to patrol, much of it remote, and because we were often the first responders to troops under fire, we were given a lot of latitude in using our firepower. We would usually put in a strike whenever any US ground commander requested one and without seeking higher-level approval. If a situation was an immediate threat, we shot first and asked questions later, especially if friendlies—ourselves included— came under fire.

During the time of my tour, there were free fire zones in the Delta, areas where—subject to certain conditions, the time of day for example—we could initiate strikes on our own without asking approval. In situations outside of free fire zones, when we found what we felt was a worthwhile target and needed permission to strike it, we were rarely denied.

## Free Fire Zones

As a single fire team roaming around the Delta, we had a lot of autonomy. At that time, there were several free fire zones within our AO. Some of them had specifically restricted activities and/or restricted times. Any persons in those areas and not conforming to those restrictions were assumed to be enemy combatants. We were given a free hand to engage targets of opportunity we found in those zones, and in our travels, we would visit them whenever we could. On the way back to Can Tho from wherever we were, if I still had armament left, I'd sometimes make a side trip to a free fire zone. Most of those times, I didn't find any worthwhile targets, but I'd shoot up my armament anyway, like a dog marking his territory.

If I had just one word to describe the Delta, a top candidate would be "flat." The Delta, most of its landmass barely above sea level, was largely a flat space of rivers, canals, and rice paddies. Trees were abundant, but because they were an impediment to rice farming, generally grew only along rivers and in tree lines bordering rice paddies. The exception was the U Minh forest and the south coastal area.

The question of how an enemy force of any size could organize, move, and conduct operations where most of the terrain offered little opportunity for concealment was a good one. It may have been the same question that frontier cavalrymen patrolling the flat expanse of western Texas asked themselves about the Comanche. Perhaps it was the same question that puzzled the British when the Zulus appeared to rise out of the ground at Isandhlwana.

There were only a few operations in which I participated where there was a force of more than a couple of companies. One was a large force operation around the Parrot's Beak that involved a reported invasion force from Cambodia. Another time there were rumored to be several companies collected in the U Minh Forest.

Undoubtedly, the relative lack of natural concealment in the Delta worked to the disadvantage of Charlie for large force operations. Not only was it difficult for Charlie to amass large numbers of people without being detected, it was also difficult for Charlie to employ larger weapons. Larger weapons were heavier and harder to carry, especially when there were only a few people to share the load and the weapons might have to be carried across open space where it wasn't wise to sit down and rest awhile.

Our unit rarely encountered anything more than small arms fire while flying. We were, though, sometimes inconvenienced by mortar shells when we parked our Cobras at some remote area.

Because of his smaller numbers, Charlie may have relied more on guerrilla tactics in the Delta than elsewhere. Charlie was constrained to smaller and more lightly equipped units, a constraint which was at least an indirect result of a shortage of natural terrain concealment. The relative lack of terrain concealment worked to the disadvantage of Charlie, but it also was a disadvantage to us. Charlie could see us coming from a long way.

As a gunship pilot and as a matter of tactical advantage, I wanted to engage Charlie. The odds were heavily in my favor. Especially in the Delta, his relatively small numbers and small arms were a poor match for our fast, maneuverable, and heavily armed gunships. I'm sure Charlie thought so, too. That's why he generally tried to avoid gunships, especially Cobras.

Because Charlie was less of a lethal threat in the Delta than in other parts of the country and because it was harder to tempt him to take us on, we may have been less cautious in our tactics than our gunship pilot counterparts in other parts of the country. For example, we could do reckless things like repeatedly flying the same pattern on a target run, and be more likely to get away with it.

I assumed my mindset was the same as any other gunship pilot; I wanted to pick a fight, but on my own terms. And that included wanting to surprise the enemy, an objective that was especially challenging in the Delta because of all the wide-open space where Charlie could see for miles and miles. In the Delta, low-level was about the only way we could hope to sneak up on anyone.

Even at low-level, it was difficult to sneak up on Charlie because, even if he couldn't see us, he could hear us coming, especially in the Delta where there weren't many natural sound barriers to blanket the noise. However, I discovered that an extremely low-level approach, when the terrain allowed it and the conditions were right, would sometimes give us the element of surprise we needed. On one particular occasion, it worked quite well.

There was a free fire zone in a remote area northeast of Can Tho. It was territory occupied by the VC. Any person there at any time was deemed to be VC. During one ten-day period, aircraft flying near the area had spotted persons there several times, but before the aircraft could get close enough to be a threat, the people disappeared. These frequent, brazen intrusions must have become an irritant to someone in command authority. The Mission Assigners From On High dictated that this blatant activity be put to a stop, and the assignment to do that fell to me and my fire team.

The free fire zone was clearly marked on my personal tactical map. It lay along a wide, deep, and relatively straight river tributary and a couple of klicks from where the tributary emptied into a larger river, the *Son Tien Giang*. It was the dry season and the tributary carried little water. Given this terrain and with these conditions, I hatched a plan with my team.

We departed Can Tho in midafternoon. It was a thirty-minute flight to the area, but we didn't fly to it directly. Instead, we skirted it to the west and when ten klicks away—far enough that any people there likely wouldn't consider us a threat—we dropped down to fly low-level. We stayed "lima-lima", intercepted the river, and turned to follow it. We skimmed above it until we reached the nearly dry tributary that emptied into the river. The tributary was a little wider than a Cobra, and because it was deep enough and the water low enough during the dry season, we could fit our gunships within the banks with just the top of the mast and the main rotor above them. Once we made the turn into the tributary, it was straight enough that we were able to average over a hundred knots while flying within it.

We flew up the tributary the two klicks until we reached the free fire zone. There, we popped out of the tributary, the sun behind us, and were rewarded to find a half dozen weapons-carrying persons. Before they could shoulder their weapons, we relieved them permanently of their military service responsibilities.

The ability to reach the zone by flying between the banks of the tributary and to use our speed there was an effective combination. It not only prevented the VC from seeing us before we got there, the banks also helped mask our sound, giving us just the extra edge we needed to catch them. They couldn't see us and by the time they heard us, it was too late. Also, unlike hunting coyotes in the flatness of West Texas, they couldn't smell us.

This whole plot never would have worked if we had missed the turn into the tributary or had misjudged the distance and zoomed out of the tributary in the wrong place. Flying up the main river some ten klicks, finding the mouth of the specific tributary we wanted, and determining when we had arrived at the free fire zone—all at low-level—required some sharp map reading. That task was handled by my front seat copilot/gunner. All I had to do after concocting this scheme was avoid flying us into the banks of the tributary and remember to turn on the hot switch.

## The Phantom Meets the Minigun

The 235th Aerial Weapons Company was a part of the 307th "Phantom" Battalion and occasionally our gunships were assigned to Phantom missions where our company provided Cobras to destroy preselected targets chosen by a US military advisor's Vietnamese counterpart or by a Vietnamese Province Chief. These targets were supposedly VC assets, but if so, I suspected they may have been selected after consultation and mutual agreement with the VC because I couldn't see much value in many of the things we were sent to destroy.

On one particular Phantom mission, I was the fire team leader for a light fire team of Cobras. From Can Tho, we flew with the Huey that belonged to our parent battalion to Ca Mau, the town that was the capital of the Ca Mau province. The slick pilot was Steve, a pilot with a smooth touch and an easygoing nature, a combination that qualified him as the battalion's VIP chauffer. Steve had picked up my team's two Cobra crew chiefs, and after a leisurely flight at Huey speed rather than our Cobra's typical cruising speed, we landed at the airstrip on the edge of the town.

The American advisor, a captain, met us in his jeep. My wingman and I got into the jeep along with Steve and his copilot and we all rode into town for a briefing at the military compound there. The two Cobra copilots and the Huey crew chief and gunner stayed to guard the aircraft, especially from the horde of kids who always collected around our helicopters in towns like this one and who invariably, even at a tender age, were accomplished thieves.

When we arrived at the compound, the advisor ushered us into the large briefing room and introduced us to an assortment of dignitaries of various grades, beginning with the province's medal-adorned military commander. No one scarcely cared who we were, or we them, but it was a social necessity before we partook of the coffee and generous tray of pastries provided for the occasion. Such delicacies were a rare treat for a bunch of gunship gypsies like us, and the advisor was kind enough to make sure some of the pastries were sent to the rest of our crews.

After some pleasant chitchat with our Vietnamese allies, none of which the two parties actually understood but nevertheless was filled with smiles and vigorous head nods, we sat down at a large table for the briefing. The advisor set up a large map of the province on an easel and, using a long wooden pointer, began identifying the targets that had been selected for us to annihilate, ones selected by the province's commander in consultation with otherwise interested political figures.

The captain dutifully pointed to each of the targets on the map and described the allegations charged against each of them. And for each one of them, he elaborated at length on its approximate size and dimensions, composition and texture, color and hue, aroma and fragrance.

These important strategic targets consisted of items such as a falling down hootch suspected of housing VC, a waterlogged sampan possibly used by insurgents to haul weapons, and a pile of brush that—no doubt, almost assuredly, probably, could be, it wasn't beyond imagination to think—concealed a cache of weapons. These weapons were—no doubt, almost assuredly, probably, could be, it wasn't beyond imagination to think—fifty-millimeter anti-aircraft weapons. Or maybe they were some small arms, or perhaps a few grenades, or at least a rusty pitchfork with a pretty long handle.

The briefing held no important information for me that I needed to know or didn't already know. In the jeep ride to the briefing room, the captain had told me that he and the Vietnamese commander would be riding in the Huey to spot the targets for us; consequently, I didn't need to be briefed on them; they could just show me what to shoot when we got there. And, because the Vietnamese commander would be along for the ride, I already knew none of these carefully selected targets would be shooting back.

As the briefing dragged on, belying the root name of the event, I was careful to make it appear to any casual observer that I was absorbed in all these details, nodding with apparent keen interest at the circles on the map. But, in fact, I was more interested in the few remaining pastries on the side table, using my gunship skills to calculate the angle of intercept and the timing necessary, as soon as the briefing was over, to outrace the dignitaries for the last sticky bun. The knack of appearing to be aptly absorbed in a discussion, one with an unlimited depth of tedium about something I had no need to know, was a military skill I had developed through the many opportunities I had to practice it.

After narrating a complete dossier on each of the targets, the advisor added other unnecessary logistical details about the mission, such as the fact that we would return to the Ca Mau airstrip whenever we needed to rearm or refuel. In the area surrounding this hamlet, there was nowhere else to go for those things.

As soon as the meeting adjourned, I was ready to make my move on the sticky bun. Yet, despite my careful planning, I failed to obtain the object of my desire. As I was about to rise from the table, the Vietnamese ally to my right grabbed my arm to catch my attention and made some comment to me, one to which I nodded my agreement although I had no idea what he had said. It took only a moment, but when I turned back, I was dismayed to see another Vietnamese ally munching the coveted bun. I suspected the two allies were in cahoots.

We rode back to the airstrip in the jeep, the advisor driving, the starched and medal-adorned Vietnamese commander in the other front seat and we pilots, along with a translator from the commander's staff, wedged in the rear.

The advisor chauffeured the jeep up to the cargo door of the parked Huey. He came around to the passenger side, and with a broad sweep of his arm, invited the commander aboard. The Huey's crew chief lent him a hand into the back of the aircraft. The translator and advisor followed him. Steve stepped into the back also to personally help the commander place a headset on his head, placing it over the commander's hat to keep it from flying off in flight. I suppose this precaution was important to prevent the hat from possibly becoming a trophy of war should the enemy ever become lost and wander into the places where our target selections lay.

We gunship pilots climbed out of the jeep and walked the short distance to our waiting Cobras. We strapped in and waited until the Huey's passengers were made completely comfortable, then all the aircraft cranked up and flew out to the target area. Only the Cobra crew chiefs remained behind.

Once over the area, the Vietnamese commander began identifying the specific targets for us. The identification began with the American advisor helping him turn the tactical map in the correct direction, pointing to a numbered circle on the map, and pointing out of the side door of the Huey to the actual target corresponding to the circled number. Once satisfied of the correspondence between the virtual and actual target, the commander pronounced it satisfactory and issued a command in Vietnamese to the interpreter, a command equivalent to "Strike the target numbered one." By the time the identification, verification, and pronouncement of these important strategic targets were made by the Vietnamese honcho, conveyed to the interpreter, translated into English and restated to the US advisor, conveyed and elaborated by him over the intercom to Steve, and eventually transmitted from Steve to us, the directive typically came out sounding something like "Say, Mac, see that tree line directly ahead of you, the one with the big dead tree that's got a limb that looks like Jimmy Durante's nose? There's a leaky sampan stuck in the embankment under the tree. Shoot it."

So, we'd do that. And in a few minutes, we would have expended some rockets, costing more money that a Texas cotton farmer could afford to spend for his kids' entire year of school lunches, so that the fact that we'd made soggy splinters out of an abandoned, waterlogged sampan would be eventually added to a tally sheet somewhere in a column labeled "Number of Enemy Waterborne Craft Destroyed by Air."

We flew several sorties that morning, shooting up stuff, returning to Ca Mau when we needed more armament or fuel, and then going back out to the area to shoot up more stuff.

About noon, we returned to the airstrip to rearm and refuel once more and to take a lunch break. The US advisor and the Vietnamese commander were met by a jeep and the two of them went to the compound for lunch. The advisor arranged to send lunch out to the airstrip for all of us. We always appreciated anyone who fed us. During the break, we rearmed and refueled and the Cobra crew chiefs had time for a thorough postflight of the aircraft.

When the advisor and the Vietnamese commander returned to the airstrip after a leisurely lunch, it was time to shoot up more stuff. However, the Cobra wing ship's crew chief had discovered a problem with that aircraft and was attempting to fix it, but he needed more time to complete the fix.

With a good meal under my belt, I was feeling better about this mission, and in the spirit of demonstrating a can-do attitude of comradery with our military allies, I agreed that I'd take my Cobra, without the wing ship, and eliminate the remainder of the targets on the list. I felt comfortable going out alone since I was sure I wasn't going to take any ground fire, and if I went down for some other reason, the slick would be there to pick me up and, in such an event, I wouldn't be overly inconvenienced. I also wanted to continue the mission because my front-seat gunner, Jim, was new and this would be more good training for him. It would give him more experience handling the turret weapons and with the benefit of a leisurely, low-stress learning environment.

The slick took off for the area and I followed it. When we got there, the slick moved up to twenty-five hundred feet and I stayed at fifteen hundred and below to work the area with the weapons.

My Cobra's turret had a minigun and grenade launcher. The grenade launcher wasn't used that often because we rarely encountered a situation that I felt called for it; however, I planned that, once Jim shot up the minigum ammo, I'd have him use the grenade launcher to gain some experience with it.

On a rocket run, the common procedure was for the pilot to start a dive toward the target and, during the dive, align the aircraft to get a good sight picture to the target, trimming the aircraft so the rockets would take a straight path. During the initial part of the target run, while the pilot was getting aligned on the target, and as soon as the target was in range of the turret's minigun, the gunner began shooting at the target. The bursts from the minigun were intended to do some damage to the target as well as dampen the enthusiasm of anyone down there who might possibly have a notion to shoot at us preemptively rather than waiting patiently until we could send a rocket for him to chew on.

Then, when the pilot was ready to fire the rockets, he would call for the gunner to cease firing while the rockets were being punched off. By observing the rockets' paths and/or their impact points, the pilot could make adjustments for another round of rockets, if necessary. Once the pilot finished punching off rockets, he began a break away from the target, and as the aircraft turned away, the gunner would open up again with the turret minigun to discourage any would-be return fire.

This was the procedure Jim was learning, and this was a good environment for learning the mechanics of the procedure because there was no enemy threat to deal with. That meant it was also an easy day for me. I could set up a rocket run directly into the wind without any concern about enemy forces or where friendlies were located. And it allowed me the added luxury of setting up a shallow dive angle with plenty of time for target alignment. I expected to set a new personal record for targets destroyed on a first run and with the least expenditure of rockets.

On the radio, Steve relayed to me the first target for the afternoon: a dilapidated hootch along the bank of a canal. I saw the one he described and maneuvered the aircraft so I could approach the target into the wind. Since there was an expanse of wide open rice paddies leading into the target from that direction, and consequently no possible place for someone to hide who might want to take a shot at us as we flew overhead, I would be able to set up an especially ideal, textbook dive that would give me generous time to get established on the target. Even if the rockets misfired or I embarrassed myself by missing the target, the shallow dive angle would allow me time to leisurely make adjustments between rounds if I needed to. However, I felt confident that it wouldn't take more than one pair of rockets to hit this target dead center. I thought this was one of those ideal situations where nothing could possibly go wrong. Jim and I both simply would be perfecting our techniques.

I turned on the hot switch, announced that fact to Jim, and glanced up to the front seat to confirm he was ready. He had the targeting device in his hands and I was sure he already had enough experience to know when to start shooting. I rounded out the lazy turn and nosed down into a shallow dive toward the target. I concentrated on the sight picture through the rocket sight and tweaked the controls to get the aircraft lined up for the rockets.

As we drew closer to the target, without any prompting, Jim pushed the trigger on his handgrip to lay down suppressing fire from the minigun. He only fired a short burst, though, before he stopped. He clicked open the intercom. "Hey, I don't see any tracers."

I was looking through the rocket sight and I hadn't seen any either. I knew the minigun had been reloaded during the lunch break from the weapons store at the airfield, and still absorbed with aligning the aircraft for the rockets, I came to an instant conclusion. I said, "Somebody probably forgot to put any tracers in the belt we loaded."

The ammo belts of the miniguns came preloaded with rounds, and it had happened before that I'd gotten an ammo belt without any tracer rounds. So, I shared with Jim what I had learned when I was a gunner and in cases like that. I told him, "Just go ahead and use the pipper and then adjust your fire from the debris you kick up." I felt good knowing Jim would be learning something new.

Jim peered through the handheld sight, and pressed the trigger. He held it and I heard the minigun spitting out the rounds.

I was lined up on the target and was ready to punch off the rockets when I heard Steve yelling on the radio, "Cease firing! Cease firing!"

When I heard the call, I instinctively looked to see where the slick was. I spotted it, a thousand feet above our Cobra and off to the right at the four o'clock position. And I was sure surprised to see a red fire hose from my very own gunship snaking up toward the slick, the rounds passing just in front of its nose.

Jim was so engaged in looking for debris down at the target area, he was still firing away. I clicked the intercom. "Jim, do you want to cease firing, please."

Jim released the trigger, but disgruntled to have been interrupted while he was concentrating so hard. "What's the matter?" he demanded.

Steve came back on the radio. "Mac, I'm sure you must have your reasons, but would you mind telling me why you're trying to shoot us down?" Steve was much calmer about this than I would have been in his position.

I asked Steve to standby. I turned off the hot switch and had Jim stow away the turret's sighting device. Then, I asked Steve to come in closer and take a look at our turret weapon. In reply, Steve asked a question that I thought, under the circumstances, to be a sensible one. "Is this just a trick to get a closer shot at us?" But he came on down anyway.

Steve took a look and reported that the minigun on the turret was pointed in its full up, full right position. Normally, when the turret weapons were turned off, they automatically stowed so that they pointed straight ahead.

Apparently, the hydraulic drive on the turret had malfunctioned, slung the weapons cockeyed, and left them stuck there in that position, causing the minigun's rounds to go astray. Jim hadn't seen any tracers because they were shooting into the air outside of his peripheral vision—as well as mine. However, Steve and everybody aboard the slick had a good look at them as the red trails raced across just in front of the slick's windshield. And, apparently, the Vietnamese commander had seen more than enough of them. Steve relayed the message from him to us.

"My backseat VIP says this mission is over and he wants to go home now."

Steve turned the slick back toward Ca Mau and I came alongside to escort him. In a moment, Steve radioed me again, "Uh, Mac, the commander told me to tell you to stay away from us. He doesn't want you to follow us. In fact, he doesn't want you anywhere near us. He's pretty insistent about it."

In the interest of good will with our allies, I turned away and flew off in the opposite direction. But I circled back, came up behind the slick in its blind spot, and took up a position there so the commander couldn't see me.

When we got back to Ca Mau, based on orders from the back seat of the Huey, I remained airborne while the slick landed and dropped off its passengers. As soon as the Huey touched down, the commander bounded out. And, as he fled the aircraft, he kept glancing up over his shoulder at my Cobra.

I talked to my wingman and discovered the problem with his aircraft had been fixed. It and the slick took off and all three of our aircraft formed up for the flight back to Can Tho.

The stuck minigun had ended the day early for us, so we went to the club to celebrate that rare event. I bought Steve's beer.

## Dog Dickering

We were working from the airstrip at Ca Mau on another Phantom mission and with the Phantom battalion's Huey, piloted by Steve. As was typical of these missions, we would shoot up designated targets in the area and return to the airstrip on the edge of the town when we needed to rearm or refuel.

Civilians wandered around the airfield, some of them peddling wares, and at any airfield like this, helicopters attracted kids. Whenever they heard us returning, they'd gather at the edge of the airstrip, waiting for us. When we hovered to the rearming stations and fuel bladders, they would edge closer. They loved to play dare with our helicopters. As we hovered, they'd leap around in the gusts from the rotor and dance around the tail rotor. We'd pick up to a high hover, when we could, to get the tail rotor away from them, but then they'd run under the aircraft. If the engine should quit, we'd come right down on top of them.

When there were kids at airstrips like this, they were nearly always a concern. Not only were we concerned for their safety; they were a potential threat. One of them could have been recruited, willingly or unwillingly, by the VC, and a grenade tossed by a kid was just as deadly as one lobbed by an adult.

Besides all that, they were beggars and thieves. Even while we were hot loading or refueling with the engines running, they'd surround us, hands outs, wanting us to give them something, preferably cigarettes. When the aircraft were parked, anything left lying around and unwatched was as good as gone. They especially valued cigarette lighters. During the time American forces were in Vietnam, we must have equipped every single kid in the country with a Zippo product.

About noon, we landed at the airstrip to rearm and refuel and to take a lunch break. Afterwards, we all hung around the aircraft waiting for the US advisor to return. Steve sat at the door of the cargo bay of his helicopter with his slick's crew chief and gunner. My team's pilots and crew chiefs gathered around the slick because its broad body provided more shade than our skinnier Cobras.

A bunch of kids had gathered around. Even though they'd apparently decided they had gotten all the handouts from us we were going to give them, they hung around, watching us as if we were the monkeys in a zoo.

They clustered in a semicircle near the side of the slick. The kids at the front squatted on their haunches and the ones further back stood, some of them with one leg over the other and leaning on the neighbor standing next to him. Some of them had their arms around each other, best-friend-like. They were all barefooted boys wearing shorts and short sleeve shirts, some of them smoking cigarettes.

Out of the corner of my eye, my attention was drawn to one boy who was pushing through the crowd of kids. I wasn't looking directly at him; I was simply listening to the conversation, but something—perhaps some ripple in the crowd as it parted, perhaps some noise—nudged my consciousness, warning me, and I turned to watch this boy who had drawn my attention. He looked to be nine or ten years old and I saw he was carrying something in his arms. Perhaps this was what had caught my attention; this thing he was carrying. I didn't know what it was. It could be a satchel charge and he was already closer to the helicopters, and us, than I wanted. When I turned to give him my full attention, the other team members also turned toward the boy.

When he kept coming, I was about to warn him back, but then I saw what he was carrying. It was a puppy: a round bellied, brown and white ball of fur, maybe six weeks old. And I knew why he was coming to us: to sell it.

Apparently, this kid had already assessed our group and had picked out the biggest sucker for this puppy he was peddling. When the boy got to us, he held out the puppy to Steve. The kid had assessed correctly. Steve took the chubby puppy and held it up his face. It had short floppy ears and it bore on its face the resigned expression of having been carried, curried, and petted so much that the adoration had become burdensome. The puppy, limply hanging from Steve's hands like a wet pair of socks on a clothes line, surveyed Steve with its sleepy eyes, yawned, smacked its lips, and then stuck out its pink tongue and licked Steve on the nose.

With that, the kid went immediately into his sales pitch. He held out his hand. "Three hundred P," he said.

Steve, under the spell of puppy love, reached for his wallet. I could see that he would have paid ten times the price. But this wouldn't do, I thought; I had to talk some sense into him. I said, "Steve, wait a minute. Think about it. You don't need a dog. What would you do with it? Where would you keep it?"

Steve rubbed his nose against the puppy's. "I'll feed him and take care of him," he said, " and I'll keep him in my hootch."

I reached out for the pup. "Let me see that dog," I demanded.

Steve reluctantly handed it to me.

I grew up on a farm and town dwellers often drove out to the country to dump unwanted dogs and cats. Many of the unwanted pets found their way to our farm. We had dogs and cats coming and going all the time. We couldn't feed them all, but as long as they didn't chase the chickens or otherwise cause trouble, they could stay. Some of the castaways stayed for a day and moved on; some of them hung around a while longer before moving on. A few of them earned a permanent home with us: the cats who were good mousers and could out bully the barn rats and the dogs who proved themselves useful, those who were natural herders or could find lost livestock, and the few who were menacing enough to scare away coyotes and door-to-door salesmen.

Those that earned their keep got regular meals and medical care when needed. As a result of having so many dogs and cats and from watching over the shoulder of the vet who regularly tended our livestock and occasionally a dog or a cat, I had become somewhat of a veterinarian intern.

I examined this mutt, holding it at arms length, giving it a thorough looking-over. Its fur was caked with dried mud and I noticed its hind paws had six toes. I held it up and looked in its ears. I lifted its head, pried open its mouth, and examined its teeth. I flopped it over on its back and poked its Buddha shaped tummy. Finally, I lifted its tail and performed a sniff test.

I stretched out my arm, holding the plump pooch by the scruff of the neck. It dangled there, droopy eyed and unconcerned. I pointed to it with my other hand, announcing the conclusions of my examination. "First," I said, "this dog is not a 'him'; it's a 'her'. Second, it's got fleas; more hoppers than Uncle Floyd's beard."

"And third," I said, poking its belly, "it's got worms."

I considered my evaluation the end of the matter; it was a flawed piece of merchandise this street kid was peddling, and I thrust it back at the kid.

The kid sneered at me, ignoring the return. Instead, he looked at Steve and gave a flick of his head toward the dog. Before I could stop him, Steve pulled the puppy from me and cradled it close to him, petting it and scratching its ears. "None of that matters," he said. "I don't care if it's a girl. I can bathe it and get rid of the fleas. And worms can be treated, can't they?"

I stared a dagger at the kid before turning to Steve. I said, "Now, think. Have you ever seen another dog anywhere at the Can Tho Airfield?"

Steve thought a moment, then gave me an I-gotcha look. "The maintenance platoon has one."

I didn't know that. But in any case, surely anyone other than Steve could plainly see that I was right; he had no need for a dog, especially one as extravagantly priced as the one this kid was trying to foist on him. I looked at the others for help.

His crew chief spoke up. "That's right," he said. "The guys in the maintenance platoon named the dog Smiley."

That wasn't the kind of help I was looking for.

I ignored the crew chief. "Now, listen, Steve," I said. "You know your boss won't let you keep a dog in your room."

I could see Steve contemplating the battalion colonel; he knew I was right about that.

My wingman snapped his fingers. "Hey, I know. We could keep her in our platoon hootch."

"Oh, yeah?" I shot back. "Who's going to feed it and take care of it?"

Steve said, "I will. Just keep her in the platoon hootch and I'll feed her."

My gunner chimed in. "We'll all look after her. We can make her our platoon mascot."

"Yeah," said the wingman's gunner, "We need a mascot."

They all gathered protectively around the puppy as Steve held it.

What was the matter with these people? Apparently, they had all lost their senses under the spell of this furred charmer. I looked at the kid; he had a smug smile on his face.

Steve pulled out his wallet. "Now hold on," I said. I needed to gain the upper hand in this transaction. Even if I couldn't stop the sale outright, I'd at least improve the deal. I wasn't going to let this kid unload that mongrel for such an outrageous price. He didn't know who he was dealing with.

I was a master negotiator. At a street shop in downtown Can Tho, I had once bargained with a vendor and whittled him down to almost a third of his asking price for a top-of-the-line coffin.

Even though I didn't need a coffin and had no place to put it, I had gotten a good price. Even back at Fort Wolters, using a new deck of playing cards and a rack of plastic chips as an under-the-counter enticement, I had negotiated a deal with a part-time bartender to pay a sharply discounted price for all the beer my companions and I could drink—even though, in hindsight, I should have stipulated that it not be Falstaff in rusty cans. More recently, I had bartered a nearly full bottle of Black Jack, three packs of cigarettes, and two pair of barely used socks for a handmade bracelet made from a bicycle chain—quite artistic I thought, and a real bargain.

I stepped between Steve and the kid. "One hundred P," I said, holding up one finger.

The kid shook his head and held up three fingers. "Three hundred P."

Behind me, Steve reached for his wallet again. I held up my open hand to stop him. I wasn't through yet. "One hundred and fifty P," I said.

The kid folded his arms. "Three hundred P."

I leaned down and looked the kid in the eye. We were practically nose-to-nose. He squinted back at me. I said, "Two hundred P. And that's our final offer. Take it or leave it."

The kid didn't blink. He shunned this ultimatum, stepped around me, and held out his hands to Steve, demanding the return of the muddy mutt.

Steve stuck the puppy under his arm and to my dismay, counted out three hundred piasters, and handed the bills toward the kid. But to my surprise, the kid shook his head, still demanding the dog back. Well, now, I thought, it appears my shrewd negotiation had busted the deal altogether. I was pretty proud of myself.

Steve, though, reached into his shirt pocket, pulled out his nearly full pack of Kools, and offered the cigarettes as boot for the deal. The kid considered the bonus a moment before accepting the consolidated offer, snatching the bills and the filtered menthols from Steve.

The kid counted the money; then, satisfied that it was all there, flipped a cigarette from the pack and stuck the smoke in the corner of his mouth, letting it dangle there. One of the hangers-on among the flock of urchins flipped the lid on a lighter and snapped a flame for this newly rich lord. The little dirty dog dealer took a slow, deliberate drag from the cigarette, blew the smoke at me, then turned and swaggered away followed by a throng of short admirers.

## The Unbearable Tightness of Being a Cobra Pilot

With the Cobra, I was convinced that the space allocated for pilots in the cockpit was an afterthought and added only grudgingly. When the folks at Bell Helicopter were designing the aircraft, I suspected the first time anyone even realized there was a problem fitting pilots into the cockpit was only after the first prototype had been built and was ready for a test flight.

I could imagine the conversation when the problem was discovered. The chief design engineer, Al, was at home early that evening, still in his white short-sleeved shirt, his thin black tie held in place with a silver tie tack. The phone rang and he answered it. "Hello."

"Hey, Al, this is Bud down at the test hangar."

"Yeah, Bud, what's up?" said Al.

"Oh, not much," said Bud. "What're you doing?"

"Just watching *Laugh-In* and playing with my slide rule," Al said.

"Yeah, I like that show," said Bud. "That Goldie Hawn is a fox."

"I suppose," said Al, "but I doubt she can hold her looks for another thirty or forty years. Now, that Joanne Worley on the other hand, she's got star talent. I expect she's going to be really big someday."

Bud said, "Not to change the subject, but we ran into a bit of a problem this afternoon when we got ready to test fly that new AH-1 prototype."

"What kind of problem?"

"Well," said Bud, "The test pilots came out to do a test flight, and they complained there wasn't any place in the cockpit for them to sit."

There was a long silence.

"Uh, Al, are you still there?"

"Yeah, I'm here," said Al. "Rats. I knew there was something I forgot."

"You mean there's really supposed to be room for pilots in the cockpit?" said Bud. "I looked in there and didn't see any place for them, so I tried to explain to those test pilots that maybe the thing was supposed to be a drone."

"That's what I wanted to design," said Al, "but those darn marketing guys said it had to have a pilot or two. They said it would give the aircraft that human touch. But, I swear, Bud, all pilots are good for is to go around breaking aircraft."

"Yeah, I know what you mean," said Bud. "I've got a Huey sitting over here right now that they wrecked yesterday."

Bud sighed. "But what are you going to do? Those test pilots said they'd be back tomorrow and insisted they would need a place to sit. And you know how test pilots are. As soon as someone hands them an orange flight suit and a white helmet, they think they're something special."

"How many pilots does it need room for?" said Al.

"Two."

Al shouted into the phone, "What do they need with two pilots? Can't they get by with just one? I mean, two people can't fly the thing at the same time, can they?"

"Well, no," said Bud. "You've got a good point there. But it may be some kind of union thing, you know, like with a train where the union says you have to have a fireman even when the engine's burning diesel."

There was another long pause.

"Well, anyway," said Bud. "What'd you want to do?"

"I'm thinking," said Al.

Al removed one of the mechanical pencils from his pocket protector and doodled on the back of the TV Guide. "What about this?" he said. "Let's put one of them, say the copilot, up in the front. Just yank one of the seats out of that wrecked Huey and set it on top of the ammo bay."

"Well, yeah, I can do that, I guess," said Bud. "Where do you want to put the controls?"

"Controls?!" yelled Al. "What does a copilot need with controls?"

"I don't know," said Bud, "but those pilots were pretty insistent that they had to have some controls for both of them."

"What a bunch of prima donnas," said Al. "Oh, alright then. For the copilot, pull the cyclic and collective out of that Huey, saw them in half, and stick one on one side and the other on the other side of that copilot's seat."

"Which one on which side?" said Bud.

"I don't know. I forget which hand those pilots use for which control."

"Do you want me to call a pilot and ask him?"

"No, don't bother," said Al. "It doesn't matter. He won't be able to fly the aircraft with those short controls anyway."

"Okay" said Bud, "that takes care of the copilot. What about the pilot?"

Al stared at his lava lamp for a moment before he spoke. "Oh, just put another Huey seat in there for him, somewhere behind the copilot."

Bud said, "You know, Al, with the instrument panel and all the radios, there'd hardly be enough room back there for anybody to scratch his butt."

"Well, that's not my problem," said Al. "The pilot will just have to scrunch up, or maybe the Army can find some midgets who want to be pilots."

"Okay, good enough for me," said Bud. "Do you want to work up some drawings for all this and run them by the QA folks?"

"Naw," said Al, "there's nothing that involves structural integrity or performance. It's just pilot stuff."

## The Legend of Dick's Deed

That day began like any other. Little did I know it would be the day a legend was born.

Our fire team's mission was to provide helicopter gunship air support for an operation near Ca Mau. My copilot in the front seat was Dave, a literate gentleman who could quote

Shakespeare. The wingman was Dick, a short timer with less than ninety days before DEROS. His gunner was Jim, who wore a perpetual grin.

In the early morning before dawn, we preflighted our helicopters by flashlight, the two Cobras parked in the revetments adjacent to each other. Dave and I finished preflighting our helicopter and I turned off the flashlight to save the batteries. In the adjacent revetment, I could see a single flashlight beam and I shouted over the head-high revetment wall, "Dick, are you ready to go?"

It was Jim who answered. "Dick is indisposed at the moment. He's taking a dump in the swamp."

Jim, who was preflighting the helicopter by himself, took a moment to offer a suggestion to Dick. "Don't let the mosquitoes bite your butt," he shouted.

From the darkness in the direction of the swamp, Dick replied with a suggestion of his own. "Why don't you kiss my butt?" he said.

We all waited until Dick completed his task.

Eventually, I saw the beam from Dick's flashlight as he made his way from the swamp back to his helicopter. I stepped part way up the side of the revetment and flashed my light over the wall. Dick was leaning against the fuselage. He looked drained.

"Are you ok?" I said.

Dick moaned, "I've got the quick trots—bad."

"I'll call Ops and have them get somebody to replace you," I offered.

Dick straightened himself and began putting on his chicken plate. "No, I'm okay. Let's go," he insisted.

I hopped down from the wall and walked to the back seat entry for my Cobra's cockpit where the gullwing canopy hatch was open. When fully extended, it left an opening about shoulder high from the ground and just big enough to crawl into, or out of, the cockpit.

As a technical side note regarding the height of the canopy hatch opening, it may have been obvious to an astute observer that the hatch opening would be higher off the ground if the aircraft were airborne. However, this proved not to be a practical design problem in terms of entering or exiting the aircraft since, for all practical purposes, it was not possible to enter the aircraft after it was airborne, and also while airborne there was rarely any desire to exit the aircraft from any appreciable altitude since the Army discouraged excursions outside of an airborne helicopter by failing to issue parachutes to the occupants.

With its tandem seating, the Cobra's cockpit was only wide enough to accommodate the breath of one person and the necessary controls and instruments. The narrowness of the cockpit, combined with the height of the hatch above the ground and its small opening, made getting into, and out of, a Cobra an exercise in dexterity. Actually, a pilot did not get into a Cobra; to state it more accurately, he conformed himself to it, like hamburger stuffed into a meat loaf mold.

After donning my chicken plate, I began conforming. Placing my right foot on the step-up, I pulled myself up to the side of the cabin and ducked under the open canopy hatch. Grabbing a handhold on the canopy, I swung my left foot over the outside edge of the cabin and placed it on the far side of the cabin floor, careful not to hit the cyclic sticking up from the floor and making sure I didn't dirty the seat by stepping on it, catch my foot on the collective lever, or kick the instrument panel. With one foot in, I hunched over with my back against the top of the canopy, and lifted my right foot into the cockpit, careful not to step on the radio console along the right side of the cockpit or bang my knee on the instrument panel. Then, cautious not to impale any of myself on the cyclic as I hunched over it, I pulled the holstered pistol on the side of my gun belt around so that it was positioned in front of one of the most precious members of my body, and from that position, I put my rear end against the back of the seat and wiggled the hindmost part of my body, gradually sinking into the seat until the aforementioned rear end touched bottom.

At last seated in the tightness of my aircraft throne with its side panels wrapped around me like the wings of the cherubim on the Ark of the Covenant, I surveyed my kingdom of controls and instruments. Satisfied that I had once again accomplished the miracle of seating myself in a Cobra, I proceeded to the task of latching myself to the aircraft. I pulled the two straps of the shoulder harness over my chest, put one end of the sturdy lap belt at my waist through the eyelets at the ends of the dangling restraining straps, joined them together with the two parts of the seat belt around my waist, and snapped the belt's lever into place to secure the whole assembly. I then activated the shoulder harness lock, testing to make sure I was girded in properly. Straining against the straps, I confirmed that I was as thoroughly cinched to the Cobra as a Frankenstein monster strapped to the board and awaiting the lightning bolt.

In the front seat, Dave labored through a similar exercise as he squeezed into the gunner's seat and latched himself to the aircraft with harness and buckle, a practice equivalent to an ancient mariner lashing himself to the mast. No papoose was ever more firmly wrapped to the means of its transportation than we were.

I called "Clear!" and pulled the engine starter trigger. The tone of the turbine engine rose in scale from a baritone to an alto as it reached its full operating rpm. With the engine running, the rotor turning, and the instrument needles where they should be, I reached up, pulled the canopy hatch closed, and latched it in place. As I always did, I visually confirmed the hatch was shut and latched. There was the danger that if a canopy hatch came open in flight at any airspeed greater than thirty knots, it could be ripped off by the force of the slipstream and be blown into the rotor. If this happened, a pilot could suffer the inconvenience of having to walk home when the aircraft quit flying, and everybody knew that pilots hated to walk anywhere. However, looking at this possibility from a positive viewpoint, a pilot was actually not very likely at all to have to walk home, since he probably would not survive the crash.

In the adjacent revetment, I saw that the rotor of Dick's Cobra was spinning and he had his position lights on. As soon as the radios were warmed up, I called on the radio. "Dick, are you ready to go?"

Dick's voice came back through my headphones, "Ready."

I took off and climbed to two thousand feet. I set the power for a hundred-and-thirty-five knots and pointed the ship in the direction of Ca Mau. I glanced behind me and saw Dick's Cobra in staggered trail to the right, a half klick behind.

There was hardly any traffic on the radios. A lone unknown voice called on the emergency channel, "Checking guard. How do you read?" This routine call was answered by a second unknown voice with the invariable response to all requests of this nature, "Get off guard, you idiot." The first voice replied cheerfully, "Thank you." After that exchange, aside from the steady drone of the engine and the comforting resonance of the rotor blades, all was quiet.

The gauges were in the green. Airspeed, altitude, and course were set and it was twenty-eight minutes to Ca Mau.

In the front seat, I could see the back of Dave's helmet, leaning to the side; he was obviously asleep. It occurred to me that I could use a nap myself, and it also occurred to me that I was the Aircraft Commander, so I used that authority vested in me by the United States Army. I leaned across the instrument panel in front of me, poked Dave on the shoulder, and spoke on the intercom, "Yo, Dave, wake up."

Dave stirred. "What is it?"

"You've got the aircraft," I said.

In a moment, I felt a wiggle on the cyclic and a pressure on the pedals. "I've got it," Dave acknowledged. I relinquished the controls and spoke to him. "See the heading? Ca Mau is straight ahead. You can't miss it. Wake me when we get there." I scanned the instruments once more, made sure the shoulder harness was locked so that I wouldn't slump forward onto the cyclic, and was instantly asleep, a babe in the cradle as the Cobra glided through the darkness.

Some time later, a mental nudge awakened me. There was an edge of lightness along the eastern horizon, the promise of the morning sun. Glancing at the clock on the instrument panel, I saw that twenty-five minutes had elapsed. Ca Mau, I thought, should be coming up in a few minutes, and I looked ahead but couldn't see the illumination barrels of the airfield yet.

I yawned and stretched as far as I could in the confines of the cockpit, then turned in the seat and looked back to the right to see where Dick was. I didn't see his aircraft, so I turned to the left, looking for him. He wasn't there either. Maybe, I thought, he was directly behind me in the blind spot.

"Dave," I said, "Crab right."

Dave pushed the right pedal, yawing the aircraft in that direction, allowing me to look directly behind us. I didn't see Dick anywhere. Maybe he had gone blackout, turning off his lights.

I pushed the radio button. "Satan One-Eight, One-Three, over."

Silence.

I called again, "Satan One-Eight, One-Three, over."

Nothing.

I took the controls and began a turn to reverse course. "Do you see them?" I asked Dave.

"Nope," he said.

My mind was racing. Where could they be? I completed the turn and started backtracking toward Can Tho.

I tried to imagine the possibilities. Maybe Dick and Jim had taken fire, had been shot out of the air, and had crashed before they could even get off a May Day. Or maybe they had both fallen asleep and had flown into the ground.

I could also imagine that this wouldn't look good on my record. I imagined my court martial, with me on the witness stand, and the prosecuting attorney asking me, "You mean to tell this court, Mister McComic, that you lost your wingman and his gunner, as well as an expensive military aircraft, while you were—and the prosecutor paused for emphasis—asleep?" I feared my momma would be mailing my cookies to Leavenworth.

The big flare in the east was just beginning to appear over the horizon as I raced back toward Can Tho, looking for my wing ship. I searched the ground, looking for burning wreckage. I searched the sky, longing to see the position lights of Dick's helicopter.

I had backtracked about ten klicks when Dave shouted, "I see them. Twelve o'clock."

It was barely daylight. I peered straight ahead through the Plexiglas canopy and saw the position lights and dark silhouette of a Cobra. It was Dick alright. My fear melted away to puzzlement.

I called to him on the radio, "Satan One-Eight, what's going on?"

The only reply was a strangled sound, as if someone were choking.

I keyed the mike again, "Satan One-Eight, are you okay?"

Again, the only reply was a gasping, breathless wheeze. And, again, my imagination was racing. Scenes of the John Wayne movie, *The Flying Tigers*, flashed through my mind, where pilots were shot and blood began streaming from their mouth. Maybe Dick and Jim had both been hit, and with blood gurgling in their throats, they were fighting unconsciousness, desperately trying to keep their aircraft flying.

As I closed on the wing ship, I noticed something curious; it was creeping along at what I estimated to be less than thirty knots.

Drawing alongside the aircraft, there was enough daylight that I could just see Dick's and Jim's forms inside the canopy. They appeared to be conscious. In fact, Dick was engaged in some desperate struggle in the back seat. In the front seat, Jim was half turned toward the back and appeared to be suffering some kind of spasms as his body rocked in the seat.

As I circled their aircraft, the aircraft slowed even more. Then I saw the back seat canopy hatch swing partially open. And as I continued to watch, I saw a dark object fly out of the open hatch. The object was swept briefly into the slipstream, fluttered away behind the helicopter, and floated toward the ground, disappearing into the shadows of the early morning. The hatch closed; the aircraft gradually nosed over; and it resumed its normal cruising speed. I flew along beside it.

Now, I was more than puzzled; I was completely perplexed. I keyed the mike. "Hey, what the deuce are you doing?" It was Jim who answered. He could barely talk. He was laughing so hard, he could only manage short, breathless gasps. "Well, ... heh, heh ... you see, ... Dick ... cackle, cackle ... wait one."

A minute or more passed. Dave and I exchanged possible theories about the reason for this unusual behavior as we waited for Jim to compose himself and provide us the real explanation.

Eventually, Jim regained enough control to talk on the radio with only a few laughing fits. "You see, here's what happened. Dick had another attack, and before he knew it, he had crapped in his pants. I mean to tell you, it was a good one, too. He really unloaded. And you wouldn't believe the smell; it was lethal. We couldn't live with it, so Dick decided he would dispose of his drawers. He took them off and threw them out. We fell behind because he had to slow the aircraft so he could open the canopy hatch. I tried to call you but, I swear, it was so funny I couldn't talk or do anything."

So, that was the explanation. It was Dick's olive drab drawers I saw flying out of the open hatch and fluttering away.

I was relieved that Dick and Jim were not victims of hostile action. I was also relieved to escape the court martial I had imagined. Relief was my immediate feeling. It was later, after we landed at Ca Mau and Jim explained completely what happened, that I experienced the feeling of awe that came to me when I realized the true magnitude of this event.

After landing, I asked Dick to tell me himself what happened, but he just shook his head and refused to say anything. Jim, however, was eager to tell again what happened. Dave and I hung on every word, occasionally interrupting Jim to ask him to repeat some elements of the event or asking him for clarification on some of the details. Jim was happy to oblige, each time adding some new relish to elaborate the drama and suspense of the story. Dick also kept interrupting, telling Jim to shut up. I'm sure this was because Dick was so humble. After all, what he had accomplished was a remarkable feat, something I thought was practically impossible.

As Jim described the details, I was amazed as I visualized what Dick had done. Within the cramped confines of the back seat of a Cobra, barely a yardstick wide at its widest point, with an instrument panel practically in his lap, a gun belt and holster around his waist, and a cyclic between his legs, Dick had managed to remove two fully laced boots, shed his socks, pull off his pants, remove his filled and sagging drawers, slow the aircraft below hatch-open speed, toss the drawers out of the aircraft, close the hatch, and—as I discovered when we landed—had put his pants, socks, and boots back on, all while flying at two thousand feet.

What Dick had done was truly an exceptional deed, something never before recorded in the annals of Cobra flying. And, surprisingly, Dick himself was apparently blind to his own greatness. He was the only one who didn't want to talk about it.

After thoughtfully deliberating upon it, all of us, with only Dick abstaining, agreed it was an achievement deserving of a medal of some kind. But we realized it was an achievement of so singular a nature that there was no Army commendation that covered it. Regretfully, we knew that Dick would never receive the formal recognition we felt he deserved. Yes, all of us—Jim, Dave, and I—agreed it was unjust, but what could we do?

Jim was the one who saw what we must do. Placing his arm around Dick, Jim assured him that he would take personal responsibility to make sure that as many persons as possible would know of Dick's deed. Moved by Jim's sincere promise, Dave and I joined hands with Jim and we too vowed to Dick that we also would do our utmost to make sure that his deed would not be forgotten. Dick, being the reluctant hero, insisted that none of us tell the story to anybody. In fact, his insistence was expressed with some violent threats about what he would do to us if we told anyone.

I am happy to report that the fire team completed its mission that day without further casualties. Dick performed his full duties despite the fact that he did so without his drawers and therefore, in a technical sense, performed them while out of uniform.

That night, back at Can Tho, the three of us were true to our vow that Dick should receive the full accolade he deserved. To his surprise, and despite his quite strenuous objections, we escorted Dick to the Can Tho Officers' Club. We escorted him with Dave holding him under the arms and Jim and I each carrying a leg. His flailing and cursing as we brought him into the club served our purpose well. Everybody looked to see what the commotion was.

As we placed Dick on a stool of honor between the club's two prized slot machines, his eyes blazed at us. And with Dick on the stool, surrounded by his loyal companions, who made sure he remained there, Jim began telling everyone the story of Dick's adventure. As Jim described the early morning events, the whole club gradually fell silent as the assembly pressed in closer to hear it all. The listeners were hushed in wonder. Even rear-echelon professionals vacated their assigned posts at the bar and at the bridge tables to come listen and marvel at the story Jim told.

Jim's story was a masterpiece of laudatory oratory. Jim praised Dick's resolve that morning and his firmness to persevere on his mission in spite of the attack upon his person, yea, a firmness more than equal to the looseness of his bowels. And Jim spared no details of the saga. In reverent tones, he told of the predawn offering Dick had made to the spirits of the swamp, much like the ancient Greek warriors had sacrificed to their gods before their odysseys. Jim told of the unavoidable calamity that befell Dick on his journey. He described to everyone, in complete and graphic detail, the product of the calamity and the toxic hazard it imposed. Jim told the hushed throng of the bold decisiveness with which Dick had acted to ensure the safety of the crew of his vessel and described Dick's dexterity and grace as he unwrapped himself of his clothing and removed the object of the calamity.

Then, at the climax of the story, Jim dramatically flung his hand into the air, demonstrating the flourish with which Dick had so deftly tossed the offending garment from the craft. At that, Dick grabbed wildly at Jim, undoubtedly overcome by emotion and wishing to embrace the one who had brought him so much attention. Those nearest to Dick, however, caught him and insisted that he remain seated on the stool of honor, having to insist with some physical force. This last event caused the crowd to break into a hearty cheer for Dick.

Everyone agreed it was an event calling for celebratory drinking. Glasses were filled, beer can tops were punched open, and everyone drank to Dick's fortitude.

After a few rounds of celebratory drinking, Dave rose to speak, and his words brought a new perspective to the deed. Dave, who was an English major in college before the Army demanded his services, observed that the climatic moment of Dick's saga, the "denouement" I believe he called it, had symbolic significance. He said it could even be considered a poetic gesture. I failed to see his point until he expressed it so artfully in verse. Dave took a drink from his beer can for added inspiration, struck a pose, gazed into the distance, and spoke these words:

"Oh, fouled underpants, dropping down to the rice lands below,

Take this message to Uncle Ho.

Let the smear which this underwear bears,

Be taken as a token,

Of our expression of the true affection,

We have for you and yours."

Some critic in the midst observed that the verse didn't quite rhyme and the meter was not measured. Dave, however, being the scholarly gentleman that he was, did not engage in unseemly argument. He explained that he had just made up the ode at that very moment and that his particular creative genius did not lend itself to rewrites; he simply took what his muse gave him.

Anyway, Dave's poetic interpretation of the event was cause for another round of celebratory drinking. Other tributes followed, too numerous to mention, each one a cause for more celebratory drinking. Toward the end of the observance, the throng raised their beer cans in salute to Dick and pledged to remember what he had done always.

The elaboration of the story that night brought fame to Dick. Those at the club who heard the story repeated it to others, perhaps embellishing it somewhat due to their enthusiasm. The story spread throughout the Can Tho Army Airfield and, eventually, beyond. The story spread across the Vietnam Delta and reached Saigon headquarters in less than forty-eight hours. It was reported, although not verified, that the story was the subject of a special White House briefing. At any rate, Dick became a legend of the 235th Aerial Weapons Company. And as becomes all heroes, Dick accepted his fame with reluctance. "I'll get you for this," he told us.

I tell this story to you, dear reader, because it is my fervent hope that wherever men may fly, and whenever they are challenged by the confines of their craft and the demands of nature, they may find inspiration in the legend of Dick's deed.

# SEALs

I was assigned to take a light fire team to a location near the east coast in the vicinity of Co Cong. The 307th battalion's Huey went with us. Before departing Can Tho, we were briefed on the operation. A SEAL team would be raiding a VC training camp with the objective of snatching key members of the camp's cadre. A half dozen SEALs would be dropped off from a boat at sea, swim to shore, infiltrate the camp, capture the VC, and whisk them away to a designated rendezvous point where the battalion slick would pick them up.

The SEALs would hit the camp just before dawn while it was still dark, capture the top ranking members of the camp's cadre, and whisk them away to the rendezvous point, arriving there at first light for the slick to pick them up. Our Cobras were along to provide cover for the slick and the SEALs and to otherwise help out, especially if things went wrong.

The timeline was coordinated so that our aircraft would arrive at an intermediate location just prior to the time when the SEALs were in position for the raid. We were to loiter at that location until the SEALs called for us. The location where we were to wait was far enough from the camp that we would be out of sight and our presence wouldn't give away the operation. We were given the push for the radio contact with the SEALs and told to maintain radio silence; the SEALs would contact us when they were ready.

With the slick, our Cobras took off in the predawn darkness and we were in position at the assigned location before daylight. We began orbiting and it soon became boring. There was nothing for us to do other than fly around in a large circle and try to keep from running into each other. At that time of the morning, even if we weren't maintaining radio silence, nobody in our team had anything to say anyway. There was little chatter on any of the regular radio frequencies we were monitoring, and the FM radio channel assigned for communication with the SEALs was entirely silent.

Eventually, a rosy glow began blooming on the horizon and daylight began gradually spreading over the Delta. Suddenly, the FM radio came alive. Someone on the SEAL channel had keyed the mike and the first sounds I heard were automatic weapons fire punctuated by explosions. Then came a voice. "Cobra fire team, this is Water Dog Alpha. Do you read? Over."

I answered. "Satan One-Three. Go."

There was nothing for a moment, and then the squelch broke again. I heard more sounds of automatic weapons and some voices shouting in the background. "Satan, be advised we're in heavy contact with a company of Charlie ..." And the radio went silent.

I thought, this wasn't good: a half dozen SEALS against a company of Chuck. I nosed the Cobra over toward the camp and keyed the mike. "Water Dog, hang on. We're coming to get you out."

Immediately the squelch broke. "Get us out? Hell, come and help us shoot 'em before they get away."

## Quick Draw

When a pilot came to the 235th and drew his initial equipment, he was issued a personal weapon. The standard issue weapon was a Smith & Wesson six-shot .38 revolver, along with a brown leather shoulder holster. But nearly all the pilots chucked the shoulder holster and bought a black, western style side holster, available at several shops in downtown Can Tho. The holsters came complete with a wide belt that had bullet loops, tin ornaments, and a leather strap to tie the bottom of the holster around a leg, gunslinger style.

When seating themselves in the tight confines of a Cobra seat, these gunslingers would have to untie the leg strap and pivot the belt so that the holster, pistol included, hung in front of their crotch, a position which serendipitously provided some protection for a part of their anatomy for which pilots have a high—some people would say, an imaginatively exaggerated—regard.

One day, a fire team of pilots was hanging around at a remote airfield, their Cobras parked nearby, and a pilot with one of these holsters was practicing his quick draw. On his last draw, the gun discharged somehow. The bullet hit the skid of one of the Cobras, ricocheted back, and nicked the thumb of this unfortunate gunslinger. It could have been much worse; the wound didn't even require stitches.

Coincidentally, the pilot in this incident happened to be the company's Awards & Decorations Officer, and attempting to put a positive spin on the incident, he wrote himself up for a purple heart and submitted the recommendation.

Though no stitches were required for his thumb, when the recommendation crossed the company commander's desk for approval, and a quick investigation led him to learn the actual facts of the case, stitches were required for the pilot's butt after the old man ripped it.

## Cluster and Rat Flubs

I learned some concepts and terms quicker than others. For example, the word "flub"—which wasn't actually the word used, but rather a different four-letter word—and all its linguistic derivatives, was a term whose use I caught onto immediately. For example, I thought it clear what someone's opinion was toward a proposed course of action when he expressed his disagreement with "As far as I'm concerned, you can just flub that!", or the depth of someone's perplexity when he preceded a question with "What the flub ...?" And I thought it equally clear what someone felt, as well as being much more succinct, when instead of commenting "Oh, my. I have just dropped a bullet catcher upon my foot", he declared more simply by yelling, "Oh, Flub!"

The word was especially common in its adjective form. For example, it was easy to grasp someone's sentiment when, confronted with the reappearance in the mess hall of chipped beef and gravy on toast, he voiced his dismay as "Oh, flub! You mean we're having flubbing SOS again?"

"Flub" and its derivatives were so versatile that many pilots, when speaking, never resorted to the occasional "uh" or "you know", or even the pause typically found in other person's speech as conversational filler. Instead, the pilots would just fill in with a "flub", "flubbed", or "flubbing" and the conversation flowed right along.

I had no problem understanding most uses of "flub", yet it took a while for me to grasp the difference between a "cluster flub" and a "rat flub." The problem was that both terms referred to an operation that produced the same degree of result. Although both definitions referred to an operation that produced so little result that it begged the question "why are we doing this?", I eventually came to learn, as a result of participating in both kinds of these operations, that the distinction between the two terms lay in the extremes of energy expended to achieve so little result.

A cluster flub was an operation executed with high ambition and intense energy. Yet it produced little result because its operational elements were so huge and the endeavor so intricately planned, that the size and complexity actually worked against achievement. It was the equivalent of the phenomenon of a helicopter's "settling with power" where the aircraft attempts to hover at a high altitude, requiring the pilot to pull more power, but the increased power thrashes the immediately surrounding air into such a state of turbulence that it can't support the aircraft, and as the aircraft begins to sink, the pilot pulls in more power, which further thrashes the air, making it even less capable of supporting the aircraft, producing the paradox that the more power the pilot pulls, the faster the helicopter sinks. Thus it was with a cluster flub; there was such a mass of resources and all of them so intricately entangled that, although energetically driven, all the energy was expended in trying to coordinate the mass, resulting in the mass becoming a mess, and thus achieving little result.

In contrast, a rat flub was at the opposite extreme. It was an operation so misguided, so aimless, and so inadequately planned and manned, that no one knew what to do—or if they did know, couldn't do—and consequently no one did anything. Oh, the participants in a rat flub went through some motions alright, but the lack of results was so predictable to everyone other than the ones whose misguided inspiration spawned the endeavor, that even though the assigned participants went through the motions, like willing rats running a maze, they had no enthusiasm for the endeavor because it was so ill conceived, so purposeless, and so inadequately invested. Thus the result from a rat flub was the same as that from a cluster flub: little.

For a novice, it was difficult to distinguish between the cluster kind, and the rat kind, of flub, yet a veteran could recognize one and label it correctly nearly a hundred percent of the time.

## The TV News Crew

One day, a two-man TV news crew—a reporter and a cameraman—tagged along with our Cobra fire team on a mission where we were assigned to shoot up various strategic targets. The targets, selected beforehand by a Vietnamese province chief, consisted of items such as abandoned, waterlogged sampans; forlorn, falling-down hootches; and others of equal strategic value. A US advisor in an overhead C & C Huey was delegated to spot the targets for us.

The news crew began by riding in the Huey, taking footage of our two Cobras as we shot up these things. When we landed to refuel and rearm, they filmed all of that as we were doing it.

When we finished and were ready to go up again, the reporter asked us to pretend we were on a scramble so his cameraman could film that. He told the cameraman to frame a wide shot of the two Cobras, one parked behind the other, and then the reporter, acting as a director, had us step behind the camera, off to the side. He directed that when he gave us our cue, we should run into the framed shot, rush toward the helicopters, jump into them, and take off with great haste.

We lounged around behind the camera while the cameraman set up the shot and then, with the camera rolling, the reporter called out, "Action!"

We ambled into the frame, strolling toward the helicopters. The reporter called "Cut!" and told us we were supposed to *run* to the helicopters.

We retreated behind the camera again while the cameraman set up the shot once more. When the camera was again rolling, the reporter called "Action!"

This time, we did run toward the helicopters. But halfway there, I pretended to trip, doing a pratfall to the ground, and the other pilots in the team, following behind, sprawled on top of me. We thought this was terribly funny. The reporter, disgusted, gave up that idea.

When we went up again, the cameraman rode in the front seat of my Cobra. He plugged a tape recorder into the headset line so he could record our air-to-air conversation. He asked me to say something that gunship pilots would say. I obliged, calling over the radio to my wingman. "Uh ... say, Ed ... uh ... I mean, Satan One-Four ... This is ... uh ... One-Three ... I ... uh ... let me see now ... uh ... over."

Ed answered in his best gunship driver style. "Yeah, what the flub do you want?"

The cameraman asked me to say something else, but I excused myself, explaining to him that gunship pilots weren't especially noted for being too articulate. I explained that, back home, we could barely express ourselves well enough to order a side of fries with a hamburger.

At our next target, the cameraman took some footage of the other Cobra shooting rockets, and then he pointed the camera back at me. But I'm sure he edited out that shot since he caught me with my finger up my nose.

One target was supposedly an arms cache hidden in a growth of trees, and as I nosed over into the rocket run, I saw that he was pointing his camera straight ahead, evidently to capture this episode from a gunship pilot's point of view. I thought this would be a good opportunity to impress the viewers back home with some gunship heroics.

At this time, I still tended to carry my rocket runs close in to the target—a compensation for a natural lack of aiming skill, I suppose—but this particular time, I decided I would carry the run even closer.

As we zoomed down toward the target, I picked up so much airspeed that when I punched off the rockets, we were in danger of passing them, and when I saw the trees getting so close I could clearly see the tiny veins in the leaves, I realized that I might have gone too far this time.

I clawed at the collective, pulling pitch, but the aircraft kept hurtling toward the ground as if a magnet was pulling it. I was already bracing myself for the impact when the helicopter finally leveled off, the skids skimming in the top branches.

As we climbed away from the near disaster, my hands shaking and my face white from all the blood pooled in my feet, the cameraman called from the front seat, "Can you do that again? I lost the focus."

## Race for the Bladder

My fire team had been working in the extreme southern part of the Delta all day, shooting designated targets. We staged from a remote airstrip, which had been stocked for the operation with additional rockets piled beside the runway. A little further down the strip, a fuel bladder had been placed there for the operation.

We worked throughout the day without a break except for a lunch of C-Rations during one of our rearming and refueling trips back to the airstrip. After the many return trips to rearm and sometimes refuel, the cache of rockets had diminished and the fuel bladder had shrunk.

When we finished our last strikes, we were nearly out of daylight; it was less than a half hour before sunset. We were also out of ordnance and almost out of fuel. We had emptied the rocket pods on the last of the targets and had shot out the turret ammo. We had some fuel, but it wasn't enough to get us back to Can Tho, so we headed for the airstrip to top off before going home.

During all of the trips to the little airstrip during the day, there hadn't been any other aircraft there, but now as I neared it, I was surprised to see an Air Force C-130 on the runway. I couldn't imagine what would bring a plane of that size to such a small airstrip as this one in such an out-of-the-way location.

Since it was at the far end of the runway and had the length of the runway before it, I assumed it was readying for takeoff, and that notion was reinforced when I saw it begin moving up the runway. The timing was good I thought; it would be gone and out of our way before we got there, making it convenient to shoot a landing to the runway directly beside the fuel bladder.

But as I rounded out on short final for a landing, I saw that the airplane, although rolling up the runway, wasn't picking up speed as it would if it were taking off. Then, it dawned upon me why that big four-engine airplane had stopped at this out-of-the-way airstrip; it was intending to refuel. That big plane could suck up a lot of fuel. Compared to it, our Cobras sipped relatively little. If that gas-guzzler took it all, we would have to divert for fuel somewhere out of the way and that would be a major inconvenience.

My wingman had sized up the situation the same as me. He was on the radio to me. "If that flubber takes all the fuel, there won't be any for us."

I didn't have radio communication with the C-130 driver. Although there was a common radio frequency designated for uncontrolled airfields like this one, in practice it was seldom used. Besides, action spoke louder than words.

As the C-130 lumbered slowly toward the fuel bladder, I sped up my landing approach and I quickly scooted the Cobra a little to the side. Rather than landing on the runway beside the fuel bladder, I'd land beside it on the bare patch of ground away from the runway.

As I flew toward the spot, I don't know if the C-130 driver heard me, but I saw he was also speeding up. As we both raced for the fuel bladder, I could see it was going to be close. The airplane was rolling fast and it had a lot of momentum.

I beat him by seconds and sat down beside the bladder just before the airplane braked to a stop beside it on the runway. Now it was a matter of who could get to the nozzle first, the C-130 crew chief or my gunner.

That foot race never happened, though, because I had a quick thinking gunner. As soon as I touched down, Jim said, "Turn on the hot switch." I hadn't thought of it, but I immediately realized what he had in mind, so I clicked on the master armament switch. Jim grabbed the handheld sight and swiveled the turret, slewing it to one side and the other a couple of times, just to attract attention to it, and then brought the guns to bear on the big airplane. It was an empty threat—we had no ordnance—and likely the C-130 driver knew it was a bluff; nevertheless, he didn't challenge us even after Jim stowed the weapon and got out to man the nozzle.

Jim hot fueled our Cobra and kept possession of the nozzle while I hovered out of the way to let the wing ship get a drink. We only took enough fuel to get us back to Can Tho and left the rest for the airplane, yet I doubt that did much to ingratiate us to the Air Force C-130 crew.

## The Black Night

Shortly before sunset, the wingman and I moved our two Cobras to the revetments near the Ready Shack, close to the west end of the runway. For the coming night, our fire team was assigned to Firefly duty, which provided an instant reaction fire team for anyone in the Delta with an urgent need for gunships. It was a nighttime equivalent to IV Corps Standby.

In the gloaming, we walked from the revetments to the alert hootch to wait with the other crewmembers for whatever the night would bring us. Barely twenty minutes later, a call came. The night clerk on the field phone told me we had a scramble to cover a medevac extraction. I knew a nighttime medevac meant a critical situation.

I copied down the coordinates for the extraction as well as the call signs and contact frequencies for both the ground unit and the medevac ship. I took a quick look at the map and noted the coordinates indicated a location seventy klicks to the northwest, and in the middle of nowhere.

The four of us ran to the waiting Cobras. While my gunner untied the rotor, I put on my chicken plate and slid my gun belt around my waist before I climbed in. By the time I was pulling on my helmet, the gunner had untied the rotor blades.

I flipped on the battery switch, turned on the aircraft's position lights, beeped down the governor, and set the throttle. I yelled "Clear!" out of the open cockpit hatch, reached under the head of the collective control, and pressed the starter trigger. The turbine engine began a low-pitched growl that grew steadily louder, becoming a higher-pitched whine as the turbine engine wound up to its operating speed. I watched the exhaust gas temperature to make sure the engine lit without exceeding its temperature limit. When the engine's N1 reached forty percent, I released the starter switch. With the engine and rotor tachometer needles spinning up, I scanned the other instruments, confirming all the pressure gauges were moving into the green. As the engine and rotor came up to speed, I turned on the radios, and as they were warming up, I strapped myself in.

As soon as I saw the wing ship's rotors turning, I radioed it. "Satan One-Eight, One-Three. Let me know when you're ready."

In a moment, I heard the wingman's voice in the earphones inside my helmet. "One-Eight's ready."

I double-clicked the radio transmit switch to acknowledge his message, then called for takeoff. "Can Tho Tower, Satan One-Three's a light fire team of Cobras, revetments one and three, on a scramble. I'd like two-five." It probably wasn't necessary for me to state we were on a scramble, a status that would give us priority over other traffic at the airfield. After nightfall, there usually wasn't much traffic to contend with at Can Tho, and the fact that we were in revetments near the Ready Shack was enough of a clue for the tower operator to know we were scrambling.

The tower operator responded. "Roger, Satan One-Three. You're cleared for runway two-five and an immediate takeoff. Winds light, south-southwest. No reported traffic."

I acknowledged the clearance. "One-Three."

I hovered quickly out of the revetment to the runway and swiveled the Cobra to align with it. I pulled in more collective, adding power, and pushed the cyclic forward. The Cobra began moving up the runway, its skids just above the surface. I held the aircraft close to the runway, allowing it to gather speed. It raced past the illumination barrels lighting the runway on both sides. When the airspeed indicator reached ninety knots, I pulled back on the cyclic to trade the built-up airspeed for some quick altitude. The Cobra zoomed into the air.

As the Cobra approached two thousand feet, I pushed the cyclic forward to level the aircraft at that altitude, let the airspeed build up to a cruising speed of a hundred and thirty-five knots, and pointed the aircraft northwest.

It was now fully dark as we sped past the few lights of Binh Thuy below, leaving them and the lights of Can Tho behind. Ahead, except for a few stars twinkling faintly in the firmament, lay the darkness of a moonless night.

When flying in Vietnam at night, the depth of darkness was immensely greater than in the States. Flying stateside, there were lots of lights. Cities had abundant lights; almost any town had some lights, even if they were only house lights; between cities and towns, car lights often lit the roads; even most rural areas in the States were dotted with yard lights. But in the Vietnam Delta, beyond the town of Can Tho and except for a few towns of similar size, the nights were as dark as primitive nature intended. Most Vietnamese lived in villages or on isolated farms, none with electricity. If a pilot was flying early enough in the evening, he might occasionally spot an outside fire or an inside cooking fire faintly cast on a thinly roofed hootch, but deeper into the night, outside the few cities, the only illumination was from the moon and the stars. When thick clouds blotted out the celestial candles, as was often the case during the monsoon season, Vietnam was a dark void. Even with a clear sky, on a moonless night like this one, the land below wasn't seen but was merely suggested by the meager starlight.

For pilots flying in Vietnam, these nights offered few visual references. Without those references, it was difficult for a pilot to determine if he was flying in the right direction, and without some reference indicating the horizon, it was equally difficult to determine if he was flying straight and level.

Without any outside visual references, a pilot couldn't rely upon seat-of-the-pants feelings; he had to depend upon instruments inside the aircraft to keep the aircraft straight and level, to make turns, to climb and descend, and to stay on course. For flying on instruments, the most intuitive instrument on the aircraft's panel for visualizing the aircraft's relation to the horizon was an attitude indicator, also called an artificial horizon. The attitude indicator's horizontal bar represented the horizon, and a pair of miniature wings mimicked the aircraft's attitude in relation to that horizon—above it, below it, or banked at an angle to it

Because of its importance in instrument flying, the attitude indicator was located directly in front of the pilot. Yet the attitude indicator on the Cobra's panel was smaller than the primary one in a Huey, and because of its smaller size, it made instrument flying in a Cobra more perilous.

Our company had lost an aircraft at night three weeks earlier when a pilot, flying over the ocean just beyond the coast, lost reference to the horizon and flew into the water. Both pilots had survived. A similar event had happened a few weeks before I arrived at the 235th. The pilot had flown into the water, but in this instance, when the aircraft hit the water, the rotor flexed on impact, dipped, and chopped through the front of the fuselage, killing the gunner.

This night, there was enough starlight to suggest the horizon, but I had to continually crosscheck the cockpit instruments to verify the aircraft's attitude, altitude, speed, and heading. Although I could keep the aircraft in level flight and steer it in a specific direction, I didn't know exactly where I was. All that lay under me was an indistinguishable blackness. I could hold a heading, but with no outside reference, I didn't know what the wind might be doing to the aircraft's ground track. It could be blowing me right or left of the intended track. I could hold a steady airspeed, but I didn't know what effect wind might be having on my ground speed; a headwind could be slowing my ground speed; a tail wind could be pushing me along faster. Without the necessary outside visual references, how was I to know if I was on track for my destination? Even if I was on track, how was I to know when I reached my destination if I couldn't see it?

In the States, there was a countrywide system of electronic ground aids for navigation. Vietnam didn't have anywhere close to such an extensive system, but the Air Force facility at Binh Thuy offered limited radar tracking service for the Delta. I dialed the UHF radio to the facility's frequency and keyed the mike to contact it. "Paddy Control, Satan One-Three."

I heard the controller reply. "Satan One-Three, Paddy Control."

"Paddy, I've got a flight of two AH-1s, about five miles northwest of Can Tho, at two thousand feet. I'd appreciate some help getting to these coordinates." And I gave the controller the grid letters and numbers I'd been given.

Paddy Control responded by assigning me a squawk code and I set it into the aircraft's transponder. In a moment, I heard, "Satan One-Three, Paddy control. I have radar contact now six miles north-northwest of Can Tho. Turn to heading three-four-five."

"Three-four-five. Satan One-Three."

Using the RFI as my guide, I adjusted my heading to that direction. I glanced back to make sure my wingman was still with me. He was an experienced pilot, but new to our unit. He hadn't had much time yet to learn the AO and I hadn't flown in a team with him before. I switched the transmit selector to the VHF radio. "Satan One-Eight, how're you doing?"

His voice came back through the darkness. "Okay."

I estimated it would take about twenty-five minutes to reach the location I'd given Paddy Control. During that time there wasn't much else for me to do except hold the heading I'd been given and keep the aircraft straight and level. As we slipped silently through the night, there was no sense of motion; it was as if we were suspended in the darkness.

Almost a half hour later, the controller's voice came over the radio. "Satan One-Three, Paddy Control. Radar indicates you're at your destination."

Below, there was nothing but inky blackness. "Roger, Paddy. I'll take your word for it."

I put the aircraft into a shallow circle, selected the FM radio for my mike, and called the contact I'd been given. "Stony Max, Satan One-Three."

There was no response. I called again. "Stony Max, Satan One-Three. Over."

I heard a voice, faint in the headset. "Satan One-Three, Stony Max. Go ahead."

"Stony, be advised I read you two by—at best. I've got a fire team of gunships for your medevac. What's your situation? Over."

"Roger, Satan. Be advised your signal is also weak. I've got one Whiskey—a Uniform Sierra—in critical condition. We have negative active contact right now, but we've got Charlie all around our position here."

"Roger, Stony. Are you prepared to identify your location when the Medevac arrives?"

"I've got a flashlight."

A flashlight wasn't much; I hoped we'd be able to spot it.

"Stony, I should be close to your location. Do you see my lights?"

"That's a negative, Satan."

That was odd. We were the only aircraft out there in this remote flatland; he should be able to see our position lights for several miles.

I keyed the mike again. "Stony, say your coordinates."

He gave me his map coordinates and I used my grease pencil to write them on the Plexiglas of the canopy cover.

"Standby, Stony."

I needed to consult my map, but I felt it wasn't a good idea to do that while also trying to fly the aircraft in these blackened conditions. I needed the gunner to take the controls, even though he would have to fly the aircraft with the front seat's shorter cyclic and shorter collective. It wasn't an extraordinary task but it would be more difficult in these conditions.

I asked the gunner if he thought he could fly the aircraft for a short while. I felt a wiggle on the controls and he said, "I've got it."

I relinquished the controls to him, turned on the red light in the cockpit to preserve my night vision, and checked the map. The coordinates Stony Max had given me placed him some eighty klicks from where we were. How pondered how that had happened as I took back the controls.

I had switched the UHF radio from Paddy Control to the contact frequency for the medevac ship, and I heard the pilot call. "Satan One-Three, Dustoff Two-One. Over."

I answered. "Satan One-Three. Go ahead, Two-One."

"Satan, I'm ETA one-five to the pickup zone. Are you on station and do you have contact with the ground unit?"

"Affirmative on contact with the ground unit, but I think there's a problem with the location. What coordinates do you have for it?"

The medevac pilot read me the coordinates he'd been given. They were the same ones I'd gotten from my Operations. Somewhere along the line of communication from the radio request made by Stony Max, relayed to the Mission Assigners From On High, then down to our units' Operations, and on to us, the coordinates had gotten relayed incorrectly. Since the medevac pilot and I both had the same coordinates, it suggested the mistake happened somewhere before reaching either of our units.

I broke the news to the Dustoff pilot. "Two-One, be advised we've got the wrong coordinates. Here are the correct ones." And I read him the coordinates that Stony Max had just given me.

After a moment, Dustoff Two-One called back. "Satan, we're marginal fuel to get there and back. I'll call my Ops, advise them of the situation, and see what they want me do. Stand by."

After a few minutes, the medevac pilot was back. "Satan, I've given them the new coordinates. Based upon that, they want me to return to base. They're sending a request to IV Corps for a medevac ship from another unit."

I acknowledged the transmission and the medevac pilot responded. "Good night, Satan. And good luck. Out."

Based on the faulty coordinates, this medevac had been dispatched from Saigon, and Stony Max's actual location placed him beyond the operating range of his aircraft's fuel load. I thought I'd better access our own fuel situation.

"One-Eight, say fuel."

"About a thousand pounds—a little less."

My fuel gauge read about the same, just at a thousand pounds. I did a quick calculation. The flight from Can Tho had taken almost a half hour, and we'd been out there in nowhere land for about fifteen minutes. It would take another thirty minutes to reach the ground unit's actual location. When we got there, we would have burned seventy minutes of fuel, leaving about fifty minutes in the tank, not counting the reserve.

Based upon the new—and correct—coordinates, I assumed another medevac ship would be dispatched from Binh Thuy, which was closer to Stony Max's actual location. I didn't know exactly how long it would take for another medevac to reach Stony Max, but from Binh Thuy, I knew it would be at least a thirty-minute flight for a Huey. And that didn't take into account how long it would take to process the request to dispatch another medevac from a different unit and to get the ship airborne, assuming there was one immediately available.

At best, I figured another Medevac might arrive just about the time our fuel warning lights came on. I didn't ever like the idea of seeing a fuel warning light unless I knew exactly where my next refueling point was and I knew I could reach it. And on a dark night like this, I especially didn't want that light illuminating my panel.

I thought I'd see if there was possibly a place to refuel that was closer than Can Tho to the extraction site. I gave the controls to the gunner and looked again at the map to find the coordinates Stony Max had given me. That's when I realized more clearly where he actually was: Nui Coto Mountain. Nui Coto was *muy* bad. Not only would a medevac ship be attempting an extraction from the mountain—and a night extraction at that—but Charlie owned that mountain at night.

Yet, that was a problem to be dealt with later; my immediate concern was seeing if I could come up with an answer for the best place to refuel. I considered Rach Gia as a refueling point. From where we were, it was farther to the little airfield there than it was back to Can Tho, but its advantage would be that after refueling there, I would be positioned thirty klicks closer to Stony Point for a rendezvous with another medevac ship than if I refueled at Can Tho. I had been to Rach Gia several times; I knew the airfield well, and I had refueled there, but that had been in the daytime. I didn't know if I could get fuel there at night. At the smaller airfields around the Delta like the one at Rach Gia, the fuel bladders sometimes weren't filled unless there was a planned operation in the area. And even so, at night, the pumps might not be turned on, or might have quit running because there was no one to tend them.

All in all, I thought the best choice was to return to Can Tho to refuel. Besides, if another medevac ship was dispatched from Binh Thuy, perhaps the Mission Assigners From On High might see the wisdom in assigning a different Cobra fire team from Can Tho to escort the Medevac, staging the fire team's takeoff from Can Tho with the medevac's liftoff from nearby Binh Thuy. That would help alleviate the problem of having aircraft on station with different fuel loads. More importantly, if a medevac ship could get off quickly from Binh Thuy, and with another gunship escort from Can Tho, they could reach Nui Coto before I could fly to Can Tho, refuel, and reach Nui Coto. In my conversation with Stony Max explaining the mistake with the coordinates, he had told me he thought the wounded US soldier couldn't survive long.

I took back the controls, briefed my wingman on my assessment of the situation, and turned toward Can Tho. I contacted Paddy Control again and asked it to keep an eye on us. I didn't really need a radar vector to get to Can Tho; all I had to do was take the reverse heading of the one that got me where I was. Can Tho was lit well enough that I could find it easily when I neared it, yet I wanted Paddy Control to keep an eye on us in case we went down for some reason.

After twenty minutes of flying, I saw the lights of Can Tho in the distance and I radioed Operations to report I was returning for fuel. Operations acknowledged the transmission but didn't reveal any further plans for my team.

Rather than the revetments, we parked the helicopters on the ramp where a fuel truck was waiting. While the Cobras were being refueled, we walked to the Operations building where the duty clerk informed us we had been directed to carry on with the mission. That was the limit of what the clerk had been told and he knew nothing about a medevac ship. We walked back to the ramp, climbed back into the Cobras, and took off for Nui Coto.

## The Dark Mountain

Nui Coto was the southernmost peak of the "Seven Sisters", a cluster of mountains that jutted from the flat Delta plain near the westernmost part of Vietnam, forty klicks from the coast to the south and twenty klicks from the Vietnam-Cambodia border to the west. Of the seven peaks, Nui Coto was the principle VC stronghold and it had held that distinction from the time the French battled the Viet Minh. During this current war, we sometimes controlled the summit and the base, but Charlie never relinquished control of the greater real estate, the slopes in between. And at night, Charlie controlled the whole mountain.

The so-called mountain, only about two thousand feet tall, was hardly more than an overgrown rock, yet this crag was pockmarked with caves, tunnels, and crevices that gave harbor to Charlie and provided him with a plenitude of concealed, protected positions from which he could mortar the surrounding lowland, snipe ground forces who ventured onto its heights, and pick off aircraft that flew too close.

Once we took off from Can Tho, I asked Paddy Control for a radar vector that would put us a couple of klicks short of Nui Coto. I didn't want to accidentally bump into it in the dark, and as an extra precaution, I climbed to twenty-five hundred feet, which would put me higher than its peak.

Paddy gave me a heading and when it reported we had arrived at our destination, I had to trust its radar again. I couldn't see it, but Nui Coto was out there, enwrapped in the shroud of darkness.

While waiting for the medevac, I flew a shallow-banked circle around the spot where Paddy had put us and contacted

Stony Max again to see if his situation had changed. I learned it hadn't, but he reiterated the urgency of extracting his wounded soldier.

I attempted to contact the medevac ship and received no answer, but a few minutes later, it called. It was the second medevac that had been dispatched for the mission, this one from Binh Thuy. He reported his ETA as one-zero minutes. I acknowledged and told him I was on station and in contact with the ground force; then I called Stony Max to inform him the medevac was on its way and would be contacting him.

When he was within range of the ground radio, I heard the medevac pilot call Stony Max. The radio operator reported he had a critically wounded American soldier and that his position was a ledge on the southeastern face of Nui Coto at the 500-foot level. The medevac pilot quizzed Stony Max for details of the landing space and then gave him instructions about preparing the patient for extraction.

Stony Max's description of the landing space revealed to me just how difficult this extraction would be for the medevac crew. The patrol with the wounded patient was on a narrow ledge jutting from the face of the mountain, a space barely big enough for the medevac ship to land. Furthermore, the pilot would have to make an approach toward the face of the mountain, and to lessen the probability of overshooting the ledge and hitting the mountain's slope, he would have to pull up short of the ledge and gradually edge onto it. Essentially, it would require him to bring his helicopter to a five-hundred-foot hover, a condition that would test the power limits of the helicopter, and from there, he would have to slowly move onto the ledge far enough to allow loading the patient but not so far that his rotor blades struck the side of the mountain. Even in daylight, this would be difficult. But it wasn't daylight; it was night. All it would take was a millisecond of vertigo, a slight misjudgment, a twitch on the controls, a gust from the wind—and the mountain would have him.

Even finding the patrol and the ledge would be a challenge. To identify the patrol's location, all Stony Max had was an Army angle-head flashlight. Its light would be only a pinpoint in the expanse of darkness. And assuming the medevac pilot could see it at all, this pinpoint would be the only reference the medevac pilot would have for judging his position and distance as he flew toward the ledge. Not only would it be difficult for the pilot to judge his approach path, flying toward a single point of light at night was a perfect setup for vertigo. His angle might vary up or down; he might wander left and right; he could unknowingly put the aircraft into a roll or dive—any of them a mistake that he might not realize he had made until it was too late.

These things were all bad enough for the medevac, but there was also the tactical situation. Charlie was on that mountain out there in the darkness. With VC around him, it wasn't a good idea for Stony Max to be shining a flashlight, yet that's what he had to do if there was to be any hope for pulling off this extraction. And, just as the flashlight beam would be a danger to Stony Max, so would the medevac ship's position lights be a danger to it. They would be a beacon for Charlie to draw a bead on.

There were *beau coup* problems, but the first one was locating the patrol. Before we could help Stony Max, we had to find him.

When I saw the medevac ship's navigation lights approaching from a distance, I radioed the pilot and he confirmed he had us in sight. When the ship reached us, I took one side of it, the wing ship the other, and we flew trailing above and behind it.

Nui Coto was some two klicks ahead. The medevac ship slowed to fifty knots and we held station with it. I peered ahead, trying to see the mountain. I shifted my focus a little to the side and under the stars, I could make out a faintly distinguishable mass looming ahead, but exactly how close I couldn't tell. Without enough visual references, everything was two-dimensional, and without depth, distances had no scale.

The medevac ship continued to slow and we slowed with it. I was tuned to Stony Max on the FM radio as he talked with the medevac pilot.

"Dust Off, I see aircraft lights."

"Roger, Stony. How close are we to your location?"

"I can't tell."

"Can you tell if we're headed toward you?"

"Uh, I think you need to turn a little left."

The medevac made a slow turn twenty degrees to the left. It was down to thirty knots.

"How's that, Stony?"

"Yeah, it looks like you're headed toward us. You sound closer."

"How close?"

"I don't know; maybe a half klick."

"Is your flashlight on?"

"Do you want it on now?"

"Go ahead; turn it on."

"It's on. Do you see it?"

"Not yet. Are we still headed toward you?"

"Maybe turn a little more left."

The medevac banked slightly and adjusted course another ten degrees. We were down to twenty knots.

"How's that, Stony?"

"Yeah, that's it. Do you see my flashlight?"

"That's a negative, Stony … wait, that's affirmative. I see it. I'm turning on my landing light."

Our airspeed was down to ten knots. The medevac ship turned on its landing light. Its thin circle illuminated a part of Nui Coto's rugged face barely two hundred feet ahead. Immediately, the darkness outside the circle sparkled from small arms fire. Muzzle flashes darted from automatic rifles. Green tracers zipped toward the medevac ship.

The medevac pilot instantly broke hard left, diving away from the fire. My ship's weapon systems were hot, but I was too close for rockets and too close to the friendlies for minigun fire; ricocheting rounds off the rocks could hit them. I keyed the radio transmit button so both my gunner and the wing ship could hear me at the same time. "Hold fire." But the command was unnecessary; my gunner had the good judgment to withhold fire and so did the wing ship. The only thing I could do was put my Cobra directly behind the medevac ship, between it and the small arms fire. I yanked the Cobra hard left to get behind the medevac and ducked the nose to pick up speed, but I had to immediately yank back on the cyclic to keep from overrunning the slower

Huey. Tracer rounds flew around us. I listened for the thump of hail on a tin roof, the signature sound of rounds hitting sheet metal. I wasn't too worried about sheet metal, though; it was the tail rotor that was most vulnerable to the small arms projectiles coming at us from behind. A hit on the tail rotor could disable it, and without it to counteract the main rotor's torque, the aircraft would begin spinning on its mast, quickly becoming uncontrollable. If I lost the tail rotor, the options for what to do raced through my head. One option was to close the throttle, disengaging the engine from the main rotor and reducing the rotor torque, but the terrain below wasn't at all conducive to a successful autorotation; we would likely hit the slope below and tumble down the foot of Nui Coto. It was the second option that I thought was the most realistic possibility for dealing with this situation: duck my head and kiss my butt a fond farewell.

The medevac pilot dove for the ground and we followed, right behind him. Tracers zipped past us, most of them now overhead. When the medevac ship leveled off, it was less than a hundred feet from the ground. Its landing light was still on, its beam reflecting on the rice paddy waters. The beam skipped over the dikes, leading our way, as we fled the dark mountain.

A safe distance away from Nui Coto, we climbed to a higher altitude and circled while we talked things over. I explained to the medevac pilot that, in this situation, we were practically toothless. The VC were too close to the friendlies for us to lay down suppressive fire; the best we could do was intimidate Charlie with our presence, and that hadn't seemed to work too well thus far. The medevac pilot acknowledged that assessment, and despite his narrow escape from the first attempt, he wanted to try again.

It was his show, so that's what we would do. We came in the same way a second time, and we got the same results; Charlie held fire until the medevac's landing light came on. Right at that moment, when it was at its closest and slowest, Charlie opened up on it. The medevac pilot dove away again, our gunships in his trail.

The medevac pilot still hadn't had enough. He made a third attempt, but this time the results were different. Even before he turned on the landing light, Charlie opened up with small arms fire and this time Charlie added a fifty-caliber gun. The medevac, and we with him, managed to escape a third time.

We didn't have enough fuel for another attempt. As he winged away to his home base, the medevac pilot bid Stony Max to hold on. My team followed the medevac and a few klicks before Can Tho, the medevac pilot broke off to land at Binh Thuy while we continued to Can Tho.

While we were refueling, I was informed that another Huey, one from Soc Trang, had been delegated as a backup medevac and was already on its way to the extraction site. As soon as we topped off, we took off, racing to catch up with it. Halfway back to Nui Coto, we overtook it.

When we reached Nui Coto, we learned that an Air Mission Commander in a Huey had arrived and we checked in with him. I learned also that another asset had been added to the operation; not only would the Command and Control Huey be dropping flares, but a truck with a searchlight was taking up a position near the foot of the mountain.

My assignment was to stand by; the AMC felt Charlie was too close to the friendlies for gunship fire, but he would call us if things got desperate enough. I moved my team a klick away, climbed higher and circled, staying out of the way.

When everything was in place, the Huey dropped flares, the searchlight truck splayed its light on the mountain, and the Soc Trang medevac went in. Apparently all that light was a big help to Charlie; he opened up on the medevac before it had a chance to get near Stony Max. After another attempt produced the same results, the AMC called off any more attempts that night, deciding to wait until daylight, which by this time was an hour and half away.

The medevac Huey left to return to Soc Trang. I didn't have enough fuel to last until daylight, so I flew back to Can Tho, landed, and topped off.

At that point, I could have waited there and timed a takeoff to put me on station at first light, but there was an ARVN outpost at the small village of Chi Lang, a few minutes from Nui Coto and from where I assumed the searchlight truck had come.

Instead of waiting at Can Tho, I decided to fly there and land at the outpost to await daylight. That turned out to be a bad decision.

## The Devil in the Dust

It was still dark when we arrived at Chi Lang, and I only knew we had arrived because Paddy Control said so. There was nothing but blackness below. I had the wing ship stay high while I went down to look for the outpost. I descended to a couple of hundred feet, as indicated by the altimeter, before turning on the landing light. I saw nothing but rice paddies reflected in the light.

I assumed I was close to the village, but I didn't know exactly in which direction it was. I guessed it was farther west and flew in that direction. Shortly, I saw a hootch in the landing light, then more. I had found the village but I still needed to find the outpost. I slowed to fifty knots and turned on the searchlight also. I knew the small outpost was on the southwest edge of the village and I made several passes over the hootches with the light on them, moving gradually in that direction.

After several passes, I saw concertina wire in the light. I swept the light along the wire; it appeared to be a perimeter, probably the one for the outpost. The beam passed over what appeared to be a narrow dirt landing strip. I held the light on the strip so not to lose sight of it, circled tight, and set up a steep approach to it. As the Cobra descended, I could see that the strip extended for at least fifty feet ahead and I didn't see any obstructions.

I was in a hurry to get on the ground and I quickly lowered the collective to descend to a hover, prior to landing. At three feet, I pulled collective to slow my descent. That's when the rotor downwash whipped the dusty strip into a man-made tornado, wrapping the Cobra and me in a swirling mass of dirt. The landing light and searchlight bounced off the grains of grit, each one a miniature mirror reflecting the lights. Blinded in that vortex of millions of mirrors, I had no ground reference. I was seconds from vertigo. In an instant, I could tilt the aircraft on its side, or tilt it too far forward causing it to tumble over its nose, or I could tilt it so far back that the tail rotor struck the ground, any of which would likely lead to the main rotor striking the ground and thrashing the aircraft to pieces, along with us who were in it.

I had to get out of this tornado—now. I had two choices. I could try to take off and fly out of it or I could try to get it on the ground without being able to see the ground. I instantly decided I'd try to put it down. The last time I saw the ground, moments ago, it was only a few feet below, but I didn't know, though, how far I may have risen or fallen or turned or tilted since I went blind. I eased down the collective and kept the cyclic centered. I would have to disregard my seat-of-the-pants senses, notoriously unreliable without an outside visual reference.

As I hunted for the ground, I found I was talking to myself. "Keep easing down the collective. Add a little right pedal. Careful, not too much, not too little. Keep the nose straight. You don't want set to set the aircraft down while it's spinning. Keep the skids level. You don't want a dynamic rollover. Keep lowering the collective. Not too fast. You don't want to hit too hard and bend the skids or bounce back into the air. Keep the cyclic centered. Steady. Be gentle on the pedal. Steady. Ease the collective down some more. Keep it coming down slowly. My body says I'm spinning to the left; ignore that. But I sense the aircraft is tilted to the right; ignore it. Just keep doing what you're doing. Keep the cyclic centered. Steady. Keep the collective coming down. Steady. Keep light pressure on the pedals. Keep it steady."

I felt a skid bump the ground. I kept easing the collective down. I felt the aircraft tilting back. Was it really, or was it vertigo? It felt like the aircraft was on its heels. I gave in to the feeling and eased the cyclic forward. I felt the skids touch at the front. I felt them scooting; the aircraft was trying to spin to the right. This was it; I had to commit: either yank the collective and hope to pull away or put the aircraft solidly on the ground. I lowered the collective and the aircraft jerked to a stop. I was down.

The man-made dirt devil still swirled around me, the lights reflecting off the spinning bits of grit. I turned off the landing light and the searchlight, rolled the throttle to idle, and sat there.

Slowly, the dirt settled. When I turned on the landing light again, the dust still hung in the air, but I could see that the aircraft, although askew, was sitting on the dirt strip. I looked down at the side of the fuselage and saw tracks scrapped in the loose earth, indicating the skids were rotating when I touched down. I had been inches from disaster.

I tried to keep the shake out of my voice. "One-Eight, I'm down. Be advised this strip has a lot of loose dirt. Be careful of going IFR in it. I'd advise an approach straight to ground. Don't come to a hover."

"Roger that, One-Three. When I saw you were going to land, I positioned behind you and turned on my landing light to help you see. I thought you were going to lose it."

I didn't know he had been right behind me all the time. "Naw," I said. "A piece of cake."

The wingman spoke again. "Why didn't you use the pad?"

"Say again."

"Why didn't you use the pad? There's a PSP landing pad twenty feet to your left."

I had no idea.

"I was saving that for you," I said.

In a couple of minutes, I watched the wing ship land on the PSP pad, a piece of cake.

We stayed in the helicopters and waited. When there was enough daylight that I felt I could lift off without going blind, I was ready to go on station, but before I took off, I thought I'd try to raise the AMC on the radio to see what the situation was.

"Panther Six, Satan One-Three."

I wasn't expecting an answer, but I got an instant reply. "Panther Six. Go."

"Panther, I've got my fire team at Chi Lang. What's the situation?"

"I'm collecting more assets: a couple of more fire teams, an LOH, and two more medevacs are on their way. We'll make a concerted effort and I think we'll have less trouble with Charlie in daylight."

"Roger that, Panther. What can I do to help?"

"Didn't your Operations contact you, One-Three? Devil Ops is sending another fire team to relieve you. You're to return to Can Tho."

Relieved? But this was my mission; I wanted to finish it. I felt disappointed, cheated. I sat there a moment absorbing it. Then I keyed the mike. "Roger. Wilco." Orders were orders.

My team flew back to Can Tho and we parked the Cobras in their revetments. As the rotors wound down, I filled out the logbook. We had logged nine-and-a-half hours of flight time since the previous evening and I felt I had accomplished nothing.

The Operations truck came to pick us up and carried us to the Operations building. I filled out an after-action report and trudged to the first platoon hootch, took a shower, and collapsed on my cot.

Afterwards I learned they got the soldier out that afternoon, and that was after an LOH was shot down, two medevac ships were shot up, and with three fire teams on station. I didn't learn if the soldier had survived.

## Can Tho Sapper Attack

During the early morning hours on the night of January 13, 1969, the Viet Cong infiltrated the Can Tho Army Airfield. Aided by sappers, they damaged or destroyed several aircraft and killed a number of persons, including a pilot from the 235th's third platoon.

Each of the three flight platoons of the company alternated weekly in providing pilots and crew chiefs for a nighttime, instant reaction fire team. The crewmembers assigned to that duty stayed in the Ready Shack, which at that time was located near the west end of the runway, and to quicken the response to a scramble, the team's Cobras were parked in revetments close to the Ready Shack.

The west end of the runway was farther from the main body of the airfield than the other end and was relatively close to the perimeter. After penetrating the perimeter near that end of the runway, the VC attack force silently killed the occupants of the nearest bunkers and turned the M60 machine guns toward the airfield, waiting while the larger body of infiltrators moved farther into the airfield, intent on destroying aircraft parked on the ramp and in the revetments along the runway. Once the sappers were inside the perimeter, among the closest aircraft for them to take out were the ready team's Cobras.

No one knew the sappers were on the airfield until the first explosion went off about 0200. With that, the alert crew in the Ready Shack started for their aircraft, unknowingly running to where some of the sappers already were. CW2 Gary Weatherhead, a fourteen-year Army veteran on his second tour in Vietnam, encountered one of the sappers and was killed.

When the first explosions went off, I was asleep on my cot in the first platoon hootch. My first reaction was to hit the floor and hug it. I thought we were being mortared. Then I heard someone shout that the airfield was being overrun. At first, I didn't believe that news, but it didn't stop me from grabbing my .38 revolver and low crawling to the door of the hootch to be in a better position to intercept any VC that might come charging in that direction. Others joined me in the doorway.

There were several explosions, all in a short span of time. We crouched in the doorway and after several minutes passed during which we hadn't heard any more explosions or gunfire, we decided to go to our aircraft. I dressed in the dark as quickly as I could, and with a flight helmet in one hand and a puny pistol in the other, two other pilots and I began making our way toward the revetments where the Cobras were. By that time, there had been no shooting inside the perimeter for some time, but we thought it possible there could another, follow-up attack, or that there were VC still on the airfield. Several buildings stood along the early part of the route and we skittered from one to another, stopping and peering around corners, wary of possibly bumping into some VC.

We eventually reached the revetments where the Cobras were parked without encountering anyone other than some other persons who had ventured out. My Cobra was parked a few revetments farther from the perimeter than the ones where the ready team's aircraft were parked, but I discovered Six-One-Four's tail boom had been mangled. I looked for another Cobra to take up and found one that appeared undamaged a few revetments farther down from where mine was parked, but someone cautioned that the VC may have booby trapped the aircraft and advised me to stay away from the Cobra until it could be checked out.

Well before then, a Huey flare ship and other aircraft were overhead, and shortly more aircraft arrived from other bases, including an Air Force AC-47 Spooky gunship. Those of us who had gone to the flight line walked to the Operations building, reported there, and hung around, waiting for orders. After an hour, we were directed to go to our hootches. All of us in the first platoon waited in our hootch until first light, and then went to the flight line to assess the situation. Crew chiefs and maintenance personnel were attending to the damaged aircraft. Cobras, Chinooks, and a Huey were among the helicopters hit. Two bodies, those of VC, still lay on the runway's west end.

It was then that we learned Gary had been killed.

## Night Crash

Before the incursion on the airfield, the Firefly team stayed in the Ready Shack near the west end of the runway and the team's Cobras were in revetments close by. As the raid revealed, those positions made the aircraft and the crews vulnerable to an attack from that part of the perimeter. Consequently, after that event, the Firefly team's Cobras were parked farther from the perimeter, at a location on the airfield's ramp close to the 235th's Operations building, and the standby crews stayed in a Ready Room within the Operations building.

Before the attack, Firefly duty had been more oriented toward responding to trouble in the Delta. Afterwards, greater emphasis was placed on providing airfield security as well as security for the aircraft and crews. Reflecting that greater emphasis, our Cobras began flying continuous cover over the airfield at night. The three flight platoons of the 235th alternated weekly in providing the crews for the patrol, and typically the same crews were assigned to the duty for the entire week. The duty began an hour before sunset when the pilots reported to

Operations to receive their aircraft assignments, to preflight the Cobras, and to move them from the revetments to the parking spots on the ramp near the Operations building. At sunset, the first of the two flight crews took up its Cobra and flew a two-hour shift. At the end of the first shift and when the other Cobra was up and on station, the first crew landed and waited until its next shift two hours later. The two crews and Cobras rotated shifts until first light.

On one night when I had the Firefly duty, Jim was the pilot of the other Cobra. Our new platoon leader, a captain, was the copilot for Jim's aircraft. At sunset, I pulled the first shift and was relieved by Jim afterwards. While he was flying overhead, I played cards with my copilot, drank bad coffee, and small talked with the officer and clerk on duty in the Operations building.

Eventually, it came time for my second shift of overhead guard duty. I took off, assumed my station overhead, and exchanged some friendly insults over the radio with Jim, who stayed airborne until I was in the air. I kept my position lights on until he turned on his lights prior to landing, and then I went lights-out.

Most of the time during a shift, I flew lazy circles around the outskirts of the airfield. Even though I was flying lights-out, I would occasionally change directions and altitude so not to establish too much of a routine for somebody who might want to take a shot at me.

At least once during a shift, as a diversion, I flew over the adjoining town of Can Tho, and on every occasion when I did, tracers shot into the air. None of them ever came that close; whoever it was could only shoot at the sound. In any case, there was little I could do about it; I wasn't going to make a rocket attack on the town because of some lone miscreant. I could even rouse some sympathy for him; maybe I was disturbing his sleep.

During a shift, when somebody guarding the perimeter suspected something, a message was relayed to the tower and the operator would call me to fly over and illuminate that area with my searchlight. I also kept an eye on the Engineers' compound directly across the Bassac River. The residents had requested our guard services at night, and I would fly there a few times each shift to run my searchlight over the compound and let my presence be known.

After midnight, as I neared the end of my fuel, I called Operations to send up the other Cobra. In a while, I saw the anti-collision light on Jim's Cobra, heard him call the tower, and watched him take off. I gave him a short report about my uneventful shift and landed. After shutting down the aircraft, my copilot and I walked to the Operations building, dropped our gear on the floor, and plopped down on the cots in the crew quarters. I fell asleep instantly.

A few minutes later, the Operations clerk woke me. He said I needed to go up again, explaining that the other Cobra was coming back down because it had a problem. I grabbed my gear and hustled out to the ramp where my Cobra was parked, only to find it was still being refueled. While I was waiting for the fuel truck driver to finish, Jim landed his Cobra on the taxiway nearby.

When he landed, I walked over to see what the problem was. As I did, a maintenance officer drove up in a jeep, parked, and walked over with me. I listened as Jim, still in the cockpit and with the engine running, described to the maintenance officer the vibration he felt in the pedals. The maintenance officer said he wanted to try some things and might take the aircraft for a test spin. Jim climbed out of the back seat to let him in. Jim asked the captain in the front seat if he wanted to get out, but the captain said, no, he was comfortable.

Jim and I walked back toward my aircraft, which had been topped off by that time. I graciously offered to let Jim fly my aircraft to finish the shift, which I felt was rightfully his, but he politely declined the offer, saying he was happy to let me do it, and strolled off to the Ops building.

After starting Six-One-Four, I began hovering toward the runway, and as I did, I could see the maintenance officer on the taxiway, experimenting with Jim's helicopter, picking it up, setting it down, and making hovering turns.

When I neared the runway, I was ready to call the tower for takeoff when I heard the maintenance officer tell the tower he was taking off from the taxiway for a test flight and would be staying in the airfield's traffic pattern. Right after his transmission, I called the tower operator to report I was ready for takeoff and he directed me to take the runway and hold until the other Cobra was clear.

As I hovered in place on the runway, I watched the other Cobra take off. After it cleared the boundary of the airfield, all I could see was its position lights. I followed them as the Cobra turned on a downwind leg. Then I saw the lights whirling around. At the same time, I heard the maintenance pilot call on the tower frequency, "Going down. Tail rotor failure." The lights plunged toward the ground and disappeared. The tower operator called the Cobra several times, but the calls drew no response.

I started my take off immediately and called the tower to report that I was on the way to the crash site. In less than a minute, I was over the location where I estimated the aircraft had gone down, but I didn't see any position lights from the downed helicopter. I held my Cobra in a tight circle, using the searchlight to comb the area, and in a moment I caught the downed aircraft in the searchlight. It was southwest of the airfield, a half klick outside the perimeter, sitting in shallow water among tall grass and reeds and near a stand of nipa palms. The Cobra was almost upright but leaning to one side. The skids were bent, the tail boom was lying at an angle to the fuselage, and one of the main rotor blades was dug into the ground on the low side. I ran the searchlight over the aircraft's canopy and I could see the maintenance pilot in the back seat. He was stirring. The captain in the front seat wasn't. In the light, I saw the back canopy hatch swing open and the maintenance pilot climb out.

I reported to the tower what I saw. The tower operator advised me that he had reported the crash and that a Huey was being dispatched to the site. I knew it would take some time to gather a crew and for the slick to get there, so I told the operator I would try to find a place to land and check on the pilots firsthand.

I circled slowly around the crash site using the searchlight to find a spot to set down. As far as I could see with the searchlight, although there were a few small spots, I didn't see a place close to the wrecked aircraft that was big enough that I could fit my

Cobra into it. All of them had nipa palms or bamboo and thick grass tall enough to damage or entangle the tail rotor. One downed Cobra was enough for the night.

I searched further out and the closest place I could find where it appeared possible to land was an open spot with shorter bamboo and grass that was some two hundred yards from the crash site. I would have to hover straight down into the opening and be careful to keep the tail rotor away from the taller grass and reeds.

I was starting down when the tower operator called with a request that I return to the runway. I acknowledged the transmission, but reminded him I intended to land and check on the crew. The tower operator then explained who wanted me to return and why.

Because it was the policy that the same platoon that provided the night flight crews also supplied an Officer in Charge for the perimeter command post, another pilot in my platoon—Ed—was the OIC that night. After he became an Aircraft Commander, Ed flew my wing more times than anyone else, and there was no one I trusted more than him.

Although the command post was capable of monitoring the tower frequency, it couldn't transmit on that frequency. Ed had heard the transmissions on the tower frequency, and by calling brigade headquarters on the command post radio, he was able to relay a message to me through the tower operator.

Ed had sent a message to have me come back to the runway and pick up him and one of the crew chiefs who was also pulling guard duty that night. Ed wanted me to carry them to the crash site. The command post was about fifty yards from the west end of the runway and Ed and the crew chief would be waiting for me at the runway's end.

It sounded like a good plan to me. I could deliver the two of them close to the crash site faster than I could land and wade a couple of hundred yards through the swamp.

I lowered the Cobra's nose and skimmed over the ground directly to the end of the runway. I saw Ed and the crew chief already there, standing near the last illumination barrel at that end. I came in obliquely to the runway, pulled back on the cyclic to slow the helicopter and, at the same time, pushed the right pedal so that I sat down aligned with the runway near the barrel. I thought perhaps the rotor wash might fan out the flames in the barrel, but it didn't. As soon as the skids touched down, Ed and the crew chief were beside the helicopter. They each opened one of the ammo bay doors on the sides of the Cobra, at the front of the fuselage. Ed got on the door on one side and the crew chief sat down on the other one.

As soon as they were on, I pulled pitch and pushed the cyclic forward for a maximum power take off. The Cobra lumbered off the ground and, as I eased it forward, it began climbing—slowly. It had a full load of fuel, a full load of ordnance, a full crew, and now two additional persons sitting on the ammo bay doors. As it came off the ground, its nose tucked low due to the extra weight at the front, and nose down, like a wagon horse lugging a heavy load, it was trying to get into the air from a standing start.

I was moving forward, and when I was ten feet in the air, I remembered that there was a commo line strung between two poles near that end of the runway. I was reminded of the line when it suddenly appeared right there in front of me, a short distance ahead.

That line had been there ever since I had arrived at Can Tho and the first time I saw it, I thought it curious that anyone would string a line that close to the end of the runway. Since that first time, the line must have crossed my vision hundreds of times—at least every time I took off to the west—but because I was always well in the air before I got to the end of the runway, I had quit giving it attention. Now, there it was—right in front of me.

The overloaded Cobra was straining to climb. I had no power to spare and the line was drawing closer. I had left the searchlight on and the line, illuminated in the glare of the light, loomed as large as a suspension cable for the Golden Gate Bridge.

I thought briefly about trying to stop the ascent and backing away, declining to the runway, but at that altitude, out of ground effect, and heavily loaded, I was afraid any change on the controls might disrupt the delicate balance I had and make things worse. So I held on to the little momentum I had. I loosened my reflexive death grip on the controls and concentrated on just keeping everything steady. I held my breath as if I were holding a rifle and about to squeeze off a shot.

The Cobra struggled, slowly rising, creeping forward, and edging closer to the line. Time seemed to slow. I was no longer a pilot; I was an observer.

With the nose abnormally tucked, the fuselage was tilted forward and I was at eye level with the line, a few feet in front of me. As the aircraft rose and inched forward, I watched the pitot tube, which stuck out from the very front of the fuselage, draw closer to the line. It occurred to me that if the pitot tube was at the line's level, it meant the main rotor had already cleared. That was good, but I still had the pitot tube to worry about. If it wasn't going to clear, I hoped it would bend easily or break off quickly rather than snag on the line, causing the nose to tilt further down. The aircraft was close to the forward CG limit and even a slight nudge could push it outside its weight and balance envelope and send it nose-first to the ground.

Then, I saw the pitot tube creep above the line; it had made it. That meant the nose was clear, but the Cobra was still rising, still moving forward, and I worried that the skids could catch the line. Unlike the pitot tube, the skids wouldn't bend or break. As the nose passed over the line, the cable moved out of the illumination from the light and slipped out of sight into the darkness below. I couldn't see the skids underneath the aircraft. After a few seconds, I was still climbing and I hadn't felt a jerk, so I knew the aircraft had cleared the line completely. I realized then that it was actually good that the nose was so low. Being that close to the line at a normal attitude, the toes of the skids would have been more forward and would have been more likely to snag the line.

With the line behind me and with a little more altitude under me, I risked nudging the nose forward a little more. The Cobra dipped lower and picked up airspeed. I didn't need any more altitude and with more air flowing over the rotor, I nudged the cyclic some more and the Cobra was cruising, flying directly above the ground. It didn't take long to get back to the crash site.

I slowed the aircraft but kept forward momentum, circling around the downed Cobra one time with the searchlight on it to give Ed and the crew chief a look at the site and the area surrounding it, bamboo and all. Ed motioned to the left and I drifted that way over a small bare spot he was pointing at, some sixty or seventy feet from the crash site. Even with two extra persons onboard, I thought I had enough power that I could come to a stationary hover over that spot if I could get down as low as five or six feet, an altitude that would gain some ground effect but still just high enough to keep the bamboo out of the tail rotor, and if I came down slowly enough that I wouldn't have to pull much collective at the bottom.

I began easing down to get as low over the tops of the bamboo as I could, but at about twelve feet, Ed bailed off. I saw him splash into the water, pick himself up, and go limping toward the wreck. I eased down another few feet and the crew chief jumped off.

With the extra weight gone, I climbed back up to a couple of hundred feet and slowly circled the site, illuminating it with the searchlight. Ed and the crew chief waded to the wrecked Cobra. I watched as the crew chief tended to the maintenance officer standing beside the aircraft and Ed examined the captain who was still in the front seat.

After about fifteen minutes, some other persons arrived at the site on foot and from the direction of the airfield. I found out later they had been on guard duty at the bunker closest to the crash site and had waded through the swamp to reach the aircraft. In another ten minutes, a Huey arrived overhead. I communicated with it on the tower frequency as requested by the tower operator so that anyone else on that frequency, including the headquarters staff, could listen in on our conversation.

The Huey pilot was looking for a place to set down so I suggested the place where I had thought to land. I flew over to it, and put the spotlight on it to help him find it. He looked it over, decided it would work, and put down there.

I flew back to the crash site and after a while, two persons from the Huey arrived there. I assumed they were the Huey's crew chief and gunner. The two of them and Ed helped the captain from the front seat and the two persons began carrying the captain toward the Huey. The maintenance officer was walking on his own and Ed came limping behind, leaning on the crew chief that I had carried on an ammo bay door. From overhead, I illuminated the path in front of them. Eventually, they all made it to the Huey and it took off. The persons from the perimeter guard stayed behind at the crash site to guard the wrecked aircraft.

I resumed my cover of the airfield, returning periodically to check on the party guarding the aircraft, until another Cobra and crew come to relieve me.

When I landed, Jim was in the Operations building. He wanted to know how the captain and the maintenance officer were. I told him everything that I had seen, but I didn't know their exact condition.

I flew another shift that night and, after daylight came, Jim and I went to the mess hall for breakfast. We found Ed there. He told us the maintenance officer wasn't hurt badly at all, but the captain had several crushed, possibly broken, vertebrae and would be returning to the States for treatment. A Chinook would lift the Cobra out that morning and, once it was dropped at the maintenance hangar, the folks there would decide whether to fix it or scrap it for parts.

While we ate, I reflected that it could have been a lot worse. No one had been killed. The maintenance officer was only shook up. The captain, although he possibly had a broken back, wasn't paralyzed—and he would be going home. Ed had a hobbling sprain but said he was good enough to fly; in other words, he kept himself on flight status because he didn't go to the flight surgeon. Jim, who had the good sense to get the aircraft on the ground when he did, was sitting there with us, still able to grin. And all of us that were in, and on, my Cobra that night had managed to escape another, potential crash, one that would have been due to pilot error on my part.

# Jim's Shoot-down

Our platoon was assigned to take two fire teams to Soc Trang. I led one fire team and our platoon leader, Captain Keys, led the other. We nicknamed Captain Keys "*Dai Uy*", Vietnamese for "captain." *Dai Uy* was energetic; boisterous; a streetwise, creative finagler; protective of his men; and an officer who pulled rank only in the most obstinate cases. I had a bunch of bosses in the Army, but *Dai Uy* was among the very best ones.

Flight platoon leaders were qualified pilots, but they were officers first and pilots second. Their other duties sometimes limited their flying time, and like most other jobs, there was a direct correlation between the amount of flying experience a person had and that person's finesse at the job. Also, because of their more limited flying time, platoon leaders didn't always gain the same degree of synergism that went along with working with the same members of a fire team day in and day out. When members of a fire team work together consistently, they learn each other's particular habits and learn to anticipate one another's actions.

On the days that he flew, *Dai Uy* often chose to fly in the front seat as copilot. But on this day, not only was he flying in the pilot position, he had also assumed the role of fire team leader for one of the teams. Jim was the pilot for the wing ship of *Dai Uy*'s team.

The two light fire teams—four Cobras in total—left Can Tho in the morning for the flight to the Soc Trang airfield. Because it was so rare that more than two of our aircraft flew anywhere together, we took the opportunity to fly in a tight formation; at least we tried to make it tight but I'm sure we must have looked pretty ragged compared to a flight of slicks.

At Soc Trang, an officer, who would be piloting a Huey and acting as the Command and Control authority, briefed us on what we were to do. A team would go out and shoot up targets that he would identify. When that team expended its ordnance, it would return to Soc Trang to rearm and the other team would go out and shoot up targets. The targets for annihilation were close enough to the airfield that a team could fly out, expend its ordnance, return to the airfield, rearm, and fly back out to the area several times without refueling; that is, if we didn't encounter any resistance, and because Intelligence had concluded the area was frequented only occasionally by the VC and only at night, we were directed to use the miniguns only if we received fire. That would speed up our turnaround since the miniguns took longer to rearm than the rocket tubes.

To expedite alternating the fire teams, the team at the airfield would monitor the radio, and when the team on station was close to expending its ordnance, the C&C pilot would call the awaiting team to come out to the shooting gallery.

After the briefing, the C&C Huey took off and my team accompanied it. When we arrived at the target area, the C&C identified individual targets one-by-one and we systematically destroyed them with rockets. The gunners kept the miniguns ready, but the area was cold. When I was down to half ordnance, I reported that status to the C&C and he called *Dai Uy*, who was waiting at the airfield, to bring his team to take its turn. After my team ran out of rockets, we flew back to Soc Trang to rearm. On the way, we passed *Dai Uy*, with Jim in trail, as they flew to the target area.

My team landed at the airfield, hovered to the stash of rockets just off the asphalt runway, and started stuffing rockets into the empty tubes. We left the engines running because we expected to be called back as soon as *Dai Uy*'s team reached half-ordnance. While my gunner humped the rockets, I remained in the back seat, monitoring the mission push.

The gunner had just finished when the C&C called to report that *Dai Uy*'s fire team was returning to the airfield and that he also was returning in the Huey. Since the C&C was coming back, I assumed the mission was at least temporarily suspended, so I hovered the Cobra to the other side of the runway and shut down the engine. I got out to stretch my legs while the gunner tied down the blades. He yelled to me from back at the tail boom, "*Dai Uy*'s coming in."

When I turned to look, I noticed *Dai Uy*'s Cobra had a shallow approach angle, much less steep than for a normal approach. And, curiously, the aircraft was cocked off to one side.

I didn't rate *Dai Uy* as the best pilot ever, but I knew he could keep an aircraft in trim better than that.

He was on short final when I realized he was going to make a running landing. He continued the shallow approach toward the runway and was still doing about fifty knots when he touched down, the helicopter's nose cocked off at an angle. The aircraft slid down the runway on its skids, slanting across the asphalt. It slid off the edge of the runway on the far side and came bumping to a stop there.

Jim, in his helicopter, had followed *Dai Uy* all the way in and fast hovered right behind him as *Dai Uy* slid down the runway and off the edge. Once *Dai Uy*'s helicopter came to a rest, Jim hovered a little farther down the runway and set down to the side of it.

When those of us in my fire team saw *Dai Uy* was making a running landing, we assumed there was a problem and we began chasing his helicopter on foot as it scooted down the runway. We wanted to be there if it flipped over or if we otherwise needed to extract someone.

We caught up with the helicopter soon after it came to a stop and clamored up to the canopy to see if anyone needed help. *Dai Uy* shut down the engine, flung open the canopy hatch, yanked off his helmet, and came storming out.

"What's the problem?" I said.

*Dai Uy* answered through clinched teeth. "Tail rotor."

I looked at the tail rotor. It was still twirling, wobbling as it came to a stop, and I saw it was littered with gashes and holes. I assumed the target area must have turned hot after I left.

"Ground fire?" I said.

"No," *Dai Uy* spat.

Although I didn't think it likely, I supposed he could have drug the tail boom through some tree branches if he'd carried a rocket run too low. "Tree strike?" I said.

Di Wi glared. "No."

"Well then, what was it?" I said.

"Him," *Dai Uy* said, and pointed.

I turned to follow his finger. It was pointing at Jim, who was walking toward us, his hands in his pockets, looking sheepish.

"What happened?" I said.

*Dai Uy* began explaining, but it took him a while because he had to stop occasionally to stomp around in a circle and cuss.

In between the stompings and cussings, I pieced together the story. *Dai Uy* had to make the running landing because the tail rotor had lost most of its effectiveness. That was because it was damaged. And that was because Jim had done it. *Dai Uy* explained that he was on a routine rocket run and just when he started a break, Jim had laid a pair of rockets right under *Dai Uy*'s aircraft. The debris from the explosion peppered the tail boom and tail rotor. Or, at least, that was *Dai Uy*'s story.

But Jim offered his version of the story. He acknowledged that he had indeed shot under *Dai Uy*'s ship when he was on a break. But he claimed it was *Dai Uy*'s fault because *Dai Uy* had turned in the opposite direction from the one he called before beginning the run.

Now, a mark of a good wing ship pilot was giving the lead ship close protection. That included putting rounds on the target to cover the lead's break as soon as he began it. Jim's intention was, as soon as *Dai Uy* made his break, to put a pair of rockets on the target, shading his aim just a scooch away from the direction of the break. And Jim was ready on the trigger alright. The moment he saw *Dai Uy*'s tail boom twitch, Jim punched off the rockets. Too late, he saw *Dai Uy* was turning in a different direction that what he expected. Rather than impacting away from *Dai Uy*'s break, the rockets hit directly under his helicopter. So, according to Jim, *Dai Uy* broke in a different direction from what he called. Besides, Jim added, *Dai Uy* had gone in too low and too close to the target; otherwise, the debris from the rockets wouldn't have damaged *Dai Uy*'s helicopter at all.

*Dai Uy*—with the benefit no doubt of having been an NCO before he became an officer and a gentleman—erupted with such a string of cussing, I learned enough new words to double my vocabulary. Sparing the colorful expressions and summarizing it all, I understood him to say, "No, I beg to differ. I did not turn the wrong way; it was you who shot the wrong way."

Jim just smiled that possum grin of his. At that, *Dai Uy* started cussing and stomping some more.

*Dai Uy* stopped cussing long enough to stomp over and inspect the tail rotor now that it had wobbled to a stop. After he examined it, he came back and cussed some more. Jim still stood there, grinning.

I estimate it took more than a quarter hour for *Dai Uy* to cuss himself empty. He finally wound down enough to ask me to contact Operations and report the status of his aircraft. Meanwhile, he put his arm around Jim and led him off for some personal counseling.

I called Operations and explained that the tail rotor of *Dai Uy*'s helicopter had been damaged and we would need Maintenance to come to Soc Trang. But when the operations officer asked me how the damage happened, I said *Dai Uy* would have to explain that to him. I wasn't going to be the one to tell him that *Dai Uy*'s very own wingman had shot him down.

## Gunship Pilots Don't Fly in Formation

Once upon a time, I took specific pride in being a gunship pilot. Formerly, when someone asked me what I did, I would lift my head and say with some haughtiness, "I, sir, am a gunship pilot." However, upon reflection, I came to realize that even though the Army was intent on making a good slick pilot out of me, it instead settled upon making me a gunship pilot because the Army conceded – after numerous attempts – that it would never be able to teach me to fly in formation, which is a prerequisite for slick pilots.

I didn't take this concession personally. A deficiency in the ability to fly in formation is a malady of all gunship pilots. No one knows why gunship pilots can't fly in formation. Perhaps it's a genetic deficiency. Perhaps it was a lapse in early childhood modeling behavior because, during school recess, they were kept inside by the teacher to write on the board a hundred times "I will not put marbles in the pencil sharpener" and therefore missed those specific play times where the other kids were playing follow-the-leader. I don't know; perhaps science can answer this question some day.

I confess I didn't immediately recognize my condition. However, the Army discovered my inability to fly in formation early in my flying career. In primary flight school, my handicap was obvious to my instructors. During the introduction to formation flying at Fort Wolters, while the other aircraft were flying in a tightly bunched pattern, like geese heading south for their winter resort, I was flapping around, up and down, sometimes ahead and sometimes behind, and a part of the flight in only the loosest sense of the term. When the other aircraft were on short final to the stage field, in a formation tighter than Dolly Parton's brassiere, I was still flopping around at three thousand feet somewhere over Possum Kingdom Lake.

At Fort Rucker, my condition was further confirmed. At the graduation ceremonies of my flight class, a civilian dignitary complimented our flight class for its missing man formation flyover. He didn't realize the empty slot in that formation was mine, and my absence was totally impromptu. The civilian may have been misled, but the Army knew the truth. Conceding that my condition couldn't be remedied, the Army did the only thing it could do to salvage its investment in me; it made me a gunship pilot.

Formation flying is not a requirement for gunship pilots. In fact, a gunship pilot's idea of formation flying is two or more aircraft close enough to see one another—or at least be in the same geographic hemisphere—and at approximately the same altitude, give or take a few thousand feet—or more.

I suppose I should have recognized I wasn't destined to be a slick pilot since I took no pleasure in formation flying. A true slick pilot relishes the discipline of formation flying. He delights in the precision of it. He takes pride in his ability to line up his aircraft by using the skid cross braces of his neighbor's aircraft. It's a confidence similar to the smugness of a pool hall hustler when he's lining up the eight ball for a sure shot to the corner pocket. On the other hand, a person who's a true gunship pilot by nature; that is, a person who lacks the ability to fly in formation, views formation flying as nothing but a disaster in the making, like noodling for sharks.

Furthermore, I came to realize that my personal inability to fly in formation must be exceptional, even for a gunship pilot. That must have been why the Army made me a fire team leader. In that position, I would be up front where a wing ship pilot could keep an eye on me and have a reasonable chance of avoiding my efforts to run into him. I'm living testimony that being a gunship fire team leader is the ultimate acknowledgment of one's inability to fly in formation.

When I first realized that the Army made me a gunship pilot, instead of a slick pilot, because of my inability to fly in formation, I felt somewhat inferior. But, with time, I came to accept this limitation and even to rejoice that I was, by nature, a gunship pilot rather than a slick pilot. Just as the ugly duckling found joy in the discovery that he was really a long-necked goose, I have found joy in discovering my own true nature, knowing that my lack of ability to fly in formation, sing on key, dress fashionably, or otherwise make any contribution to polite society is because I am, by nature, a gunship pilot. And knowing this, I have come to feel so much better.

## Swamp Landing

Most aviation units in Vietnam probably had at least one "hangar queen", an aircraft with chronic maintenance issues. At Can Tho Army Airfield, among the 235th Aerial Weapons Company's fleet of Cobras, ours was Six-O-Eight.

Pilots avoided Six-O-Eight whenever they could because it was notorious for being a weak ship. Often, when a pilot discovered he had been assigned Six-O-Eight, he would find some reason during preflight to red-X it; that is, mark an X in its logbook, effectively grounding the aircraft, along with a note about some condition that made it unsuitable to fly. And whenever pilots did fly Six-O-Eight, they would often red-X the aircraft after the flight with a note that the aircraft was underpowered.

However, the maintenance folks never found enough evidence to substantiate these claims, and it must have become an irritation for them to constantly investigate a problem so vague they couldn't correct it. It must have been a particular nuisance to the maintenance officer because a red-X required him to test fly the aircraft before signing off the mark and returning the aircraft to flight status.

On one fateful day, the wing ship pilot of my fire team had been assigned Six-O-Eight. He couldn't find anything during preflight to justify grounding it, so he was stuck with it. He flew it that day and as we were returning to Can Tho, he told me he was going to red-X the aircraft because of its anemic performance. As we neared the airfield, I radioed Operations the status of our aircraft, including the information that Six-O-Eight was being red-Xed.

We usually parked our Cobras in the revetments along the side of the runway. The revetments were a collection of head high sandbag walls arranged perpendicular to the runway and a few yards from it, sort of like hash marks along the sideline of a gridiron field. Each revetment had two open ends, one of which fronted the runway. A few yards behind the rear ends of the revetments lay "the swamp". To park our Cobras in the revetments, we made our approach to the swamp, coming to a hover over it, and then turning and hovering into the revetments from the rear so that the Cobras faced the runway.

The swamp was a piece of stagnant marsh trapped inside the airfield. It was rectangular shaped, about thirty yards wide, and its length extended the entire distance behind the revetments that lined the runway, separating them from the larger parking ramp on the opposite side of the swamp.

Dumping anything into the swamp was officially prohibited, but it proved too handy a place not to tempt mechanics working on the ramp to pour used aircraft fluids into it. People on the ramp with pressing business also found the swamp to be more convenient than walking all the way back to a latrine.

Loathsome waste of almost every kind imaginable had been dumped into the swamp. And it reeked. Its foul composition ranked among the top five worst smelling things that ever affronted my snout. It enjoyed this distinction along with—in no specific order of odoriferous rank—the distinctive aromatic assault that wafted from my grandpa's fungus infested feet; the eye-watering stench of sun ripened, congealed coyote wretch; the almost visible waves of gag inducing vapor radiating from a rancid vat of Vietnamese homemade *nuoc mam* sauce; and one particular, unforgettable episode of passed gas emitted by my front seat gunner inside the Cobra's enclosed cockpit on a hot day in July that rendered me almost unconscious.

Even the vapors from this corrosive pool of slimy, oil-slicked semi-liquid could blister the warts on frogs that lingered too long near its festered shores. Among the superstitious, this abomination of filth and putrescence was rumored to be the womb of demons.

This day, we had just parked our helicopters in the revetments and were gathering up our gear when the maintenance officer came racing up in his jeep. He screeched to a halt near the revetment where Six-O-Eight sat and jumped out of the jeep. He appeared aggravated because he had to deal with Six-O-Eight again, and he didn't say anything to us before he jumped into the aircraft and took off.

We shrugged and began walking to the Operations building, but we only got as far as the crossway connecting the runway with the ramp when I saw him returning in Six-O-Eight. He had simply taken off, flown an abbreviated traffic pattern around the airfield, and was already bringing the aircraft back, apparently in a hurry to get the test flight out of the way, return Six-O-Eight to its revetment, and sign it off as flight ready.

I watched his approach to the swamp. He was coming in fast, way too fast. And because he had so much airspeed, he had to flare the aircraft way back, practically standing it on its tail, to stop it. The result was, that by the time the aircraft came to a stop, it had ballooned another fifty feet higher. And so, there he was, with no forward airspeed, fifty feet too high, and—as he discovered when he tried to pull in more power—too little to hover. As soon as I saw him come to a stop, dangling there above the swamp, I knew he was in trouble. He was in a predicament that pilots described as "out of airspeed, altitude, and ideas all at the same time".

Six-O-Eight began settling toward the swamp. As it did, I could imagine the maintenance officer desperately pulling up on the collective, practically ripping it out by its roots, and despite it all, feeling the aircraft sinking lower and lower, and him with it.

Six-O-Eight kept dropping, slowly and surely, toward the swamp. Its skids touched the surface, slipped underneath, and kept on going. Ol' Six-O-Eight settled into the swamp like a tired pig in a hog wallow, sinking down until its skids reached the bottom, finally coming to rest with the swamp's slimy surface half way up to the bottom of the canopy lid. I hadn't known exactly how deep the swamp was until that maintenance officer provided Six-O-Eight as a measuring stick.

As Six-O-Eight sat in the swamp, bubbles bigger than a bullfrog's bellows belched around it. Oozing from the putrid depths, the thick blisters burst open, flinging forth fresh floods of fetid fumigation.

The Can Tho Airfield was always a beehive of activity during the day. Aircraft, vehicles, and people were everywhere. As soon as Six-O-Eight began sinking into the swamp, all the activity came to a standstill. Vehicles stopped. Maintenance personnel and flight crews paused to watch. People stood suspended in slack-jawed amazement, watching Six-O-Eight slip slowly into the swamp. Then, as soon as it came to rest and as if with a common cue, everyone grabbed his camera. Practically everybody in Vietnam carried a camera with him wherever he went.

The maintenance officer, at the helm of Six-O-Eight, went down with the ship. When it settled into place, he sat there a while before he finally shut down the engine. Then he removed his helmet, raised the canopy, stuck his head out of the cockpit, and examined his plight. Eventually, he stood up and placed one foot out of the cockpit and tentatively onto the step-up at the side of the fuselage, which was just above the filth line. He pulled his other foot out of the cockpit and tried to place that foot also on the step-up, but the short, narrow platform was only made for one foot, so there was only room for the tips of his boots. He stood there, pigeon toed, trying to decide what his next step would be. Inevitably, he concluded what it had to be; there was no other choice. He must abandon the ship.

Like a man walking a short plank, he stepped off the perch and plunged into the morass, landing in it chest deep. He stood there a while, feeling for footing. Then he began wading slowly through the quagmire, struggling as he slogged through the bog, the bottom muck sucking at his feet. Eventually, he reached the shore of the swamp, and when he came wading out, there were more cameras snapping him than McArthur when he returned to the Philippines. Covered with black, slimy swamp goop from his nametag down, he went trudging off across the ramp, dripping a trail of slime behind him.

All of us in our fire team stood mesmerized by the spectacle of Six-O-Eight landing in the swamp and could only gawk as the maintenance officer emerged from the aircraft, splashed into the gooey lagoon, and waded out. But when he began walking away, leaking evidence of the misadventure from his soggy bottom, we started laughing so hard we had to plop down right there on the crossway.

It was a while before we could compose ourselves enough to get out of the way so we wouldn't be run over by a C-123 that had just landed. It turned out, though, we weren't in any danger; its pilot had stopped and was aiming his camera out of the side window to get a picture of Six-O-Eight sitting out there, forlorn, in the swamp.

## The Flashing Red Light

The 235th's new CO wanted to improve things. One of the first things he thought needed improvement was how we crossed the road.

Our company normally provided one or more fire teams each day for IV Corps Standby duty where Cobras and their crews were assigned to be a ready-reaction force, prepared to take off immediately in response to a call for gunship support from anywhere in the delta. When a call came, the pilots ran to the helicopters, cranked, and took off. The tower gave us priority clearance when we announced we were on a scramble. To help ensure the team got off quickly, the flight crew was stationed in the Ready Room of the company Operations building and the helicopters were positioned on the airfield's parking ramp and as close as possible to Operations.

A road separated the ramp from the Operations building. The narrow road, connecting the ramp area with maintenance hangars, living quarters, the mess hall, and a larger part of the remainder of the base, was a busy one. Furthermore, every driver treated this road as if it was a raceway where he was intent on setting a new world land speed record for his particular category of vehicle.

When going between the Operations building and the ramp, the pilots had to cross the road on foot. Normally, that meant waiting for a break in the stream of vehicles before darting across in front of would-be record setters. With all that traffic on the road, the CO felt we pilots should have some priority when on a scramble, so he decided he would do something about that. His solution was a flashing red light.

He had a six-foot pole planted beside the road directly in front of the Operations building, and mounted atop the pole, a flashing red light. Except that it was red, the light resembled one that K-Mart used to attract shoppers to the site of a blue-light special. Below the light, a sign explained to anyone who bothered to read it that vehicles should stop when the light was flashing.

A wire stretched from the light to the Operations building where it connected inside to a switch. When there was a scramble, the Operations clerk, or whoever else was on duty, could flip on the switch, causing the light on the pole to start flashing.

When I first heard about the plan for the flashing red light, I had considerable doubt about the effectiveness of this pilot-crossing scheme. With my assessment of the state of mind of the maniacs who drove on that road, I didn't place much trust in the expectation that a flashing light, even though it was a red one, would halt their single-minded rush to get to wherever they were going. In fact, rather than causing drivers to stop for pilots crossing the road, I feared it was more likely to give those drivers an unnecessary tip-off that we were about to cross and provide them an even better chance of running us over. I heard no more about the plan until one evening at the Officers' Club when someone mentioned that the red light had been installed just that afternoon.

The next day, my fire team had IV Corps Standby duty, but before assuming standby status, we had a preplanned early-morning mission. We completed that first assignment—covering the insertion of Ruff-Puffs for a search-and-destroy operation—and flew back to Can Tho. We didn't have to shoot any of our ordnance during the insertion. The LZ was cold and the Air Mission Commander hadn't asked us to prep it.

It was standard policy, upon returning to the airfield and before landing, to contact Operations and report the status of the aircraft and their needs, specifically whether or not any of the aircraft needed maintenance, ordnance, or fuel. As we neared Can Tho, I radioed Operations that we would be landing shortly and that the aircraft only needed refueling. The Operations clerk acknowledged.

I shot the approach to the near crossway connecting the runway with the ramp, and with the wing ship behind me, hovered to the spot on the ramp directly across the road from our Operations building. After we shut down the aircraft, we climbed out, leaving our chicken plates in the seats of the aircraft and our helmets hung near the open canopy hatch, the cords plugged in to the communications panel. Having those things in place would save time in the event of a scramble. And as much as we could for all the aircraft's gadgets, we dialed, set, and cocked them to further reduce time getting airborne when a scramble came.

Leaving the aircraft poised for an instant takeoff, we walked across the ramp toward the Operations building. When we came to the road, there was the usual heavy traffic and we waited for a gap in the flow of vehicles. Eventually, an opportunity came and we walked across the road as a deuce-and-half bore down on us. As it rumbled past, the driver blasted his horn.

When we walked into the Operations Building I discovered the person I had talked with on the radio was a new Operations clerk. It was his first day on the job. I tried to strike up a conversation with him because I was curious to learn what the other teams in the Delta were running into that day. Also, from chats like this, I could sometimes gather a piece of information about someone, a bit of under-the-table intelligence that I could use to plague that person when opportunity presented itself. For example, there was the time I learned about the incident involving a pilot in the second platoon. This pilot was casually leaning against the Operations counter, smoking, when the lit end of his cigarette accidentally fell into the pouch on the front of his chicken plate. He learned of this accident only when the codebook in the pouch began to smolder. Another pilot, upon seeing the smoke, filled a cup from the water cooler to extinguish the fire. However, by the time he had filled the cup, the victim of the accident had already beaten out the fire himself. The pilot with the cup, discovering he was too late to be of assistance to the victim, and disgruntled by that fact, threw the water on the victim anyway. But I didn't get anything from the clerk. He had been left alone on the job and he was having a hard enough time just trying to figure out what he was supposed to do.

I walked out to the Operations' new Ready Room where the rest of the team was. The Ready Room was actually a small travel trailer that had been pulled up close behind the Operations building, something the new CO had added. To reach it, we only had to step out the back door of the Operations building and walk a few steps to the door of the trailer.

In the Ready Room, my gunner picked up a worn deck of cards and we began playing pinochle. After a hand or two, the game broke up, and for the same reason that ended every game of pinochle. After playing for a while, we all remembered that we actually hated the game.

Instead, we took up poker. We had no chips; we carried no cash on us; and we had nothing to write on; so the pots were verbal IOUs. The bets started off modest, but soon we were betting things like cattle ranches, a thousand acres of Oklahoma oil land, the offshore mineral rights to the California coast line, Big Ben, the bottom nineteen stories of the Empire State Building, the publicity rights to the Loch Ness monster, a personally autographed photograph of the Abominable Snowman, and all the gold teeth in Vietnam. One pot went up to an estimated billion dollars. But the game fell apart when the betting went too far. When the wingman bet a paperweight made from a genuine moon rock, my gunner slapped down his cards in disgust. "That's just crazy," he said. "As if a man would ever walk on the moon!"

The other gunner kept the deck for himself and began playing Solitaire; my wingman began regaling my gunner about Kentucky coonhounds; and I picked up a dog-eared paperback to read.

Some time later, we were called to scramble. I glanced at my watch and saw it was nearing noon, so I wasn't especially surprised to learn that the Ruff-Puffs we had helped insert earlier that morning were the ones who had called. They were suspicious that there might be some VC in a nearby tree line and wanted gunships to shoot up the trees. I sighed to myself; it was show time for the Ruff-Puffs, which meant we weren't going to have a hot lunch that day. Sometimes, during IV Corps Standby, we were allowed to go to the mess hall for a quick lunch. But I knew that by the time we finished this performance and returned to Can Tho, the mess hall would be closed. It looked like another meal of C-Rations.

We piled out of the Ready Room, and hurried through the Operations building, the most direct route to the aircraft. I was in the rear and about to follow the rest of the team out the door when the clerk called to me. "Here," he said, "I'll write down all the contact information for you." Often, to save time on a scramble, that information was radioed to us after we were in the air, and in this case, I didn't need the information since I had already gotten it when we covered the insertion that morning. But the clerk was new and still learning, so I went back and waited a few seconds while he copied down the information onto a slip of paper. When he finished, I snatched the paper and ran out the door.

I saw the rest of the team across the road, already at the aircraft. When I came to the road, I stopped, waiting for an opening in the traffic. I saw an opportunity and was about to dart across, but the clerk yelled from the door of the Operations building, "Wait. I forgot to turn on the light."

That was the first time I had thought about the light. Although the other members of the team had apparently crossed the road without the aid of it, and I felt I was no less brave than them, I decided to wait for the clerk to go back inside and turn on the switch. He was new, I thought, so I would help him do things by the book. Shortly, the light started flashing.

To my surprise, the vehicles that had been flying past were suddenly stopping. As they came to a halt, I noticed that the pedestrians walking along the side of the road were also stopping. They were looking to see what was stopping the traffic. Then, the people who were on the parking ramp across the road stopped what they were doing to see what it was that was stopping traffic on the road and that was gathering a crowd by the Operations building. I was flabbergasted; the flashing red light was really working. Even I was stopped, watching the traffic stack up.

As I stood by the flashing red light, I noticed all the stopped drivers were looking at me. The pedestrians were looking at me; all the people on the ramp were looking in my direction. And with all this attention, I suddenly felt like a person of some importance. I had an audience. Well then, I thought, I'll just show these folks what a real gunship pilot looks like in action. Setting my cap at a jaunty angle on my head and checking the gig line of my uniform, I prepared for my moment of glory.

I put on a stern face appropriate for the drama of the moment and began jogging across the road, careful to keep my tongue from hanging out the way it normally did when I ran. I felt I was the perfect image of the intrepid gunship pilot, dashing to my awaiting aircraft, there to mount my aerial charger and fly away to rain terror and destruction on the forces of evil.

When I reached the other side, I thought I had performed the jog across the road in rather good form. And I felt the flashing red light had no small part in this accomplishment, providing as it did an especially dramatic touch to the jog. I hoped someone in the throng of admirers was getting this on film. What a thrill it would stir in the heart of anyone who would later view the image of this fearless aviator who was now so briskly—even handsomely—racing across the ramp to his awaiting helicopter gunship.

When I got to my Cobra, I allowed myself a small glance from under the bill of my cap. Vehicles were still stopped on the road and people were still watching me. Most likely, I thought, it was because they were awe-struck by my performance; although, I suppose this suspension of any productive activity on their part might have been due to the new clerk's forgetfulness in turning off the light. It was still flashing.

Putting my best foot forward, I planted it on the step-up at the side of the fuselage and gracefully pulled myself into the cockpit, seating myself in my chariot of war. Jutting my chin like a true air warrior, I deftly flipped on the battery switch. My eyes swept the instrument panel to confirm I had battery power for the start. I did, and I reached for the engine starter trigger. But then another one of the instruments caught my attention: the fuel gauge. Its needle was near empty; the aircraft hadn't been refueled.

I sat there a moment, comprehending this situation. While I sat there, coming to the realization that I wasn't going anywhere anytime soon, the ego leaked out of me until I was as empty as the fuel tank.

I turned off the battery switch and slowly climbed out of the aircraft. I began walking back to the Operations building to have a word with the new clerk. The drivers, the pedestrians, and the spectators on the ramp were still watching me as I crossed back over the road, slouched with my hands in my pockets and my cap bill pulled down low on my forehead to hide my face. The red light was still flashing.

## Tan Son Nhat Debacle

US political figures who came to Vietnam sometimes took a tour of the Delta or some part of it, and when they did, the tour often included a ride in a Huey, which required gunships to escort it. For the helicopter part of the tour, lesser figures of prestige might fly into one of the Delta's more prominent airfields, like Can Tho or Soc Trang, aboard an Air Force plane and then hop aboard a Huey from one of the units at that airfield. However, that was for lesser figures who perhaps were considered more expendable and could be allowed to hazard such airfields. For persons of greater renown, the helicopter tour originated from Saigon and gun teams were required to fly there to rendezvous with a spit polished Huey that had been prepared for the excursion.

I had flown a few of these local escort missions, meeting up with a slick at some airfield in the Delta and trailing along behind the slick at an altitude well out of effective ground fire range, but not so high as to cause the dignitary to suffer chill.

A few months after becoming President Nixon's Secretary of State, William Rogers traveled to Vietnam. I'm sure he had his reasons for doing that, but he didn't tell me what they were. I only learned about his trip after he had arrived. In the evening, my platoon leader, Captain Keys, dropped by my cubicle and informed me that the Secretary was in Saigon and that part of his itinerary the next day was an aerial tour by helicopter of a vicinity of the Delta near the capital city. I found that information remotely interesting, but I didn't know why Captain Keys would bother telling me about this. Then he mentioned that, in addition to fixed wing aircraft circling overhead, helicopter gunships, Cobras specifically, would directly escort the Huey carrying the Secretary and that the 235th would be supplying those Cobras. Although no one had asked me, it seemed to me the most logical choice for an escort of Cobras would have been those belonging to the 334th's Playboys. They were closer to Saigon than we were, but perhaps the Playboys had already provided so many of these kind of escorts that these notably named pilots had become bored from such an abundant amount of prestige.

Captain Keys further informed me that pilots—but only select ones—from all three of the 235th's flight platoons would be part of the armed escort, and then he added that I was among those selected. I found that mildly flattering, but it held no great allure for me unless possibly the assignment involved a barbeque for the Secretary and I was also invited to participate in that.

Captain Keys said that the 235th would be taking a total of six Cobras—including two crews from each flight platoon—to Saigon's Tan Son Nhat Air Base, and from there, they would take off with the Secretary's Huey for the one-hour sightseeing flight. My opinion was that the assignment would take half a dozen Cobras away from more urgent missions in the Delta, yet I would be content to tag along, and I even became a little bit enthusiastic about the prospects for the trip when it occurred to me that it might offer me a chance to visit the big PX in Saigon.

My enthusiasm was dashed, however, with the next piece of news that Captain Keys had: out of all the pilots in the 235th, I had been chosen to lead this flight. He obviously thought I would be thrilled by this selection, perhaps he had even lobbied for it, but I suddenly felt like a condemned man to whom the warden had announced the honor of being the first person to try out the new electric chair.

Tan Son Nhat Air Base, in the heart of Saigon, rivaled Chicago's O'Hare Airport as the busiest airport in the world. For a farm boy like me, flying in the Delta suited me; it was like driving in the country. But flying into Tan Son Nhat would be like driving on a Los Angeles freeway at rush hour. Hundreds of aircraft, and of all kinds, trafficked the airport daily. Tan Son Nhat landed not only military aircraft like B-52s, F4s, F-100s, and other big or high performance things, but it also handled top-of-the-line commercial airplanes, big ones like DC-8s, Boeing 707s, and 727s. Not only was the air traffic there thick, it was fast. Compared to most of the aircraft that habited Tan Son Nhat, even a speedy Cobra would be like a ranch horse on a racetrack full of Kentucky Derby contenders.

My specific dismay, though, lay in having to lead the flight through the maze of aerial corridors that surrounded Tan Son Nhat. Flying into that air base wasn't like flying to the other airfields in the Delta where I simply spotted it and landed, or maybe had to talk with only a lonesome tower operator whose most excitement for the day was having more than one aircraft arrive at the same time. Tan Son Nhat had elaborate air traffic patterns that demanded adhering to strict corridors with little tolerance for error and that required precise navigation to conform with. It was like an urban city hub surrounded by intermingled freeways and mix master intersections, all filled with vehicles ranging from Mac trucks and Greyhound busses to Aston-Martin DB5s and where, in comparison, a helicopter was a motor scooter.

Captain Keys gave me the briefest of details about the flight itself. The six Cobras would depart Can Tho the next day at 1030 hours, fly to Tan Son Nhat, and meet up with the slicks at the airport's Razorback Pad—wherever that was. Then Captain Keys slapped me on the back with his congratulations and left.

I had flown into Tan Son Nhat one time before. That was on a day off and riding in the jump seat of the company's slick, which was piloted by the company's armament officer. I had left the driving to him, not bothering to pay attention to how he got in and out of there. I never expected to need to know that.

I did remember him mentioning that there were several different landing pads for helicopters and that each pad had its own traffic pattern with convoluted approach procedures for getting to it, designed so that a helicopter bound for one pad didn't wander into the path of another helicopter bound for a different pad and that helicopters, no matter where they were bound, didn't blunder into the path of faster and bigger airplanes. Each of the patterns involved numerous checkpoints and severe altitude restrictions. He had mentioned that at the first checkpoint a helicopter had to be at a precise altitude, then when flying from that first outer checkpoint to the next one, a helicopter had to stay under some specific altitude but above another, and that the upper and lower altitude restrictions changed between the successive checkpoints. He had explained that the approach patterns were a series of specifically placed checkpoints, each requiring a report of a pilot's progress to a controller, designed so that an arriving helicopter reached a first checkpoint at a precise altitude and flew to the next stepped-down checkpoint, gradually lowering, until it reached a last checkpoint at a precisely lower altitude where the helicopter would be properly positioned for landing.

The armament officer had elaborated all this as I had so blissfully rode along that day, no more concerned about retaining this specific information than a checker player listening to a chess master. Yet I had grasped the overall concept; it was all an elaborate maze of aerial stepping-stones designed to bring a helicopter increasingly lower and closer to its final destination, suggestive of how a Venus flytrap might draw a victim into its folds.

Now saddled with the honor of the assignment, my first thought was to go to the armament officer and have him explain the details of these procedures, but I couldn't; he was off on R&R. So I immediately went to anybody I could find who had some experience with Tan Son Nhat and wring from that person anything I could learn about navigating that airspace. I found two persons. The first person, like me, had simply ridden along on a leisurely day off, but who, due to a pressing hangover, was even more oblivious than me about how he got there. The second person, though, was an old pro at it. He assured me it was all a piece a cake and, as he left to go to the club, he tossed me an approach plate that described the checkpoints, altitudes, and procedures. I grabbed it as if it were the key to my salvation and went to my cubicle to study it. My first glance at the approach plate substantiated my perception that the procedures were indeed complicated, but although they first appeared somewhat confusing to me, I thoroughly studied the plate until well after midnight, by which time I was completely confident that I was more confused than when I started.

By the morning, though, I knew how I could handle the problem. I went to the copilot who shared the distinction of being selected for this assignment as well as the dubious prestige of sharing the cockpit with the chosen leader of the flight, tossed him the approach plate, and told him I was granting him the honor of navigating us into Tan Son Nhat. I expressed my confidence in his ability for the job and added the assurance, although from a second-hand source, that it was all a piece of cake.

At the appointed time, we all took off together from Can Tho, me at the front, riding point for this herd of Cobras bound for Saigon. In time, I saw the city in the distance as we neared it. I was satisfied with how well I had handled the navigation to this point, albeit the route had been a simple straight line. The rest I the navigation I would hand over to the copilot.

"Where's the IP?" I said, remembering from the approach plate that getting into the air base began by flying to an Initial

Point and reporting our arrival there. The copilot promptly replied. "I have no idea."

"What do you mean you have no idea?" I said.

The copilot clarified his answer. "I mean I don't know."

"Didn't you study the approach plate?" I said.

"Yeah," he acknowledged, "but it didn't make any sense to me."

"But what difference does it make," he added. "You know your way in and out. You said it was a piece of cake."

For a moment, I panicked, but then I remembered the inspiring words of my high school football coach who had shared with me his observation that, although I was otherwise one of the most inept players he had ever coached, I always performed well in a game. Well, it was game time, I thought.

"Give me that approach plate," I said.

He handed it back to me and, while flying, I looked at it again. It might as well have been an Egyptian scroll filled with hieroglyphics—bird headed persons, lotus blossoms, and such— yet I did recognize a few symbols, one of which marked the IP. I approximated where it was, flew in that direction, and when I estimated I was close to it, I keyed the mike, gave my call sign, and reported that I had a flight of six Cobras at the IP.

One thing I had learned the night before from the old pro was that helicopters, going into and out of Tan Son Nhat, talked to the air base's ground controller rather than the tower operator who handled fixed wing traffic, and I had pre-dialed the ground control frequency into the radio before I keyed the mike. However, the old pro hadn't informed me that the ground controllers were all Vietnamese, rather than the other tower controllers who were American.

The response to my reported position had a decidedly Vietnamese accent, but was otherwise unintelligible to me.

Again, I relied on the copilot. "What'd he say?" I said.

The copilot, as helpful as before, said, "Beats me."

I glanced at the approach plate again. I noticed another symbol that suggested it was where I should go next, and a number beside it that hinted it might be the altitude I was expected to be at when I got there. I turned toward where I thought that point might be and began dropping down to that altitude. When I approximated I was at that point, I keyed the mike again to report my supposition as a fact. Back from the radio came another incomprehensible reply.

Periodically glancing at the approach plate, I hop scotched form one supposed checkpoint to another. As I wound a convoluted path toward the airport, I dutifully reported my questionable progress and received equally questionable responses.

There were aircraft everywhere. It reminded me of the return flight to the main heliport at Fort Wolters where all the aircraft, nearly all of them with shaky student pilots at the controls, converged at the same time at the end of a flight period. It was like the swallows returning to Capistrano, except thicker. But at least at Fort Wolters there were only three paths to the heliport and each of them was clearly marked with prominent, brightly painted cross arms mounted on poles in the ground. At Tan Son Nhat, though, aircraft of all kinds appeared to me to be flying randomly at every altitude imaginable, yet somehow they were all managing to stay out of each other's way.

I finally reached what appeared to be the last checkpoint before landing, which surprisingly to me also appeared to be a good place for turning a base leg in preparation for turning another ninety degrees that would align for a final approach leg toward the main runway, which was the widest and longest runway I had ever seen. It was at least five times wider than the farm-to-market road that ran through Climax and longer than the well traveled gravel road that led to the bootlegger's den on Tickey Creek.

At this point, the course seemed simple. I turned on the base leg, flew until I was in line with the runway, and then began turning directly on the final approach leg that would lead to a landing on that long, wide runway. As I turned toward the runway, I could see over my shoulder the other five aircraft behind me, all of them following me, the chosen leader who had brought them through the bewildering wilderness of checkpoints to this landing upon a giant runway. As I completed the turn, the huge runway stretched before me, its wide breadth as open arms inviting us all to come hither.

To expedite things, I had pushed my airspeed to a hundred-and-fifty knots and I was proud of my followers who had stayed close behind. Now, with the approach and landing assured, I allowed the airspeed to slow to zero and hovered to a stop right over the bright stripe that ran down the middle of the huge runway. Holding that position, I pedal turned upon the runway so I could better view and admire the other Cobras hovering there on the runway, nose-to-tail, in perfect alignment. It was a sight to behold; I wished I had remembered to bring my camera.

From the radio came the now familiar, yet equally un-understandable Vietnamese voice. I supposed it was congratulations of some sort for this display of airmanship. Then came another call on the radio, this one clearly an American speaker. "Flight of six Cobras on the active, clear the runway—now!"

Since it appeared there weren't six other Cobras anywhere around, I assumed he must be talking to us, and when I looked further back, in the distance behind the last Cobra, I saw a DC-8 airliner, the intakes of its big jet engines like the open mouths of a school of sharks, coming wheels-down toward the very runway we were on. It was on short final, bearing down on us, closing faster than a red-tailed hawk diving on a covey of quail. I didn't need any more urging and the other Cobra drivers must have sensed the same urgency. We all scattered off the runway faster than fleas from a dunked dog.

The jet's tires squeaked onto the runway. From the safety of the grass beside the runway, I watched the big bird as it rolled to a turnoff toward a taxiway and imagined what the mess might have looked like had we not cleared the runway.

I keyed the mike, and with as much dignity as I could muster, politely asked if someone could please tell me where the Razorback pad was. This time, it was an American voice that answered and that gave us clear, precise directions, carefully directing our course there. I supposed some higher authority had assigned him to us with the admonishment that he should never let us out of his sight. This special treatment was, no doubt, because we were the honored escort for the Secretary of State.

## Flattop Army Aviator

Even though I was an Army helicopter aviator, I felt I was qualified for Navy aircraft carrier operations. That's because I was trained to land on, and take off from, the deck of a Navy LST. In fact, I think I could make the case that I was more than carrier qualified because, with an LST, it was harder to land and take off than it was for a carrier's large waterborne airfield. Not only was an LST deck smaller, it bounced around more. And as a practical matter, I was convinced that an LST was a much better vessel than an aircraft carrier for satisfying the Navy's desire to exterminate Army helicopter pilots.

At one time in my young life, I considered becoming a naval aviator, and for plenty of good reasons. Not only did I think I would look good in one of those white dress uniforms, it was my observation that girls were attracted to those uniforms. Also, it was my understanding that the Navy had the best food of all the services. I could just see myself as a naval aviator, dressed in a spotless uniform, Miss April clinging to me, while I dined on lobsters and clams.

Then, my dream was shattered when I learned that naval aviators spent a considerable amount of their career flying over large bodies of water. I didn't like large bodies of water. As far as I was concerned, they were unnatural, something to be feared. I attributed that strongly held opinion to the influence of my West Texas relatives upon me when I was a child.

In West Texas, where it precipitated only every third May, large collections of water existed only as mirages, and children on those barren plains marveled when granddads in rocking chairs told those youngsters about the one time when it actually rained two days in a row. Since water there was such a precious commodity, children weren't taught how to swim; there was no need. Furthermore, in order to prevent youngsters from polluting the few, small bodies of water that did exist, they were encouraged to avoid those bodies. Adults told them stories of drownings and other watery hazards that convinced youngsters that bodies of water were more dangerous than rattlesnakes. Consequently, according to my mindset, flying over water was as terrifying a thought as Prohibition.

So, instead of becoming a Navy pilot, I became an Army helicopter aviator. But I felt this was no second-rate outcome. On the contrary, I was grateful that fate placed me in this position of superiority among all aviators.

We Delta Devils of the 235th Aerial Weapons Company sometimes supported Navy Riverine Operations, and I surmised that it came to someone's attention—likely some official whose job bore the heavy responsibility of deciding whether a sheaf of papers placed on his desk ought to be bound together by a paper clip or a staple—that because these operations used an LST as an offshore support craft, there could be times when we might be called upon to park a Cobra or two on an Navy LST. Then this official must have found a regulation somewhere stating that pilots had to be instructed and qualified in order to perform such a feat.

Only a few of us Devils were selected for this LST instruction. It appeared to me the Army selected us because we were the ones who had the most flying time; that is, we were the ones nearing the end of our tours and hadn't yet been eradicated. I suspected the Army, holding that against us, must have sought other opportunities to get its money's worth out of us, and since we had proven so resistant to the Army's normal means of accomplishing our demise, it must have seized upon this instructional requirement to collaborate with its sister service, the Navy, to serve that end. And, thus, from these precepts, the adventure began.

For our instruction, we were told that we would receive a ground school (or was it a water school?) on Navy aviation operations, followed by flight instruction involving landing on, and taking off from, an LST.

Late one afternoon, the Army gathered us together, and a Navy officer, not even an aviator, conducted the school, beginning with Navy terminology, explaining things like "port", "starboard", and "poop deck."

It was during this school that I learned the principle difference between an LST and an airfield: an LST moves. This concept of a moving landing site was an eye-opening revelation to me. Generally, my experience had been that airfields stayed in one place when I left them and they didn't tend to move someplace else the minute I turned my back. I could usually find an airfield right where I left it. Oh sure, just like any other helicopter pilot, I had on a few occasions misplaced an airfield or two, but I had never had one get up and move of its own volition. Furthermore, unlike an LST, land-based airfields didn't try to run away from me when I was attempting to land on them.

In the school, the Navy officer explained some of the communications protocol in contacting an LST. For example, a typical radio contact might be, "Navy LST One-Two-Three, this is Satan One-Three. I would like to land now, and by the way, where are you?"

He also informed us that an LST deck could hold only two helicopters. Then, as an afterthought, he mentioned that, as we were making an approach to an LST, if we happened to notice there was already another helicopter on the deck and we intended to occupy the other spot, we should take an interest in observing whether the preceding helicopter's rotor was turning or if it was tied down. If it was tied down, he assured us we could hasten to proceed with the landing. However, if this earlier arrival's rotor was still turning, he suggested we might reconsider our intention to land since the deck of an LST didn't have enough room to accommodate the diameters of two turning helicopter rotors; at least, without causing vital parts of both helicopters to be cast upon the waters. We pondered that for a moment.

Then someone looked at the time and commented that the club was about to open so we rushed the Navy officer through the remainder of the school. He fluttered his hands in the air, simulating the flight pattern for a landing to an LST. On the approach, he said we should come in perpendicular to the length of the LST and terminate the approach in a hover over the deck. Regarding the height of the hover, he urged us to keep an open mind on that subject since it depended upon the depth of the waves on which the LST was riding. Some of those swells could make an LST bob up and down like the cork on a fishing line with a hooked a turtle. The actual termination of the landing—that is, putting the skids on the deck and making them stay there, all without bending them—he left to our imaginations. Finally, the Navy officer assured us that there was really nothing to worry about, citing the statistic that almost half of those who attempted a landing to an LST did, in fact, achieve this goal.

When the school ended, we chosen few retired to the club. There, we discussed the perils of LST operations. After a few drinks, the unanimous conclusion was that if Navy helicopter pilots could do it, it couldn't be that hard for us.

The next morning, we were up early for our required flight instruction. All of us—except one—were picked up by a Navy slick helicopter and deposited on an LST in the ocean off the coast from Soc Trang. The plan was that these pilots would wait there so that they could practice take offs and landings in the Cobra that the one other pilot would fly out to the LST. A key component of this plan was that the person who initially flew the Cobra out to the LST would actually be able to land on the craft to begin with. And it was me who was the one who would fly the Cobra out to the LST and, supposedly, make the first landings and takeoffs.

The day was full of rain and the wind gusty. In fact, the Army probably selected this day for our LST training because the Viet Cong wouldn't let their boys go out on such a miserable day.

With an instructor pilot in the front seat of the Cobra, I departed Can Tho. I found my way to Soc Trang, passed over it, and then headed out over the gray watery expanse where, the instructor assured me, there was an LST somewhere beyond the mist shrouded horizon. I think I knew what Lindbergh felt like as he left New York behind.

Flying over the ocean, I discovered that a helicopter sounded different than when flying over land. I found myself hearing surges in the engine, grindings in the rotor, and whistlings in the cracks of the canopy that I had never noticed before. And I had never before noticed so many twitches of the gauges' needles; each one, I was sure, a prelude to an engine failure and a plunge into the eternal sea.

Eventually, I was relieved when the LST appeared straight ahead. I keyed the mike to make contact with the radio operator. I identified myself and asked for landing directions. He replied with some nonsense about "stern" this and "port quarter" that, which I suppose was somehow related to landing on the LST, but as far as I could discern, might as well have been directions for making porcupine gumbo. Besides, who was the Navy to try and tell an Army aviator how to do things?

I simply set up an impromptu landing pattern, flying toward the tail end of the LST, then turning away from it for a downwind leg, and eventually rounding off the corners to make a hundred-and-eighty-degree turn back toward the vessel. This actually worked out better than I anticipated. I was flying parallel with the LST's length, and when things looked about right, I turned another ninety degrees so I could make an approach perpendicular to the length of the ship. This was going to be a piece of cake.

I began my descent toward the deck and that was when something unexpected happened. The spot on my sight picture to the deck began slipping away. I turned the aircraft to line up again, and just when it looked right once more, the spot moved away again. That's when reality met theory; I realized the LST was moving. Oh sure, I knew that it could move, but I had assumed they would at least start me out on this training by anchoring the thing down. I was a little aggravated with the Navy for this oversight on their part.

I soon discovered, though, that I really didn't have to re-aim the aircraft at the deck. Instead, I could set up the approach, get the sight picture, and just let the helicopter drift sideways with the moving LST. With this discovery, the rest of the approach went well. I was lined up on the deck, sliding along sideways at the same rate as the LST was moving forward, and at just the descent angle to clear the railings around the deck.

I was feeling pretty good about the whole thing until I got about fifty feet from the deck. That's when I noticed that the deck was moving up and down faster than the sucker rod of a West Texas gooseneck oil pump when the spot price for crude jumped to over fifty dollars a barrel.

I brought the helicopter to a stop over the LST's landing deck, which from my perspective appeared to be about the size of a card table at a church bingo party. I held the helicopter at the highest hover I could maintain and waited for the oscillating deck to come meet me at its earliest convenience. Shortly, the deck rose to the occasion, pitching up toward me. It stopped briefly at its apex and I pushed down on the collective to land. But before I could light, the deck plunged down again, leaving me suspended in the air.

Then I saw the deck coming back up toward me faster than I could spend money on payday. In a panic, I pulled as much collective as I could to escape it, and by the time I looked down again, the deck had fallen away once more as the LST hit a trough, and there I was, suspended so high above the deck I could barely see the sailors down there. However, I could still see them well enough to determine that they thought my predicament was terribly funny. And I could see also that money was exchanging hands between them regarding the outcome of my predicament.

I lost track of time as I alternately chased and fled from the plunging and lunging deck. During this time, the instructor up in the front seat offered encouraging comments such as "You know, you're not being paid by the hour to do this."

Just when I thought I would never get the skids of my aircraft and the deck to agree upon a common altitude, I felt the deck knock gently on the skids. Quickly, I seized the opportunity and shoved down the collective to latch onto the deck before it could drop out from under me again. Immediately, I felt the aircraft falling as the LST plunged into another trough, but this time the skids were on the deck and we were all—man and machine—riding the waves together.

At this point, I had logged one LST landing and there was so much sweat in my flight gloves they were sloshing. But I had done it. I let out a sigh of relief and rolled off the throttle to flight idle in preparation for letting another victim have a shot at this torture. That's when the instructor said, "Now, make a takeoff."

Although I was drained from the landing, I thought to myself, how difficult can it be to make a takeoff? I would just get the aircraft light on the skids, wait for the LST to rise up on the peak of a swell, pull pitch as the deck bottomed out again, and I'd be on my way. It seemed simple enough, and once I was airborne, I would simply refuse to return to the LST. I would fly back and land at Can Tho, where the ground stayed put under me.

Having thus resolved, I was ready to begin when I noticed this sailor standing a few feet in front of the helicopter, between it and the railing, watching me intently. I suppose he had been there all along, even while I was trying to find the deck earlier, but I was so engaged in that quest that I hadn't noticed him.

He stood there and I waited patiently for him to move out of the way. After a while, he hadn't moved, and I began to suspect that he might have some purpose related to me, so I asked the instructor about him. The instructor explained that he was there to direct my takeoff. His purpose was to give me signals designating when to come to a hover and when to take off. I had never had someone do this for me before. I considered him to be a sort of cheerleader for helicopter takeoffs.

I rolled on the throttle and waited for him to signal something. He simply stood there with his hands on his hips. The instructor said I should give him a thumbs-up when I was ready to go. So I flipped him a digit, and in response he began waggling his arms up and down, which I took to be the Navy signal encouraging me to come to a hover. Either that, or he was attempting to become airborne himself.

The Cobra strained to lift off the deck and I managed to get it up to a four-foot hover with the torque meter almost pegged. I was struggling to maintain even that height, yet the sailor still stood there in front of the helicopter, flapping his arms, and insisting on more altitude before he would give me the signal to take off. I did the best I could and managed to coax the Cobra another inch or two higher before the rpm began to bleed off. The sailor still stood there, flapping.

I considered the situation. I estimated the railing behind the sailor to be about three feet high and I calculated that, from a four-foot hover, I could just clear the railing. So, neglecting for my purpose the fact that the sailor in front of me stood six feet tall, I nudged the cyclic forward and headed for the open sea.

As the skids cleared the railing by a foot, I looked back and saw the sailor sprawled on the deck. Fortunately, for a man his size, he could move pretty fast. If he hadn't ducked when he did, he would have had a shortened naval career. Based upon that experience, for years I thought the term "midshipman" referred to a sailor who had been chopped off at the waterline—so to speak—by an Army helicopter pilot attempting to take off from an LST.

To shorten the story, I did in fact return and managed to make a second landing on the LST. Thereupon, I gratefully gave up the aircraft to the next person. After that training, I was never again called upon to land on an LST, something for which I was profoundly grateful.

# The Riverine Patrol

Dawn marked the end of the night's Firefly duty for the four of us in my team and we had some time off before we were to report for the next mission in the early afternoon. I used part of that time to go to the base's tailor shop and arrange for the Vietnamese proprietor to make a tropical worsted uniform I planned to wear home when my tour ended in less than two months. After that, I made a meal from the assortment of goodies I had been sent from home and I had time for a lengthy nap.

When the alarm clock went off, I rolled off the cot, slapped on my cap, strapped on my gun belt, hung my chicken plate over one shoulder, and rather than waiting for a jeep, walked to the Operations building. The ten-minute stroll would help loosen me up before being confined to a cockpit for what would likely be several hours.

The airfield was busy, people scurrying about, either afoot or on wheels. Jeeps, trucks, and other Army vehicles played chicken with one another on the narrow, intertwined streets without signal lights or stop signs. As I neared the Operations building, I enjoyed watching vehicles clattering across the PSP-clad ramp, weaving around and dodging the parked and taxing aircraft there: slender Cobras; broad Hueys; boxy Chinooks; sleek single-engine Air America PC-6s; raised-tailed, twin-engine Caribous; haughty, four-engine C-130s; tail-dragging Bird Dogs; and OV-1s with their large, round, side canopies that reminded me of giant, bulge-eyed dragon flies. What appeared to be anarchy when I had first arrived at Can Tho now seemed to be orchestrated choreography.

I arrived at the Operations building before the rest of the team, and since the Operations personnel were too busy for chitchat, I used my time while waiting to study the wall-mounted Area of Operations map. Its plastic cover was spotted with handwritten notes and symbols indicating the locations where the 235th's fire teams were currently operating and the hot spots of reported enemy threats. Those areas included the chronic ones: Nui Coto mountain near the Cambodian border, the U Minh forest just south of Can Tho, and the area around Rach Gia near the southwestern coast of Vietnam, all places that had become familiar to me.

When the rest of the fire team arrived, we loaded into the Operations truck and the driver took us to the Cobras, the same ones we had flown the previous night and had parked in revetments not far apart. I expected the crew chief to be at the revetment with the aircraft, but he wasn't. Normally, the crew chief was present for the first preflight inspection of the day, but those preflights were usually in the morning; I assumed he had been placed on other duty this afternoon.

Our assignment would take us to the southernmost part of Vietnam, the Ca Mau Peninsula. A large triangular area with the South China Seat on its east and the Gulf of Thailand on the west, the peninsula extended south from the Delta's plain of canals, giving way as it neared the coast from cultivated rice paddies to a wild marsh of dense mangroves threaded with meandering streams.

Our mission was to provide air cover for a Brown Water Navy patrol. A trio of boats was scheduled to come in from the sea, enter the mouth of a small river on the east side of the Ca Mau Peninsula and navigate a maze of writhing waterways before exiting from the mouth of another small river and returning to the South China Sea, a route six klicks long. Typically on these patrols, the twistings and the narrowness of the channels forced the patrol boats to creep along the waterways when searching for VC, a pace that invited ambush from the continuous hiding places within the thick mangroves.

Our rendezvous with the boats was a point southeast of the town of Ca Mau, which was a hundred-and twenty klicks south of Can Tho, and the rendezvous point was another twenty-eight klicks beyond the town. I calculated that with a flight time of thirty-five minutes we could provide about an hour and a quarter of cover. The Ca Mau airfield would be less than ten minutes away from the operation area and was a reliable refueling point. I felt the timing was important. I didn't want to arrive late and hold up the operation, and I didn't want to arrive too early either, possibly burning fuel needlessly and reducing our time on station.

The assigned rendezvous time was 1300. To be on station at the scheduled time, we needed to be airborne by 1225. But there was a problem; during the preflight, the wing ship was discovered to have an oil leak, one beyond what the wing ship AC was willing to accept.

I called Ops on the radio, explaining the wing ship was Red-Xed, and the Operations clerk gave me the tail number of a replacement. With the additional time required to preflight another aircraft, it was going to take us past the planned departure time, so I informed the clerk we would miss our ETA for the rendezvous by an estimated half hour and to pass that information along to the Mission Assigners From On High.

By the time the wingman completed the second preflight and we cranked for takeoff, we were a little more than a half hour behind schedule. I typically cruised at a hundred and thirty-five knots, but to make up some time, I added more power to bump our cruise speed to near its limit. I assumed our delay had been communicated to the Navy and it would be waiting on us.

Ten minutes before our ETA at the rendezvous point and within range of radio communications, I keyed the transmitter to check in with the lead boat. There wasn't an immediate answer, which didn't surprise me; I anticipated the operation might have been canceled with the realization that it wouldn't have air cover at the scheduled time.

I called again. "Zeus Adam, Satan One-Three. Over."

The squelch of the FM receiver broke. I could hear what sounded like a heavy caliber gun and loud voices before another voice spoke. "Satan One-Three, Zeus Adam."

"Zeus, I've got a light fire team of Cobras. ETA ten."

"Roger, Satan. Be advised we're in heavy contact, taking fire from both sides of the stream. We have three men down."

The boats had obviously started the patrol without us. As soon as I had heard the firing over the radio, I had pulled more power for more speed. "On our way," I said.

I immediately called the team to go hot and flew toward the rendezvous point at the maximum speed Six-One-Four could give me. I was focused straight ahead, trying to pick up muzzle flashes. It was my gunner who redirected my attention. "Two o'clock," he said. In the distance, still some six klicks away, I saw the flashes, lots of them.

I swung the aircraft to point in that direction, racing toward the flashes. I leaned forward in the seat, like a rider on a horse, urging it on. Every second seemed an eternity. The number of flashes was increasing; any one of them could mean a Navy man's death. Even though we were still well out of rocket range, I felt I had to do something immediately to suppress the fire. I thought, even if I couldn't hit the ambushers, I might be able to scare them off. Rockets made a lot of noise, even from far away.

I raised the nose and punched off a pair. The rockets streaked from the tubes, trailing brief plumes of flame. They made a long arch skyward before curving down and plunging into the heavy growth beyond, the impact marked by small geysers from underneath the thick foliage.

Another ten seconds and a half klick closer, I triggered another pair of rockets. These reached farther than the first ones, yet still way short of the cluster of muzzle flashes. However, after the second pair, the volume of flashes lessened, and as we drew closer, I could see it was only the boats that were firing. Either the ploy worked or Charlie had broken off contact as the result of the boats slipping by his position. When we arrived overhead, all the shooting was over.

While the boats sped away as fast as they could in these back streams, we worked over the ambush spot with our rockets and miniguns. If we did any damage, it wasn't evident; the overgrowth was too thick.

We shot out half our ordnance before we broke off to follow the boats, saving the remainder in case the boats ran into more trouble. We followed them, circling overhead, until they returned without further incident to the safety of the sea.

I never learned if the Navy had been informed we would be late, but in any event, the operation had gone ahead without us. In my parting conversation with Zeus Adam, he informed me he had three wounded seamen; he feared the one hit in the leg would lose it.

# Rach Gia

Among the places we frequented was the airstrip at the edge of the town of Rach Gia. Pronounced "Rock Jaw", the town and airstrip were near the western coast of Vietnam, off the Gulf of Thailand, and seventy klicks almost directly west of Can Tho.

The airstrip was considered relatively secure because Vietnamese White Mice policemen were present during the day, yet so were civilians and in greater number. Anyone of them could have been a VC in peasant's clothing, and I saw the policemen there only in the daytime, never at night. My more memorable experiences at the Rach Gia airstrip were at night or near night.

One of our missions that took us to Rach Gia was shrouded in mystery. At Operations, I was told that my assignment was to take a team to the airstrip, arriving near sundown, and wait there in case our gunships were needed for a nighttime Navy operation that was being conducted near the coast. I wasn't given any other details about the operation; I was simply given directions on how to operate the battery-powered radio that was handed to me and told the frequency to monitor. If I was called, whoever contacted me on the radio would give me whatever information I needed to know.

We landed at Rach Gia before dusk, topped off with fuel, and parked along the side of the airstrip to wait. I wasn't at all comfortable with our situation. Not only did the overall tactical situation change in Charlie's favor at night, I was especially concerned about where we were. And not only was this a remote airstrip, it had no perimeter protection; in fact, no protection at all. By dark, there was no one else at the airstrip except us.

My team had already had a full day of flying. As darkness set in, I set up shifts to monitor the radio for a possible call and I took the first shift. The other members of the team went to find a place to sleep wherever they could; we didn't even have bedrolls. After my shift ended, I stayed with the radio; my hackles were too high to sleep. Among the things that troubled me about this situation was how little I knew about why we were here, and I thought it unusual to place four pilots and, more especially, two valuable helicopters in such a vulnerable situation as this. For all I knew, maybe the Mission Assigners From On High had staked us as bait at the airfield; perhaps we were a diversion to attract Charlie's attention from whatever the other operation was. I remained with the radio all night, my six-shooter beside me, but I never heard a peep from the radio. At first light, I considered us relieved from this duty and we flew back to Can Tho, arriving to discover we had been assigned IV Corps Standby duty for the day.

On another occasion, I took a fire team to Rach Gia, which was the staging point for a Navy operation we were to support. Perhaps it was the same kind of operation as the earlier one because that's all I was told about it. But this time, we weren't alone; there were also Navy UH-1 gunships. And this time we stayed airborne, flying orbits near the airfield, apparently so we could respond faster if we were needed. We came down only to refuel. During one of those hot refuelings, in the middle of the night, I was startled when an old Vietnamese lady appeared beside the running helicopter where I sat with the canopy hatch open. She offered me tea, holding up a pot and cup. It seemed to me a godsend; I was starving for a drink and my canteen was empty. She poured the tea into the cup and handed it up to me. I gulped it down and thought it was the best tea I had ever tasted. I wanted a refill, but the gunner had finished the refueling and it was time to go airborne again, so I handed the empty cup to her and nodded my thanks. It was only after I left that it occurred to me I had not paid her. Yet I had no way to pay her. Sometimes I carried loose piasters in my pocket, but I hadn't this night. And although my wallet held a little military script, I never carried it when I flew, not did I carry any other personal effects. If I were captured or if my remains fell into the wrong hands, it was better that there be nothing to learn about me other than what was on my dog tags.

It also occurred to me that if that stranger who had suddenly appeared beside my helicopter had been a VC rather than an old lady peddling tea, I wouldn't be having this conversation with myself. Then it occurred to me that the old lady could have been a VC sympathizer and the tea I had just drunk could have been poisoned. And immediately another thought crossed my mind, a question: how had I become so suspicious that I would consider an old, kindly lady like that to be a threat?

On yet another occasion at Rach Gia, I missed the opportunity of being dismembered by a grenade. My fire team had landed at the airstrip at dusk, refueled, and positioned the aircraft to a place beside the runway a little further away. After the two-minute cool-down, I had shut down the engine and the wingman, parked behind me, had shut down his. Both of us climbed out of the back seat and we met behind my Cobra where we talked briefly before walking a short distance away onto the runway to look around. As far as we could tell, we were the only ones there. After the wingman's gunner had tied down the rotor of the wing ship, he joined us on the runway and my gunner joined us shortly after he finished tying down the blades of our ship. That's when the grenade landed. With the explosion, we all flattened ourselves on the runway. At that point, we weren't certain it wasn't a mortar round and those were usually followed by more. The explosion had come from where the helicopters were parked nearby and it wasn't uncommon for Charlie to chuck mortars at helicopters parked at remote airstrips, an experience I had enjoyed beginning early in my tour. After a while, when nothing else had come our way, we got up and went to the helicopters to see what damage may have been done. We discovered a small depression in the soft earth where the explosion had occurred, and the size of the depression convinced us the explosion resulted from a grenade rather than a mortar. Supporting that conclusion was the fact that none of us had heard the characteristic swoosh that accompanied a mortar round. The grenade had landed between the tail of my helicopter and the front of the wing ship. We surmised that we had parked the aircraft close enough together than it must have been a two-birds-with-one-shot opportunity that some part-time Viet Cong couldn't pass up. I suspect that, like Deputy Barney Fife who carried only one bullet in his shirt pocket, this VC had one grenade he had been saving for just the right occasion and we gave him the chance he had been waiting for. The explosion had sprinkled some shrapnel underneath the tail boom of my Cobra and put a few small holes underneath the nose of the wing ship, but neither of the aircraft was seriously damaged, and neither were we. In retrospect, I considered it odd how unconcerned I was about this; I had come to feel things like this were simply a part of the job.

It was near Rach Gia that a 235th pilot, WO-1 Larry Bodell, was killed, shot in the head while flying as gunner in the front seat of a Cobra. That was in February. The previous month, CW-2 Gary Weatherhead had been killed during the attack at the Can Tho Airfield. The month after Larry was killed, CW-2 Glenn Fetterman, who had barely escaped being killed during the attack at Can Tho, was shot and killed, also hit in the head, while flying in the back seat of his Cobra. His gunner managed to land the aircraft.

## A Ball of Fire: The End of the Beginning

A ball of fire was rushing up toward me, seconds away, and there was nowhere to go, nothing I could do. With the realization that the outcome was out of my hands, the ball of fire became a wondrous object to observe. I marveled at its brilliant flames and its graceful arch. And when it passed overhead, a few feet above the rotor, I pondered the mystery of how this marvelous thing could have missed.

I felt the Cobra's controls in my hands and I snapped to my senses. I had time for one shot and I took it, punching off a pair of rockets before breaking away and letting Six-One-Four carry me to safety. As I sped away, I watched the rockets impact. They had gone long; I had missed and would have to go back. As I moved the cyclic to make the turn, I saw the wing ship's rockets impact. They were right on target, and from where they hit, I saw a secondary explosion. He had nailed whatever it was.

I radioed the outpost that I thought their worries were over, at least for this coming night, and we flew away, staying at low level, the sun setting behind us.

As we sped over the Delta's rice paddies toward Can Tho, I realized how lucky I had been to escape the ball of fire this day and, just twenty-seven days from going home, how lucky I had been all along.

Ahead, I saw a young boy herding a water buffalo. I rolled the helicopter slightly in that direction to better see him, and suddenly the sun's reflection upon the paddy turned the dirty water to gold, the power of that image's beauty magnified because it was so unexpected. As I flew over the boy, he waved and I waved back.

Three weeks later, I flew my last mission in Vietnam. I had remained lucky; I was a survivor.

After parking Six-One-Four in its revetment, I gathered my map of the Delta, the one I had pieced together during my tour, from its familiar place tucked aside the instrument panel. That evening I would give the map to the new fire team leader I had helped train.

I lingered a moment in the Cobra with my name on it, watching its rotor winding to a stop. I tried to freeze the moment in my mind, the familiar arch of the instrument panel, the feel of the cyclic, the engine fumes lingering in the air, the smell like the coal oil lanterns I remembered when I was a kid. I felt thankful, thankful for the privilege I had been given to fly, and even more thankful to fly Cobras. Six-One-Four and I had done things together too terrific to fully describe.

I had walked away that day dry-eyed, too tough for tears. I was young then with plenty of other things yet to come. I'm no longer that young, and I'm not that tough anymore.

# Glossary

**AC:** abbreviation for Aircraft Commander.

**AH-1:** a two-man-crew, tandem seating helicopter gunship produced by Bell Helicopter. The first production model was the AH-1G.

**Air Cavalry:** an airmobile unit that combines scout, gunship, transport helicopters, and its own infantry.

**Air Mission Commander:** the on-site command authority for an airmobile operation; often rode in the back of a Huey; generally synonymous with "Command & Control."

**Aircraft Commander:** the pilot responsible for the operation of an aircraft.

**AMC:** abbreviation for Air Mission Commander.

**Army of the Republic of Vietnam:** South Vietnamese ground troops.

**anti-torque pedals:** a helicopter's controls that change the pitch of the tail rotor. In a hover, they control the helicopter's yaw (left-right) movement.

**AO:** abbreviation for Area of Operations.

**Area of Operations:** the geographical area for most of a unit's operations.

**ARVN:** abbreviaton for Army of the Republic of Vietnam.

**ash and trash:** a helicopter operation, usually single-ship, that transports supplies or personnel to or from a ground unit.

**assault helicopter company:** an Army aviation unit, typically consisting of Hueys, with the primary purpose of transporting troops.

**autorotation:** the state of a helicopter's main rotor when it's turning as a result of air rushing up through it rather than being powered by an engine. It's a means of allowing a helicopter to land in the event the engine quits.

*beau coup:* a lot; many.

**Bladder:** see fuel bladder.

**Bingo fuel:** when the quantity of fuel reaches the amount considered "reserved."

**Brown Water Navy:** US Navy units that conducted inland boat patrols.

**C-4:** a pliable plastic explosive.

**C-7:** a twin-engine transport airplane; originally part of the Army's fleet of aircraft and later transferred to the Air Force.

**C-130:** a four-engine, turboprop Air Force transport airplane.

**C&C:** abbreviation for Command & Control; can refer to a person in command of an operation or the aircraft from which that person operates.

**C-Rations:** boxed meals; generally, a box of canned portions was intended as one meal for one person.

**call sign:** an alias for a unit asset, often consisting of a name and a number.

**Caribou:** the Army's name for a C-7.

**CH-47:** a twin-engine, twin-rotor Army transport helicopter.

**Charlie:** 1) the phonetic for the letter "C"; 2) a nickname for the Viet Cong.

**check ride:** a flight with a "standardization" pilot that usually includes an assessment of a pilot's capability.

**chicken plate:** nickname for a vest with a solid armor plate in front.

**Chinook:** the name for a CH-47 Army helicopter.

**chunker:** nickname for a helicopter gunship's grenade launcher.

*co*: Vietnamese for a young, unmarried woman.

**Cobra:** the name for an Army AH-1 helicopter.

**collective:** a helicopter control that adjusts the concurrent pitch on all rotor blades. In a hover, a collective controls a helicopter's up-down movement.

**Command and Control:** See Air Mission Commander.

**commissioned officer:** military officers with broad personnel command authority.

**crew chief:** an enlisted person responsible for the upkeep of an individual aircraft.

**cyclic:** a helicopter control that controls pitch and roll in flight. In a hover, it controls forward, backward, and sidewise movements.

**cyclic grip:** the handgrip part of a cyclic. It has numerous buttons and switches to activate certain aircraft systems; for example, radios and armament.

*Dai Uy*: Vietnamese for "captain"; pronounced DI WEE.

**Date Eligible to Return from Overseas (DEROS):** the projected date for returning home from an overseas assignment; for example, the date for completing a tour in Vietnam.

**Delta:** 1) the phonetic for the letter "D". 2) the southernmost part of Vietnam.

**DEROS:** abbreviation for Date Eligible to Return from Overseas.

**deuce-and-a-half:** a 2.5 ton truck.

**DI WEE:** Anglicized spelling for *Dai Uy*.

**doghouse:** the enclosure covering a helicopter's rotor system below the rotor blades.

**Dustoff:** a common term for a medical evacuation or the helicopter and crew that performed a medical evacuation. (see Medevac).

**E&E:** abbreviation for Escape and Evasion.

**Escape & Evasion:** actions for surviving, and avoiding capture, when in enemy territory.

**FFAR:** abbreviation for folding fin aerial rocket.

**flechettes:** dart shaped projectiles packed in an explosive warhead.

**flub:** a term used in this book for another four-letter word that begins with an "F."

**folding fin aerial rocket:** an unguided rocket used by helicopter gunships and other aircraft primarily as an air-to-ground weapon.

**free fire zone:** generally, an area where it wasn't required to seek permission before firing on targets, sometimes subject to certain conditions.

**friendlies:** troops who were not enemy forces.

**F\*\*king New Guy:** a person newly arrived in Vietnam.

**FNG:** short for F\*\*king New Guy.

**Fox:** short for "Foxtrot", the phonetic for the letter "F".

**fuel bladder:** a heavy-duty, collapsible fuel container made of rubber.

**grenade launcher:** a turret-mounted helicopter gunship weapon that fires 40-millimeter grenades.

**gunship:** an armed helicopter.

**H-34:** a piston-engine Sikorsky helicopter originating in the 1950s.

**HE:** an abbreviation for high explosive; can refer to a rocket warhead packed with shrapnel and explosive material.

**high explosive:** explosive material that detonate with great velocity.

**hot fuel:** refueling while an aircraft's engine is running.

**hootch:** generally, a dwelling; can be either civilian or military.

**hover:** the state of a helicopter when operating off the ground but not in flight.

**Huey:** the name for an Army UH-1 helicopter.

**Initial Point:** a geographical location for beginning a designated flight pattern.

**Instructor Pilot:** a pilot who trains other pilots.

**IP:** abbreviation for Initial Point or Instructor Pilot.

**IV Corps:** pronounced "Four" Corps, the southernmost of South Vietnam's four tactical zones.

**Jesus nut:** the large retaining nut that holds the main rotor of a helicopter to the mast.

**jungle boots:** combat boots made of leather and canvas.

**KBA:** Killed by Air.

**KIA:** Killed in Action.

**klick:** shorthand for a kilometer; approximately six-tenths of a mile.

**KP:** Kitchen Police; mess hall duty.

**Landing Zone:** a place designated for an air assault landing to carry in assets.

**lift ship:** a transport helicopter, usually one that carries troops.

**lima-lima:** 1) landline, telephone communications using wires. 2) low-level, flying close to the surface.

**Loach:** nickname for an LOH.

**LOH:** Light Observation Helicopter, generally used for low-level scouting.

**LST:** "Landing Ship, Tank"; a naval vessel supporting amphibious operations.

**LZ:** short for Landing Zone.

**Medevac:** a medical evacuation or the helicopter and crew that performed a medical evacuation.

**minigun:** a machine gun with rotating barrels.

**Mohawk:** the name for the Army's OV-1 airplane.

**mortar:** a short-tubed muzzle-loaded canon.

**nails:** a nickname for flechettes.

**nipa palm:** a sharp-edged palm that often grew in dense concentrations.

**newbie:** Someone new to Vietnam; a more respectful term in place of FNG.

*nuoc mam*: Vietnamese fermented fish sauce.

**OH-13:** a piston-engine, bubble-domed, Korean-War-vintage helicopter used by the Army for primary flight training.

**OH-23:** a piston-engine, three-place observation helicopter, first flow in the 40s, and used by the Army for primary flight training.

**ordnance:** weapons and ammunition.

**OV-1:** An Army photo observation and electronic reconnaissance aircraft.

**Operations:** A part of a military unit that directly coordinates and manages the logistics of military operations.

**P:** short for piaster.

**P-38:** a small can opener with a foldable blade used to open C-Rations.

**Pedal turn:** a turn to the left or right by a helicopter when hovering; initiated by pressing the anti-torque pedals.

**Pedals:** see anti-torque pedals.

**Perforated Steel Plate:** steel plates, about three-by-eight feet, designed to lock together and when laid on the ground, provided a hard surface.

**Plexiglas:** a strong, lightweight, transparent material enclosing the upper part of an AH-1's cockpit.

**Piaster:** Vietnamese currency; during the Vietman war it was worth about one cent.

**Pickup Zone:** a place designated for an air assault landing to carry out assets.

**pipper:** used for aiming, a lighted pattern that appears on the transparent plate of a turret weapons' sighting device.

**platoon:** a unit within a company.

**poncho liner:** an insert for a rain poncho, sometimes used as a bed covering.

**Popular Forces:** South Vietnamese local militias, usually ranging only near the villages where they resided.

**Post Exchange:** a military store.

**Prick 25:** nickname for a PRC-25, a portable, backpack FM transceiver.

**Province chief:** Governor, sometimes a high-ranking military officer, of a Vietnamese province.

**PSP:** abbreviation for Perforated Steel Plate.

**Push:** a radio frequency.

**PX:** short for Post Exchange.

**PZ:** short for Pickup Zone.

**R&R:** abbreviation for Rest &Recuperation.

**Real live officer:** refers to a commissioned officer rather than a warrant officer.

**Recon-by-fire:** putting ordnance into a place suspected of concealing combatants as a means of having those combatants reveal themselves.

**Regional Forces:** South Vietnamese military forcers similar to National Guard units.

**Revetment:** a barrier or partial enclosure made of sandbags and often reinforced with PSP.

**Roger:** a radio communication term acknowledging "received and understood."

**Ruff-Puffs:** Regional Forces-Popular Forces; a collective reference to both South Vietnamese Regional Forces and Popular Forces as opposed to other members of the South Vietnamese Army (ARVN).

**Rest & Recuperation:** vacation time during a tour, usually about a week.

**salvo:** several rockets fired at the same time.

**sampan:** a small Vietnamese boat, most of them about the size of a canoe.

**sapper:** a Viet Cong or NVA solider armed with explosives who penetrates a perimeter, usually under stealth.

**satchel charge:** a pack with explosives.

**SCAS:** abbreviation for Stability and Control Augmentation System.

**SEAL:** Navy special warfare team members.

**search-and-destroy:** a military offensive to find and destroy enemy forces.

**short-timer:** a person nearing the end of a tour in Vietnam.

**shrapnel:** metal pieces expelled by an explosive.

**slick:** a transport helicopter; generally, a Huey used to transport troops and supplies rather than rigged as a gunship.

**smoke grenade:** a device about the size of a hand grenade; when the pin in pulled, it releases a colored smoke.

**Signal Operating Instructions:** a booklet containing call signs of units and their associated radio frequencies.

**SOI:** abbreviation for Signal Operating Instructions.

**SOS:** "S**t on a Shingle; creamed meat on toast.

**Specialist:** an Army rank above Private First Class.

**Stability Control and Augmentation System:** an electromechanical system designed to smooth aircraft motions not induced by the pilot.

**States:** shorthand for the United States.

**steel pot:** an Army helmet with a metal covering.

**tandem:** fore and aft; inline.

**throttle:** a control that regulates fuel to an engine.

**TAC officer:** Training, Advising, and Counseling officer who helps train, develop, and evaluate Warrant Officer Candidates.

**TH-13:** a more modern version of an OH-13 helicopter, used by the Army for instrument flight training.

**TH-55:** a piston-engine, two-place helicopter produced by Hughes Aircraft and used by the Army for primary flight training.

**traffic pattern:** a defined path for controlling air traffic, often associated with an airfield. An airfield's traffic pattern usually includes upwind, crosswind, downwind, base, and final legs.

**Uncle Ho:** nickname for North Vietnam leader Ho Chi Minh.

**Viet Cong:** combatants with allegiance to North Vietnam.

**warrant officer:** officers who are highly trained for a particular specialty and generally exercise authority primarily within that specialty.

**white phosphorous:** the most volatile form of phosphorous; burns readily and produces a great volume of smoke; can refer to a rocket warhead packed with this material.

**Wobbly-One:** a WO-1 warrant officer, especially a new warrant officer.

**WOC:** Warrant Officer Candidate; a person in training to become a Warrant Officer; rhymes with "rock".

**WORWAC:** Warrant Officer Rotary Wing Aviation Course; an Army helicopter pilot training program that leads to a student pilot becoming a Warrant Officer.

**UH-1:** an Army utility helicopter produced by Bell Helicopter used mostly for transport, but sometimes adapted for other purposes; for example as a gunship.

**Uniform Sierra:** the phonetics for the letters "U" and "S"; can refer to a US soldier as opposed to a Vietnamese soldier.

**VC:** abbreviation for Viet Cong.

**VNAF:** South Vietnamese Air Force.

**Whiskey:** the phonetic for the letter "W"; can refer to a wounded casualty.

**White Mice:** South Vietnamese police who wore white helmets and gloves.

**Willie Pete:** nickname for white phosphorous.

**WP:** abbreviation for white phosphorous.

**Zippo:** a popular brand of cigarette lighter.

YB 23

Printed in Great Britain
by Amazon

81799896R00169